La Ligne d'écume

Pavement Books
London, UK
www.pavementbooks.com

First published 2016 © Gilles Chamerois, Christopher Collier, Patrick ffrench, Sophie Fuggle, Nicholas Gledhill, Fiona Handyside, Áine Larkin, Claire Launchbury, Thérèse De Raedt, Zoë Roth

Cover Photograph by Emmanuelle Groult. Reproduced with permission from the artist.

The authors have asserted their right under the Copyright, Designs and Patents Act 1988 to be identified as the authors of this work.

All rights reserved. No part of this publication may be reproduced, stored in a retrieval system, or transmitted, in any form or by any means, electronic, mechanical, photocopying, recording or otherwise, without the prior permission of the authors and the publisher.

British Library Cataloguing in Publication Data.
A catalogue record for this book is available from the British Library.

ISBN: 978-0-9571470-7-2

La Ligne d'écume:
Encountering the French Beach

edited by
Sophie Fuggle and Nicholas Gledhill

STRANDS book series

A strand is a thread, a trajectory, a train of argument or thought. It is also a road, a promenade, the place where beach meets cityscape. It is a limit as well as a line. It is the site of encounter, conflict and confrontation. As borders are reinforced and sea levels rise, spaces of inclusion become those of exclusion. The strand gives way to the stranded, marooned, isolated, imprisoned and alienated. This series presents a range of perspectives and critical methodologies aimed at questions of space and our sociocultural engagement with it. As such it incorporates studies and approaches from cultural studies, literature, film and media studies, anthropology, political science, architecture and human geography.

Current titles

Return to the Street edited by Sophie Fuggle and Tom Henri

Taking Up Space edited by Jamal Aridi and Jessica Glendennan

La Ligne d'écume: Encountering the French Beach edited by Sophie Fuggle and Nicholas Gledhill

CONTENTS

Acknowledgments	vii
Notes on Contributors	ix
Note on Translations	xi
Introduction SOPHIE FUGGLE & NICHOLAS GLEDHILL	1
I. Beach Archaeologies	11
Beneath the Cobblestones, the Beach: An Idea in Everyone's Mind? CHRISTOPHER COLLIER	13
Devant la mer: Thresholds of Fiction and Theory PATRICK FFRENCH	35
Death on the Sand: From Tragic Humanism to Depressive Realism NICHOLAS GLEDHILL	49
II. Framing the Beach	65
Proust and the Beach as *Écran* ÁINE LARKIN	67
Vacance: vacancy and vacation in the films of Jacques Rozier GILLES CHAMEROIS	89

III. War Zones   111

Bodies on the Sand: Corporeality and the Beach in the   113
Films of Catherine Breillat and François Ozon
FIONA HANDYSIDE

Colonies de Vacances   133
SOPHIE FUGGLE

'Elle ne sera bientôt qu'une épave soudée à ses rochers':   159
Women Writing the Wreck of Beirut
CLAIRE LAUNCHBURY

IV. Eroded Identities   175

Between Real and Ideal Space: Writing, Embodiment and   177
the Beach In Michel Houellebecq
ZOË ROTH

The Beach as Liminal Site in Abderrahmane Sissako's   193
Heremakono
THÉRÈSE DE RAEDT

Index   217

ACKNOWLEDGMENTS

The idea for this collection emerged from a series of discussions between the editors while they were both based in the Centre for Cultural Studies at Goldsmiths, University of London. Preliminary thoughts on this were further developed during the *Taking Up Space* Conference held at Goldsmiths in 2012 which led to a film night dedicated to the French beach organised by Jessica Glendennan. Additional encouragement for the project was provided by friends in the French department at King's College London including Patrick ffrench, Johanna Malt and Sanja Perovic and subsequently by colleagues in the French department at Nottingham Trent University especially Enda McCaffrey and Chantal Cointot.

Special thanks also go to John and Theodor Hutnyk and to Emmanuelle Groult for her cover image.

NOTES ON CONTRIBUTORS

Gilles Chamerois is Associate Professor at the University of Brest, France. He was a student at the French Louis Lumière National Film School and has written articles on film and adaptation (Terrence Malick, Robert Kramer, Ken Loach and John Huston) and co-written two books on novels and their adaptations, *Jane Eyre* with Élise Ouvrard and *The House of Mirth* with Marie-Claude Perrin-Chenour. He has also edited or co-edited two collections of essays on Thomas Pynchon, and written a number of articles on this author.

Christopher Collier is completing a doctorate in the School of Philosophy and Art History, University of Essex. His research examines the re-emergence of the avant-garde practice of 'psychogeography' during the 1990s. He has several articles on the topic in print and forthcoming. He also teaches part time at Essex Business School and the Centre for Interdisciplinary Studies in the Humanities. At the time this text was written Christopher was precariously employed as a somewhat psychogeographical travel writer - producing marketing copy about beaches he had never visited, and possibly never will.

Sophie Fuggle is Senior Lecturer in French at Nottingham Trent University. She is author of *Foucault/Paul: Subjects of Power* (Palgrave, 2013) and has co-edited various collections on space and culture including *Word on the Street* (IGRS, 2011) and *Return to the Street* (Pavement Books, 2015). Her current research focuses on cultural representations of incarceration.

Patrick ffrench is Professor of French at King's College London. He is the author of *The Time of Theory: A History of Tel Quel* (Oxford UP, 1996), *The Cut: Reading Georges Bataille's Histoire de l'œil* (British Academy, 1999) and *After Bataille: Sacrifice, Exposure, Community* (Legenda, 2007), co-editor (with Roland-François Lack) of *The Tel Quel Reader* (Routledge, 1998) and (with Ian James) of *Exposures: Critical Essays on Jean-Luc Nancy* (Oxford Literary Review, July 2005). He is currently working on two book length projects - *Proust's cinemas* - on how *A la recherche du temps perdu* might allow us to imagine cinema differently, and *Spasms: the Politics of Moving Bodies*, on late 19th- and 20th-century discourses around bodily movement.

Nicholas Gledhill is a London-based writer, musician, teacher and intercultural training consultant. He has postgraduate degrees from the University of Leeds and the Centre for Cultural Studies, Goldsmiths, University of London. He is also an editor of the arts and cultural theory journal *Nyx*. His current research is focused on the development of modernist themes in the European novel.

Fiona Handyside is Senior Lecturer in Film Studies and French at the University of Exeter. She is the editor of *Eric Rohmer: Interviews* (2013) and co-editor with Kate Taylor-Jones of *International Cinema and the Girl: Local Issues, Transnational Contexts* (2015). She has written *Cinema at the Shore: The Beach in French Cinema* (2014) and is currently completing a monograph on Sofia Coppola.

Áine Larkin is Lecturer in French at the University of Aberdeen, and author of *Proust Writing Photography* (Oxford: Legenda, 2011). She has contributed chapters to a number of books, including *Marcel Proust in Context* (ed. Adam Watt, CUP, 2014) and *Cent ans de jalousie proustienne* (eds. Erika Fülöp and Philippe Chardin, Classiques Garnier, 2015). She co-edited a special issue of *Romance Studies* (2014) entitled *Unsettling Scores: Proust and Music*. Funding awards include a Postdoctoral Research Fellowship from the IRCHSS (2008) and an RSE Workshops award (2014). Her research interests include Proust studies, medical humanities, and dance in the modern novel.

Claire Launchbury is Research Fellow in French and City Studies at the Institute of Modern Languages Research and the Centre for Metropolitan Studies, Institute of Historical Research at the University of London. Her research focuses on issues of memory and representation in postwar Lebanon and on francophone voices of resistance in the Middle East more broadly. Her second monograph, *Beirut and the Urban Memory Machine* will be published by Amsterdam University Press in 2016.

Thérèse De Raedt is Associate Professor of French at the University of Utah in Salt Lake City. Her research has focused around the theme of 'otherness'. Her publications include several articles on the novel *Ourika* by Mme de Duras, on the film *Vers le Sud* by Laurent Cantet, on the Holiday resort Club Med, on Franco-Senegalese mixed race couples, and on the film *Congo River* by Thierry Michel. She has published several interviews with African writers and artists.

Zoë Roth is Lecturer in French at Durham University. Her work broadly addresses the relationship between lived experience and aesthetics in twentieth- and twenty-first century comparative literature and visual culture. She has published in such journals as *Word & Image* and *Philip Roth Studies*.

NOTE ON TRANSLATIONS

The French beach as site of encounter has been subject to multiple readings, writings and translations. As the essays in this collection attest, it is a site that is inhabited, occupied, appropriated and exported globally. The use of English translations alongside original French citation throughout the book is intended to reflect such appropriations beyond a Francophone community. However, the editors have as far as possible respected the varied translation formats of the book's contributors, some of whom have provided their own translations to the French original, others who are working primarily with established translations.

INTRODUCTION

Sophie Fuggle & Nicholas Gledhill

I. Mapping the French Beach

According to a well-worn anecdote, Louis XIV complained that, with the advent of new scientific methods for calculating the coastline, he was conceding more territory to the astronomers than he was to his enemies.[1] To attempt to map any coastline is perhaps always an exercise in futility. Castles in the sand will be washed away at high tide. The same applies to the beach as site of creative inspiration and cultural production. Consequently, this collection resists an affirmation of the French beach as fixed space giving rise to a coherent set of themes. Instead, the aim is to explore the trope of the beach within the French cultural imaginary from both inside and beyond the parameters of the *Hexagone*. As such the real and imagined beaches featured in the book exceed those making up the coastline of mainland France. In addition to France's seaside resorts of La Baule and La Ciotat, Marcel's Balbec and Roquentin's Bouville, our beaches include the Beirut shoreline, the desert city of Nouadhibou in Mauritania, the multiple Club Med villages across the globe and the future desertscapes of Michel Houellebecq's *La Possibilité d'une île*.

At the end of François Truffaut's *Les 400 Coups*, Antoine Doinel arrives on the beach. The camera turns back from the waves to focus on Antoine's face crossed with the realization that there is nowhere else to go. In Jean-Luc Godard's *Weekend*, the Parisians never make it as far as the beach. Again, it seems to embody the frustration of urban desire to go or be somewhere else. However, a shift has occurred in which the idea of the beach as total limit or unattainable escape has been displaced or at the very least, eroded. The overriding message of Godard's 2010 cinematic offering, *Film Socialisme*, is that Europe is over. The fixed yet perpetually shrinking space of the beach has been replaced by a cruise ship, cast adrift alongside the coastlines of Odessa, Palestine and Egypt. If the

---

[1] As recounted in Dava Sobel, *Longitude: The Story of a Lone Genius who Solved the Greatest Scientific Problem of his Time*, London and New York, NY: Penguin Books, 1996 [1995], 27.

beaches of Southern Europe and beyond defined the post-war French imaginary in terms of leisure, travel and freedom, these must be reimagined in late capitalism in terms of voluntary and involuntary migration, border control and global capital.

More recently, images of refugee children washed up on Mediterranean shores are circulated as a form of 'poverty-' or 'victim- porn' provoking a form of moral outrage which is always already redirected towards the preservation of the Western bourgeois family and the safeguarding of the spaces it inhabits. Consequently, claims to expose Western hypocrisies towards the refugee 'other' such as the one made by satirical paper *Charlie Hebdo* via a juxtaposition of a cartoon rendering of Aylan Kurdi with that of 'animal-like' Arabs chasing women in Cologne,[2] are already framed within a politics of fear which sees both sets of images and events in terms of the threats they pose to European domestic comfort and well-being. Whether framed as an urgent call for charity or as satire masquerading as critical discourse, the use of such images does little to interrogate let alone transform the underlying socio-economic and political systems which have led to the dispossession of millions through war, economic crisis and climate disaster.

II. Encountering the French Beach

Rather than simply reduce the beach to a point on a trajectory or an area on a map, how might we resist this type of cultural mapping, focusing instead on the French and Francophone beach as a space which has taken its meaning and value from the encounters it has produced and engendered? To clarify what is at stake in defining the beach in terms of its 'encounters' here, we might identify three modes of encounter which have provided an organizing function to French sociologists such as Alain Corbin and Jean-Didier Urbain writing the social history of the European beach.[3] Again, this is not simply a question of the beach in its topographical/topological specificity but the beach as it is presented and represented within popular consciousness as narrative, symbol, myth and brand. As such the beach is implicated in a social history of looking, at once

---

[2] Aylan Kurdi was a 3 year old Syrian refugee who drowned on 2 September 2015 trying to reach the Greek Island of Kos with his family. The image of him lying face down in the sand was widely circulated by international media. Following the sexual assaults which took place outside Cologne cathedral on New Year's Eve 2015, the satirical paper, *Charlie Hebdo* published a cover image by Riss with the question 'Que serait devenu le petit Aylan s'il avait grandi?' [What would have become of little Aylan had he grown up?].

[3] Alain Corbin, *The Lure of the Sea: Discovery of the Seaside 1750-1840*, translated by Jocelyn Phelps, Berkeley and Los Angeles, CA: University of California Press, 1994; Jean-Didier Urbain, *Sur la plage: Mœurs et coutumes balnéaires XIXe-XXe siècles*, Paris : Payot, 2002.

subject to changing aesthetic techniques and their objects and, at the same time, implicated in the production of such techniques. The beach is simultaneously canvas and frame. It is also a battlefield.

The first encounter involves human conquest over nature and, in particular, the terrifying, unforgiving power of sea and ocean. Charting the emergence of the beach as a site of pleasure and relaxation, Corbin links this development with individual and collective ways of seeing and looking. The radical shifts in perception of the beach between the classical period and modernity resulted from a complex range of images and discourses and the varying influences these possessed. Thus, fear of the sea prior to the eighteenth century had as much to do with biblical narratives of the Flood as it did to authentic stories of shipwrecks and drowning.[4] What is important to note here is the symbiotic relationship between visual culture as lens for seeing the beach and the representations of the beach subsequently produced and mapped back onto public perception.

The second encounter concerns that of the dangerous, subversive other. The site of initial encounter, it constitutes a threat as much as a promise. A threat or menace of erasure, the beach is a space, *the space*, where survival may well only depend on the elimination of the other. Thought temporally, it represents the moment where all life becomes, if only fleetingly, bare life, *homo sacer*. But it is also the site of potential friendship, allegiances, deals and trade agreements all of which require the appropriation and assimilation as opposed to the elimination of the other. The beach is thus also a dropping off point where the drowned, the shipwrecked and the enslaved all wash up to be handed out new identities, roles and chains.

Over the past two hundred years, a process has occurred whereby the beach has ceased to constitute the space of encounter with the dangerous other both in the form of the sea and also those that obtain their livelihood from it. This other has been transformed into (imported) slave, servant, spectacle, souvenir – a presence relegated and regulated to serve the needs and pathologies of the wealthy (white) visitor. The beach is emptied of these 'other' figures who disappear into villages and ghettos inland, living and working unseen in hotel kitchens, cleaning guestrooms or, disguised as cheap parodies of themselves and those who preceded them, performing 'tradition' as evening entertainment. A presence, a livelihood, an identity and a culture all rendered invisible by their own spectral spectacle.[5]

---

[4] Corbin. Op. cit., 1.

[5] Urbain, Op. cit., 90-1. In a lecture given on Albert Camus at the Institute Français, London in September 2011, the novelist Geoff Dyer suggested that for Camus and other *pieds-noirs*, the Algerian beach was essentially conceived as a long strip of playground 'facing backwards towards France.'

As Urbain points out in *Sur la plage*, it is precisely the 'aestheticization' of this 'other', the fisherman, as subject of eighteenth and nineteenth century art and literature that signals his disappearance or erasure from the beach.[6] This aestheticization cannot be uncoupled from the processes of industrialization reconfiguring the rural landscape as much as that of the cities. Embodying the exoticism of the sea as well as the romanticism of the rural, artisanal worker in contradistinction to the reviled urban working classes, the representation of the fisherman on canvas designates the possibility of the beach as site of exotic, romantic encounter precisely at the cost of such an encounter.[7] 'The beach would become a scene without these indigenous: emptied of these Savages.'[8]

It is at this point that we find the third encounter. Even before the development of mass tourism in post-war Europe, the beach represented a space in which one came into violent confrontation with oneself. Yet, this is a violence all the more dangerous for the Western complacency and privilege it has come to affirm. The idea of losing and finding oneself on the beach has been claimed by artists, writers, students and luxury brand managers alike. Running parallel to the romantic discourse of beach as limit experience, is that of the beach as space where one goes precisely to remain the same. The beach provides a site in which to replicate bourgeois domesticity and consolidate social hierarchies.[9] Here, one encounters one's self not simply in the repeated banality of the annual trip to the same guest house or holiday apartment, the same spot on the beach, but in all those who like us have had the same idea, are undertaking the same 'vacation.' A violent confrontation composed of traffic jams, check-in lines, crowded restaurants and littered beaches. Here, the beach provides the backdrop to an aesthetics of the self in which radical self-transformation is short-circuited by a narcissism of small differences embodied in the micro-colonization of individual plots of sand by the careful positioning of towels and umbrellas.

Reflecting further on this third encounter, we might identify a form of inertia produced as the most recent outcome of this violent encounter with ourselves. Augé terms this 'l'inaction propre à la vie de la plage' [the inaction specific to life on the beach].[10] For him La Baule represents 'une immense sale d'attente sans espoir de départ' [an immense waiting room with no hope of departure].[11] Moreover, to remain the same yet different we go to greater lengths, travel fur-

---

[6] Ibid., 73. For an account of the 'capturing' of the beach by French impressionists, see Lena Lenček and Gideon Bosker, *The Beach: The History of Paradise on Earth*, London: Pimlico, 1999, 127ff.

[7] Urbain., Op. cit., 76-7.

[8] Ibid., 80. Our translation.

[9] See in particular Chapter 6 of Lenček and Bosker, *The Beach*.

[10] Marc Augé, *L'Impossible Voyage: Le tourisme et ses images*, Paris: Éditions Payot et Rivages, 2013, 41. Our translation.

[11] Ibid., 43. Our translation.

ther in search of the beach. 'The seaside tourist might go as far as the ends of the earth. But precisely in order to stop. The aim of his displacement is interruption'.[12] The 'immobility' which defines the beach vacation for Urbain is the very same inertia described by Paul Virilio who identifies its intensification with the increased speeds by which individuals and images alike can now travel.[13] In the opening to her semi-autobiographical novel, *L'Amant*, Marguerite Duras articulates a similar transformation of the lived experience of long-distance travel and the sense of separation and absence it is no longer able to produce:

> Pendant des siècles les navires avaient fait que les voyages étaient plus lents, plus tragiques aussi qu'ils ne le sont de nos jours. La durée du voyage couvrait la longueur de la distance de façon naturelle. On était habitué à ces lentes vitesses humaines sur la terre et sur la mer, à ces retards, à ces attentes du vent, des éclaircies, des naufrages, du soleil, de la mort.

> [For centuries, because of ships, journeys were longer and more tragic than they are today. A voyage covered its distance in a natural span of time. People were used to those slow human speeds on both land and sea, to those delays, those waiting on the wind or fair weather, to those expectations of shipwreck, sun and death.][14]

The distances we travel have long ceased to correspond to an embodied experience of movement and instead have resulted in the severe limitation of our physical activity and range of gestures.[15] After 8 or 12 hours spent in an airplane seat, we climb into a taxi for another half an hour before lying down on our towel or sun lounger at another beach resort with the explicit intention of staying put, remaining the same, for the duration of the week or fortnight. Journey and departure have been eliminated and we find ourselves in a state of 'generalized arrival'.[16] Yoga on the beach or aerobics in the pool compounds rather than alleviates this inertia. Violence assumes a form of voluntary paralysis here.

Such paralysis, and its symbolic co-location with the hedonistic beach resort, runs as a central theme throughout the writing of Michel Houellebecq, arguably the most influential French novelist working today. In late-twentieth century works such as *Les Particules élémentaires* and *Lanzarote*, Houellebecq depicted a French – and by extension European – culture struggling to find purpose in the face of a profound lassitude. The pervasive image of the body beautiful on the beach served to compound a sense of existential crisis in the

---

[12] Urbain, *Sur la plage*, 15. Our translation.

[13] The notion of 'dromology' runs throughout Virilio's work. For a specific discussion of the shifting (eroding) relationship between space and time, see *Open Sky*, translated by Julie Rose, London and New York, NY: Verso, 1997.

[14] Marguerite Duras, *L'Amant*, Paris: Editions du Minuit, 1984, 132-3. Translated as *The Lover* by Barbara Bray, London: Flamingo, 1986.

[15] Virilio, *Open Sky*, 17.

[16] Ibid., 16.

individual, reduced to a condition of absolute materialism by the intersecting forces of late-capitalism, moral liberalism and secularisation. More recently Houellebecq has developed this idea of a French cultural collapse still further, in his controversial 2015 novel *Soumission*. In the near future, in a politically deadlocked France crippled by post-modern inertia, a radical Muslim party gains power and imposes Islamic law. In Houellebecq's wry and troublingly ambivalent vision France, a weary and decadent 'failed state', inevitably succumbs to the single-mindedness and vigour of its former subaltern. Empire has come full-circle, the cultural tide has turned.

*

Rather than organizing the chapters of this collection according to the particular cultural artefacts – art, literature, film, philosophy – they take as their objects of analysis, the book is organized thematically. However, a series of arbitrary lines drawn in the sand, such categories are only one possible way of setting out the different approaches to reading the beach. The first section, 'Beach Archaeologies', explores the beach as literary, political and philosophical concept along with the shifting role of the beach in relation to French thought and cultural identity from Sartre to Houellebecq. In Chapter One, Christopher Collier explores the story behind one of the most famous slogans of twentieth-century French political struggle, *Sous les pavés, la plage*. In Chapter Two, Patrick ffrench identifies the trope of the beach as a shifting signifier in twentieth-century French thought, analyzing its role in the texts of Sartre, Barthes and Foucault. Nicholas Gledhill considers the beach's persistent appearance as site of potential violence and transgression, mapping key moments in the French beach's recent literary history.

The second section, 'Framing the Beach' comprises two essays which both look at the way the beach is both framed and itself operates as literal and figurative screen. Áine Larkin's analysis of Proust's Balbec in Chapter Four uses the idea of beach as 'écran' to explore Proust's use of visual imagery as well as the different ways in which his novel has been transposed and reappropriated in contemporary cinema. Examining the role of the beach in Jacques Rozier's films, in Chapter Five, Gilles Chamerois situates Rozier's work within a wider cinematic tradition taken up with capturing the beach as site of freedom and pleasure.

Section Three, 'War Zones' returns to the theme of violence evoked in earlier chapters. In Chapter Six, Fiona Handyside analyses the *cinéma du corps* of François Ozon and Catherine Breillat, focusing on their construction of the beach as site of female subjugation and rape. Chapter Seven takes the link between war and tourism as its starting point. Sophie Fuggle considers how the creation of a series of myths around the holiday resort, Club Med, have since its opening in the 1950s legitimized a neo-colonial agenda as intrinsic to French national identity. Women's narratives as both response to war and as affirmation of identity constitute the focus of Claire Launchbury's study of the war-torn coastline of Beirut in Chapter Eight.

The fourth and final section, 'Eroded Identities' picks up the theme of the beach as site of construction and erasure of the self. In Chapter Nine, Zoë Roth provides a comparative analysis of Michel Houellebecq's beach narratives, considering how the beach provides Houellebecq with a salient example of postmodernism's quest for 'embodied experience' and his shifting reflections on this quest within his œuvre. Chapter Ten explores a key example of 'migration cinema', Abderrahmane Sissako's *Heremakono*. Thérèse de Raedt offers a detailed analysis of the film's imagery, its affirmation of the beach as space of possibility and hope as much as it is one of fear, risk and treachery. The shore elsewhere makes its claim upon the shores of Europe's Mediterranean coastline.

III. Reimagining the French Beach

Where several of the essays included in the collection provide an analysis on the beach as site of violent confrontation whether this be conceptual or physical (real or imagined), implicit throughout is a call for different encounters. Encounters which are perhaps less productive and more creative. How might the beach be reimagined as an ethical as much as aesthetic space? Here, Agnès Varda's *Les Plages d'Agnès* might provide some brief insight. The beach has long represented a site of sexual encounter between youthful, naked bodies. Such encounters have been exoticised by Gauguin's paintings and Henri Charrière's alleged stay with an indigenous tribe on a Venezuelan beach during his escape from the *bagne* in Guyane in *Papillon*. Using the beach as an anchor point for a retrospective on her life, Varda reclaims the beach as a constant. Appearing in various guises, the beach is a site of return and reflection embodied most poignantly in the images of Jacques Demy, her long-term lover, shortly before his death in 1990. Thus, as a fully-clothed octogenarian, Varda is able to rewrite and reframe the space of the beach as a site of enduring love alongside casual sex, family ties alongside adventure and risk. Varda quite literally holds up a mirror to herself yet instead of being overwhelmed by the banality and vacuity of what she finds is able to celebrate her life through this reflection.[17]

Varda's beach, like Proust's novel, involves a form of blurring, embodied by the *ligne d'écume*, between the autobiographical and a series of fictional framings. Perhaps this might be considered in terms of a self-writing attesting to an ethics of the self via an aesthetics of the self. However, here we might argue

---

[17] For a detailed study of Varda's retrospective, see the chapter, 'The Old Woman at the Sea: Agnès Varda's Beachscapes' in Fiona Handyside, *Cinema at the Shore: The Beach in French Film*, Oxford; Bern: Peter Lang, 2014.

that the ethical stakes should be higher still. If the beach provides us with a raw space in which to encounter both ourselves and the other, we must not only rethink the human encounters taking place here but, at the same time, the impact of such encounters on the raw space itself. This is no longer the question of conquering nature which defined beach encounters in previous centuries but a more symbiotic relationship with our ever-shrinking coastline. How might we therefore reimagine the beach beyond its existing status as site of late-capitalist alienation, postmodern sexual violence or neocolonial plundering? As Patrick Chamoiseau's 2012 rewriting of the Crusoe narrative, *L'Empreinte à Crusoé*, attests, without ignoring or denying humanity's problematic relationship with the beach, this can nevertheless be rewritten as a space of ecopoetics and, indeed, *poesis*.

References

Augé, Marc, *L'Impossible Voyage: Le tourisme et ses images*, Paris: Éditions Payot et Rivages, 2013.
Chamoiseau, Patrick, *L'Empreinte à Crusoé*, Paris: Gallimard, 2012.
Charrière, Henri, *Papillon*, Paris: Robert Laffont, 1969.
Corbin, Alain, *The Lure of the Sea: Discovery of the Seaside 1750-1840*, translated by Jocelyn Phelps, Berkeley and Los Angeles, CA: University of California Press, 1994.
Duras, Marguerite, *L'Amant*, Paris: Editions du Minuit, 1984, 132-3. Translated as *The Lover* by Barbara Bray, London: Flamingo, 1986.
Handyside, Fiona, *Cinema at the Shore: The Beach in French Film*, Oxford; Bern: Peter Lang, 2014.
Houellebecq, Michel, *Les Particules élémentaires*, Paris: Flammarion, 1998.
———, *Lanzarote: et autres textes*, Paris: Librio, 2008.
———, *Soumission*, Paris: Flammarion, 2015.
Lenček, Lena and Bosker, Gideon, *The Beach: The History of Paradise on Earth*, London: Pimlico, 1999.
Sobel, Dava, *Longitude: The Story of a Lone Genius who Solved the Greatest Scientific Problem of his Time*, London and New York, NY: Penguin Books, 1996 [1995].
Urbain, Jean-Didier, *Sur la plage: Mœurs et coutumes balnéaires XIXe-XXe siècles*, Paris : Payot, 2002.
Virilio, Paul, *Open Sky*, translated by Julie Rose, London and New York, NY: Verso, 1997.

Filmography

Les 400 Coups, directed by François Truffaut, France: Les Films du Carosse, 1959.
Les Plages d'Agnès, directed by Agnès Varda, France: Ciné Tamaris and Arte France Cinéma, 2008.
Film Socialisme, directed by Jean-Luc Godard, France: Vega Film, 2010.
Weekend, directed by Jean-Luc Godard, France: Comacico, 1967.

I. Beach Archaeologies

1.

BENEATH THE COBBLESTONES, THE BEACH: AN IDEA IN EVERYONE'S MIND?

Christopher Collier

It is not 'historians' who do the judging, but history, that is those who make the latter.
– Guy Debord[1]

'Sous les pavés, la plage' - 'beneath the cobblestones, the beach' - so quintessentially '68', so typically situationist. What few words could better sum up, in the minds of many, what these things - May '68, the situationists - were all about? In fact, it's such a classic strapline, one could almost believe it was dreamed up by an ad agency, or in the brainstorming session of a couple of marketeers. One little known version of events suggests that it actually was.

*

Ten years after the event, Jacques Baynac's classic account of May 1968 began with an introduction entitled 'Sur les pavés, la Page'.[2] The title was a play upon what has become the definitive slogan of those tumultuous spring days. It suggested the events of 1968 had been occluded by the very abundance of their representations, their historicity paradoxically erased by a proliferation of commentary.[3] The proposition bears superficial similarities to the work of Guy Debord, the most prominent member of the 1957-72 avant-garde organisation the Situationist International (SI).[4] In fact, a central thrust of Debord's *La Société du*

---

[1] 'Communiqué from the SI concerning Vaneigem' (1970), trans. John McHale in *The real split in the International: theses on the Situationist International and its time (1972)*, London: Pluto, 2003, 168.

[2] Jacques Baynac, *Mai Retrouvé – Contribution à l'historie du mouvement révolutionnaire du 3 mai au 16 juin 1968*, Paris: Editions Robert Laffont, 1978.

[3] Baynac's insistence on verifiable documentation has led him to address some controversial historical territories. It is also worth noting that Baynac was previously published by Gérard Lebovici, Debord's close friend and confidant.

[4] The SI were an avant-garde organisation who sought a total artistic and social critique of alienation, the commodity economy, hierarchical power structures and the 'pseudo-activities' of both work and leisure. After a slow start, a number of English commentaries on this movement are now available. For an intellectual contextualisation,

spectacle, published six months before May '68, is the idea that history has been arrested in representations.

As representations go, the scope and breadth of May '68's complexity is frequently reduced to fragments, abstracted mnemonic markers, two of which I have somewhat predictably already introduced to evoke it – *that* slogan in particular, and the ideas of the SI. In popular Anglophone commentary, these two metonymic articulations have become intrinsically linked - with each other, and with the May upheavals themselves. Whether or not they were at the time, within this pseudo-history, they have become the ideas in everyone's minds.[5]

*

Forty years after the event, in 2008, a little-known doctor from Tours, Bernard Cousin, published a largely overlooked memoir. *Pourquoi j'ai écrit: sous les pavés la plage* was a pithy attempt at settling an historical account frequently overdrawn in the intervening near half-century.[6] He convincingly claims that it was he, along with his friend Bernard 'Killian' Fritsch, the co-founder of an advertising agency, who delivered the famous slogan into the world. Yet somehow this daydream of a 25-year-old medical student, part-time marketer and self-defined Platonist became definitively associated with the events of '68 and with the ultra-left critique pursued by the situationists.[7] In many ways this short slogan came to stand in the place of - and take its place in - 'history'.

For some this reductionist foregrounding of slogans is a deliberately ideological move, a method of recuperating the radical history of '68 for liberalism,[8] yet even from the beginnings of their slow and tortuous academicisation, the SI's critique is often erroneously equated to this 'one phrase' in which 'one can see, all at once, the political idealism of the group, its realism about transforming a society'.[9]

---

see Anselm Jappe, *Guy Debord*, Berkeley, CA: University of California Press, 1999. The first half of Sadie Plant's *The Most Radical Gesture: The Situationist International in a Postmodern Age*, London: Routledge, 1992, provides an historical account, whilst McKenzie Wark, *The Beach Beneath the Street: The Everyday Life and Glorious Times of the Situationist International*, London and New York, NY: Verso, 2011, offers a broader historical introduction to various participants.

[5] For example, the two are connected in the titles of books such as: Dark Star, *Beneath the Paving Stones: Situationists and the Beach, May 1968*, London: AK Press/Dark Star, 2001, or Wark, op. cit.

[6] Bernard Cousin, *Pourquoi j'ai écrit: sous les pavés la plage*, Paris: Rive Droite, 2008.

[7] Ibid.

[8] Kristin Ross 'Establishing Consensus: May '68 in France as Seen from the 1980s', *Critical Inquiry* 28:3, Spring 2002, 650-676.

[9] Edward Ball, 'The Great Sideshow of the Situationist International', *Yale French Studies*, 73, 1987, 22n.

The slogan's incorporation into an SI œuvre arguably centres on its mention in situationist René Viénet's historical account of the May events. Importantly, he repeats it in a passage concerning the overcoming of alienation through the sublation of both work and leisure into creativity and play. Yet he does so, not to claim situationist authorship of the phrase, but instead to directly contrast the *autonomous* and *spontaneous* creativity of the May revolt with cynical positioning by the organised left. The French Communist Party, its unions and interlocutors had, in the eyes of the SI, attempted to encourage those participating in the mass wildcat actions to renounce revolutionary demands for the sake of wage increases, incentivising them with the prospect of Club Med holidays.[10] For the SI, revolution would be a realisation of those very desires, desires both manufactured and *falsely* placated in the burgeoning beach holidays of a nascent leisure and tourism industry. Capital would not and could not meet the demands it had unwittingly unleashed, instead this 'beach' would lie in, and under, the streets.

*

Twenty years after the event, and apparently sourcing his attribution of the slogan solely from Baynac, Laurent Joffrin credits Killian Fritsch, 'a student of poetic soul', with its creation.[11] For Cousin, aside from the attribution, Joffrin's account is 'roughly correct', although he holds that 'the truth seems more helpful for the future than any judgment on the poetic form'.[12] In the following chapter I will readdress 'the truth', as Cousin has it - i.e. the circumstances in which the slogan came to be written - reopening this fragment, covered (over) by the pages of so many commentaries back out onto history. Yet to do so is not simply to relay these circumstances as I find them, but to draw out the 'poetic soul' of these now famous words, proposing that their resonances within their contemporary socio-economic and cultural situation - their poetry - is what makes them stand so readily for that moment in history. This resonance, I aim to demonstrate, has lead to the slogan's conflation with a certain misconception of 'Situationism'. Yet I also argue that examining the slogan via an engagement with the situationist programme might ultimately lead to a clearer understanding of the ambiguities of that programme, of '68 itself, and ultimately, why these words became the

---

[10] René Viénet, *Enragés et situationnistes dans le mouvement des occupations*, Paris: Gallimard, 1968.

[11] Laurent Joffrin, *Mai 68: Historie des Événements*, Paris: Éditions du Seuil,1988, 115. My translation.

[12] Bernard Cousin, testimony sent both to *Libération*, and the website of amateur historian Daniel Dzierzgowski on the 25/2/2008. My translation. Available:
http://users.skynet.be/ddz/mai68/temoignages/souslespaves.html. Accessed 1/7/2012.

most famous situationist slogan they never wrote.

Beneath

Turning from the May sunshine momentarily, towards the darkness beneath the stones, the famous slogan begins to evoke something of both 1968 and the SI's writings through its most seemingly inconspicuous component - the notion of 'beneath'.

A preoccupation with the beneath, the underside and unconscious haunts the French poetic tradition and frequently finds articulation through recourse to the satanic. The strong association of Satanism with more secular forms of revolt had coloured the work of artists and writers in France at least since the 1789 Revolution and was to characterise their representations throughout the nineteenth century. From Lamartine, Vigny and Hugo, to Rimbaud and Baudelaire, the devil was frequently evoked in connection with rebellion. This ambivalent 'Romantic' fascination with the satanic arguably articulates a subjective rejection of contemporary social organisation.

As the SI's ultimate precursor (via Letterism), Surrealism, as much as it can be labelled a coherent entity and despite various attempts from 1925 onwards to marry such an approach with more materialist orientations, drew heavily on this 'satanic' tradition, manifesting a degree of continuity with the approach found in French nineteenth century literature.[13] Likewise, in the writings of the SI one might identify a similar motif, what Michael Löwy called a 'dark romanticism'.[14]

If this heritage lends the SI an identifiable thematic shade however, it was also precisely Surrealism's subjective or Romantic approach that for Debord meant it must necessarily be superseded. As he stated in 1958, ten years prior to the composition of Cousin's slogan:

> [T]here was in surrealism - comparable in this regard to Romanticism - an antagonism between the attempt to affirm a new use of life and a reactionary flight beyond the real.[15]

---

[13] Ibid. Breton conceded Surrealism was 'the amazingly prehensile tail' of Romanticism, a movement which was 'only at the beginning of making its desires known through us' - André Breton, 'The Second Manifesto of Surrealism', in André Breton, *Manifestos of Surrealism*, trans. Richard Seaver and Helen R. Lane, Ann Arbor, MI: University of Michigan Press, 1972, 153.

[14] Michael Löwy, 'Consumed by Night's Fire - The Dark Romanticism of Guy Debord', trans. Marie Stewart, in Michael Löwy, ed., *Morning Star*, Austin, TX: University of Texas Press, 2009, 97-104.

[15] Guy Debord, 'Contribution to the Debate "Is Surrealism Dead or Alive?"' (1958) trans. Tom McDonough, in Tom McDonough, ed., *Guy Debord and the Situationist International: Texts and Documents*, Cambridge, MA: MIT, 2004, 67-68.

Debord sought to both transcend and sublate Surrealism's idealist contradictions, not by posing a 'satanic' liberatory impulse as something mystical, exterior or prior to the rational. Instead he expresses it as an immanent negativity within contemporary social organisation, a force that would combat the boredom engendered by the current relations of production, specifically by exploiting their contradiction with advancing mode of production. His methodology is indebted to Hegel and Marx, yet Debord professes his wish to overcome what he sees as the idealist error of Surrealism, arguably inherited from Hegel, precisely by seizing 'the superior technical means' of the era in order to experiment 'with new environments and behaviours.'[16] Therefore, whilst he considers 'Romantic' and subjective impulses reactionary in isolation, generalised they might act dialectically upon the mode of production, resulting in a resuscitation of history and a dissolution of the collective subject *in* and *as* the terrain of that history.[17]

Hence Debord does not reject the 'satanic' outright, yet his evocation of a satanic 'beneath' differs importantly from Romanticism. Ten years after 1968 he released the film *In girum imus nocte et consumimur igni*, titled from a Latin palindrome meaning 'we go wandering/circling at night and are consumed by fire' - an incantation known traditionally as 'The Devil's Verse'.[18] The word '*girum*' conjures up both the nocturnal drifts of the *dérive* - in the sense of the English phrase, 'to go for a turn' - but also the nefarious necromancer, drawing a protective magic circle when ritually raising up underworld spirits. Here Debord suggests the lumpen youth and social outcasts of the letterists/SI 'enlisted irrevocably in the Devil's party', becoming 'the "bad side" that makes history by undermining all established satisfaction'.[19]

The SI sought to push the contradictions between the advancing productive forces and the lagging conditions of social organisation to breaking point. As Löwy attests,[20] 'the secret of dividing what was united' of which Debord speaks, was to draw up from the spectacle a dialectical movement poetically evoked by the satanic - a critical 'historical evil which leads existing conditions to their destruction'.[21] In this much the SI attempted an ambitious, if somewhat ambiguous

---

[16] Ibid.

[17] For the debt Debord's thinking owes to Lukács, and his disagreement with the early Lukács' reading of Hegel, see Jappe, 20-43.

[18] *In girum imus nocte et consumimur igni*, dir. Guy Debord, Pairs, Simar Films, 1978, transcript in Guy Debord, *Complete Cinematic Works*, trans. Ken Knabb, Edinburgh and Oakland, CA: AK Press, 2003.

[19] Ibid.,173. The notion of the 'bad side' of history is a reference to Marx's invocation of negative dialectical progress in opposition to the affirmative stance he identified in Proudhorn - Marx here, and after him Debord, identify the negative with history itself. See Karl Marx, *Karl Marx: Selected Writings*, ed. David McLellan, Oxford: Oxford University Press, 2000, 227.

[20] Löwy, 103-4.

[21] Debord, 2003, 172-173.

compromise in which the poetic and subjective spirit of satanic revolt might be reconciled with the dialectical progressions of a more classically historical materialist account.

Fellow letterist and situationist Michèle Bernstein's thinly-disguised depiction of Debord in her détourned novella *Tous les chevaux du roi* prefigures his assertion that the letterists were 'emissaries of the Prince of division'.[22] She arguably associates him, via the character Gilles, with the wandering, satanic envoy of the 1942 film *Les Visiteurs du soir*.[23] Bernstein's darkly seductive portrait also appears to recall Rimbaud's Infernal Bridegroom in *Une Saison en Enfer*, the satanic character who can 'turn infamy into glory, cruelty into charm,' and who famously proclaims, 'I will never do any work!'[24] This strongly echoes words Debord was to immortalise in an instance of 1953 graffiti on rue de Seine – *NE TRAVAILLEZ JAMAIS* ('never work') - a slogan he self-consciously identifies with, including it in his autobiography *Panegyric*.[25] Indeed, later he describes it as his greatest offering, one that summed up the entire Situationist programme.[26] This slogan was key for the Letterist International[27] and in fact transcends a libertine refusal of work - that Rimbaudian sloth and vagabond spirit lionised in Surrealism,[28] or even an existential 'authenticity', - it arguably prefigures the development of the refusal of work as a domain of struggle within autonomist Marxist currents but also the outright rejections of a positive worker identity which followed within French ultra-leftism and beyond. For Debord, seizing 'the superior technical means' of the era would be to abolish work, hence reconstituting the already fragmentary and abstracted, subjective impulse toward play and free creation through a new unity with objective conditions.

As Baudelaire had done in the opening poem of *Les Fleurs du mal*, the SI presented an ambiguity regarding the relation between boredom and this sub-

---

[22] Ibid.

[23] See Odile Passot, 'Portrait of Guy Debord as a Young Libertine' (1999) in Michèle Bernstein, *All the King's Horses*, trans. John Kelsey, Los Angeles, CA: Semiotext(e), 2007, 123.

[24] Arthur Rimbaud, *Poems*, Peter Washington, ed., trans. Paul Schmitt, London: Everyman, 1994, 226-227.

[25] Panegyric Vol.2, in Guy Debord, *Panegyric*, trans. John McHale, London and New York, NY: Verso, 2004, 84.

[26] See Guy Debord, *Œuvres*, Paris: Gallimard, 2006.

[27] See Jean-Michel Mension, *The Tribe*, trans. Donald Nicholson-Smith, London and New York, NY: Verso, 2002.

[28] For example, Louis Aragon's 'I will never work, my hands are pure' – 'Fragments of a Lecture given in Madrid at the Residencia des Estuiantes' (1925), in Maurice Nadeau, *The History of Surrealism*, trans. Richard Howard, London: Plantin, 1987 – echoing Rimbaud's denunciation of a 'century of hands'.

jective, 'satanic' revolt. For Baudelaire, we cannot tell if the monster *Ennui* consumes us because we are at the mercy of the devil's whims, or whether in fact *Ennui* itself grants such whims their seductive power.[29] Likewise for the situationists and their proposed battle for everyday life, if 'boredom is counterrevolutionary'[30] it is also through the overcoming of boredom that revolution will occur, through 'the invention of games of an essentially new type'.[31]

However, in an attempt to go beyond existentialist diagnostics of freedom realised through struggle with angst - their success at which is debatable - for the SI this subjectivation is, as stated, the revolutionary overcoming of contradictions between productive forces and social organisation.[32] The SI saw boredom as manifesting these contradictions. As Vaneigem states, perhaps analogous to, but also politicising Baudelaire's sentiment:

> The spectacle-commodity economy produces both the conditions that repress subjectivity and – contradictorily, through the refusal it provokes – the positivity of subjectivity.[33]

If the conditions of the spectacle condemn us to boredom, boredom also provokes the dissolution of the proletariat as a specialised subjectivity, generalising the condition of proletarianisation and opening the potential for new subjectivations.

Perhaps May '68 in France became so readily associated with the SI's analysis, precisely owing to the lack of a conventionally acute capitalist crisis; wages, consumption and living standards had reached an historic high in the post-war decades. Thus the SI's diagnosis of a generalisation of the proletariat, their defining of leisure as inseparable from work, but most of all their analysis of the boredom and banality of contemporary life, appeared a feasible explanation for the unexpected and unprecedented revolt.

Understood simplistically as a subjective demand for liberty and the rejection of inauthenticity, such a reading of the SI correlates with what Boltanski and Chiapello identified as the 'bohemian' critique of capitalism evident in '68.[34] Cousin's slogan clearly suggests such an explanation, and from a characteristically Romantic position - here was a man who throughout his memoir

---

[29] Jonathan Culler, 'Baudelaire's "Satanic Verses,"' *Diacritics*, 28:3, Autumn 1998, 92.

[30] 'The Bad Days Will End', *Internationale Situationniste* 7 (1962), trans. Ken Knabb, in Ken Knabb, ed., *Situationist International Anthology*, Berkeley, CA: Bureau of Public Secrets, 112.

[31] Ibid. 39.

[32] I refer here to existentialism's programme in general rather than simply Sartre's specific engagement with Baudelaire.

[33] Raoul Vaneigem, 'Notice to the Civilized Concerning Generalized Self-Management,' *Internationale Situationniste* 12 (1969), in Knabb, 2006, 365.

[34] Luc Boltanski and Ève Chiapello, *The New Spirit of Capitalism*, London: Verso, 2005, 39.

compares the '68 rebellion to Hugo's demonic '*Djinn*'[35] and who held Vigny, Rimbaud and Baudelaire amongst his favourite writers.[36] This may explain why the slogan and '68 appear to resonate with the satanic motifs evident in the work of the SI. However, whilst symbolic resonances certainly exist between Cousin's Romantic sentiment and the SI, the SI's dialectical Satanism begins to suggest something that leads in quite another direction - off the page and onto the street.

The Cobblestones

The cobbles of the slogan are again particularly evocative of the events of May 1968, yet also the situationist programme. That the SI were interested in the streets goes without saying: psychogeography, unitary urbanism and the practice of *dérive* are amongst the most thoroughly discussed elements of their œuvre. Likewise cobblestones are also strongly resonant with '68, particularly with its radical point of escalation - the street battles during the 10th May 'Night of the Barricades'.

I have already touched upon the link between a 'dark romanticism' and the SI, something evident not least in their practice of psychogeography. Even from its beginnings, when Ivan Chtcheglov references Baudelaire and Poe in psychogeography's seminal text, his *Formulaire pour un urbanisme nouveau*,[37] there is a 'gothic' dimension to the practice. Like the surrealists before them, the SI were interested in Baudelaire's 'Old Paris' and their psychogeographic experiments flirted with the outmoded as a potential qualitative means of throwing spectacular innovations into relief.[38] Yet this deliberate archaism of psychogeography also parallels a spectre of past urban revolts that haunted '68, meeting in the symbol of the cobblestone.

Taking a cue from Engels, one might acknowledge the construction of barricades as psychogeographic architecture.[39] Ripping up cobbles to form these structures, as well as to throw at police lines, was both an evocation of the past - an attempt to escape the twentieth century via the backdoor - but also a new

---

[35] Cousin, 15. See Victor Hugo, *Les Djinns*, a poem in which a host of devilish spirits, the Jinn, attack a town and drive out its inhabitants.

[36] Bernard Cousin, personal correspondence, 24/7/12.

[37] Gilles Ivain (Ivan Chtcheglov), 'Formulary for a New Urbanism' (1953), *Internationale Situationnist* 1, (1958), in Knabb, 2006, 1-8.

[38] For example, in *In girum...* he laments 'Paris no longer exists,' echoing Baudelaire's famous statement: 'The old Paris is gone' see David Pinder, '"Old Paris is no more" Geographies of Spectacle and Anti-spectacle' *Antipode*, 32:4, 2000, 357-386.

[39] Engels argues that the building of barricades is an important psychological as well as physical tactic of urban revolt. Friedrich Engels, Introduction to, Karl Marx, *The Class Struggles in France, 1848-1850* (1895), edited by Clemens Palme Dutt, New York, NY: International Publishers, 1934, 14.

urbanism, both a psychogeographical and physical tactic. Whether barricades of '68 were initially constructed out of immediate, practical necessity or as a performative iteration of past struggles remains conjecture, yet their construction can surely be seen to conform, probably unwittingly, to the SI's notion of 'unitary urbanism' - that end goal of psychogeography. The barricades echo unitary urbanism's call for the spontaneous and collective appropriation of the built environment for the realisation of everyday life: intersubjectivation via a dialectical interaction with material form. Compare this barricade building with one-time situationist Constant's description of unitary urbanism for example:

> A deliberate intervention in the praxis of daily life and in the daily environment [...] which recognizes no goal in life, but which makes life itself the goal.[40]

This is what Alastair Bonnett labelled the 'revolutionary re-appropriation of the landscape', a certain *détournement* of urban form that took place during the May events.[41] The constructions symbolically echoed the barricades of 1848 and the Commune, which was in the words of the SI, 'the only implementation of a revolutionary urbanism to date'.[42]

Whether the symbolic resonances of the barricades motivated their construction is irrelevant. Such resonances clearly existed. Interestingly, in Baynac's version of events, the initiation of barricade building, the material appropriation of the streets, begins with boredom. Two friends, Jean-Yves Mignochon and William Panfield, park by Luxembourg in the Latin Quarter, '[t]hey are bored' states Baynac. In an attempt to uproot a sign, a cobble comes loose and soon everyone is tearing up the cobbles just 'to do something'.[43] Baynac states there is 'the idea of building a barricade [...] as in the last century', but no one does until a former Renault worker begins to help pile the cobbles. Others join and the friends slip away, discovering the rue Gay-Lussac already half-exposed.[44] Bored in the city, this psychogeographical play autonomously takes on an insurrectionary character.

Solidarity carries a similar account from rue Gay-Lussac[45] and following the night of 10th May, *Le Monde* reported that although 'it appears that the building of barricades wasn't part of [the] plan' to occupy the Latin Quarter, immediately

---

[40] Constant, *Unitary Urbanism*, lecture at Stedelijk Museum, Amsterdam, 20/12/60, trans. Robyn de Jong-Dalzeil, in Tom McDonough, ed., *The Situationists and the City*, London: Verso, 2009, 115-116.

[41] Alastair Bonnett, 'Situationism, Geography and Poststructuralism', *Society and Space* 7, 1989, 136.

[42] Guy Debord, Attila Kotányi, Raoul Vaneigem, 'On the Commune' (1962) in Knabb 2006, 399.

[43] Baynac, 79. My translation.

[44] Baynac, 79-80. My translation.

[45] Darkstar, 65.

groups began to 'tear off the fences around trees and traffic signs and use them to rip up the paving stones'.[46]

It is possible to speculate that the symbolism of such barricades, with their resonances of nineteenth century revolution, played a part in the unprecedented militancy seen that night, a militancy that in turn catalysed events that followed, particularly the escalatory strikes called in solidarity against police brutality on the following Monday 13th. The effect of the barricades on the behaviour of the combatants, though it cannot be proven, would place them firmly within the theoretical framework of a situationist psychogeography – 'the precise laws and specific effects of the geographical environment, consciously organized or not, on the emotions and behavior of individuals'.[47] In this respect, both the events of '68 and the writings of the SI appear at least associatively connected through the mediation of the cobblestone. This would perhaps account for the way in which the cobble as a symbolic object, and by extension the slogan containing it, became resonant with both.

It is also worth noting however, that the Parisian cobblestones carry a specific, historical symbolism in addition to that of the barricades. The widespread surfacing of the streets in this manner evokes Baron Haussmann's notorious nineteenth century domestication of the labyrinthine passages of Paris, widening, opening and cutting new boulevards. These boulevards functioned as both an apparatus of control and a facilitation of capital, thus arguably what these stones were for Haussmann's time, so analogously, the beach holiday became in the twentieth century. In this respect, the beach holiday never offered some authentic space, beneath, beyond or in opposition to the centralised planning of Haussmann, or for that matter, the similar approach the SI saw recast in the technocratic urban planners of their own time. It offered rather a false promise of freedom and vital authenticity, founded in false opposition to the restrictive, planned environs of capitalist urbanism. Thus it was the spatial figuration of that wider false opposition the SI identified between work and leisure. The beach by the 1960s was already equally subsumed in such a domestication of space by capital and as an apparatus of control, just as much as the newly surfaced and subdued streets had been for Haussmann. Those who saw the beach as a way out in '68 were aiming at the ideologies of another era, and thus though the situationist project has often been characterised in such terms, I would argue in fact it differed in this important regard.

---

[46] 'The Night of the Barricades', *Le Monde*, 12-13 May 1968, trans. Mitchell Abidor. Available: http://www.marxists.org/history/france/may-1968/night-barricades.htm. Accessed: 12/7/2012.

[47] Guy Debord, 'Introduction to a Critique of Urban Geography', *Les Lèvres nues* 6 (1955) in Knabb 2006, 8.

It is no overstatement to claim the slogan pivots on its comma. The weighting, the rhythm and its mnemonic quality centres upon this inconspicuous oratory pause. This was not accidental. Indeed Cousin describes how the comma was added after some reflection, as the final touch to the line.[48] Such a considered technique of writing might once have been the preserve of poets, but Cousin was of a new breed of 'poets' strongly emergent in the 1960s, those the SI equated with the 'bards of conditioning' - the marketers.[49] I propose that Cousin's background writing marketing copy is one important reason this slogan resonated with both May '68 and the SI's programme.

Sacked from his job at Les Halles, Cousin obtained work with a small advertising agency, Internote, becoming friends with its co-founder Bernard 'Killian' Fritsch. Here he studied the techniques of advertising, its subliminal messages, learning to speak to what Vaneigem called 'the ideas in everyone's minds'.[50]

Debord identified an 'ideological absence in which advertising has become the only active factor', arguably proposing that advertising had sublated ideology, both overcome and uplifted it in a Hegelian sense.[51] As early as *Internationale Situationniste #1*, the SI state they are engaged in 'a sprint between artists and the police to test and develop the use of new forms of conditioning'.[52] Yet the ambiguity they attached to such modern technologies of control is made plain seven years later:

> The path of total police-state control over all human activities and the path of unlimited free creation of all human activities are one: it is the same path of modern discoveries.[53]

Importantly, the situationist approach to spectacular alienation was not an existentialist quest for subjective authenticity, but rather about realising a revolutionary potential existent in the class position of a generalised proletariat:

---

[48] Cousin, 34.

[49] Raoul Vaneigem and Attilia Kotanyi, 'Basic Program of the Bureau of Unitary Urbanism,' *Internationale Situationniste* 6 (1961), in Knabb, 2006, 89.

[50] Raoul Vaneigem, 'Basic Banalities I', *Internationale Situationniste* 7 (1962), in Knabb, 2006, 122.

[51] Guy Debord, 'Report on the Construction of Situations' (1957) in Knabb, 2006, 32.

[52] 'The Struggle for the Control of the New Techniques of Conditioning', *Internationale Situationniste* 1 (1958), trans. Reuben Keehan. Available: http://www.cddc.vt.edu/sionline/si/struggle.html. Accessed: 14/4/2012.

[53] 'Now, the SI', in *Internationale Situationniste* 9 (1964), in Knabb, 2006, 175-6.

> We did not put our ideas 'into everyone's minds' by the exercise of some outside influence [...] we gave voice to the ideas *that were necessarily already present* in these proletarian minds.[54]

Although as in existentialist thought, subjectivation occurs through an interaction with situations, for the SI these situations could be actively created by disseminating the latest psychological tools to a generalised proletariat via 'the liberatory use of the superior technical means of our times'.[55] Spectacular alienation was something historically specific to modern society's mode of production, as was the praxis by which it would be overcome - a 'propaganda for new desires'.[56] This would be the realisation and suppression of art that Surrealism and Dada had failed to achieve. Their innovations had, as Vaneigem noted, been subsumed into advertising - as representational techniques.[57] The SI sought to invert this, and realise them in life. The superior technical means that advertising had developed, would now be used to propagate in favour of new desires.

After the eruptions around the Sorbonne, Cousin relates how his bosses at the agency confided in him their revolutionary sympathies. Killian in particular, Cousin notes, had situationist leanings. He describes his bosses as 'revolutionaries,' yet uniquely for him, 'engaged in a critique of the modern society of the sixties.'[58] He states that this caused him to listen with interest, intrigued that they sold advertising, at the same time as criticising its ends.

Cousin relates that as he and Killian became friends, Fritsch attempted to convert him to 'Situationism'. He had read a few issues of their journal, *On the Poverty of Student Life* and Vaneigem's *The Revolution of Everyday Life*, as well as delivering situationist pamphlets during the May events. However, unlike Killian, he was no 'pro-situ'.[59] Self-defining as a 'Platonist', his memoir speaks continually of his strong attraction to the metaphors of childhood, prehistory and the natural world. It was this divergence of opinion that provoked the emergence of the slogan - he recalls that he and Killian wanted to compose a piece of graffiti on which both would agree.

---

[54] Guy Debord and Gianfranco Sanguinetti, *Theses on the Situationist International and Its Time* (1972), trans. John McHale, in McHale, 2003, 9.

[55] McDonough, 2004, 68.

[56] 'The Dark Turn Ahead', *Internationale Situationniste* 2 (1958), trans. Reuben Keehan. Available: http://www.cddc.vt.edu/sionline/si/darkturn.html. Accessed: 14/7/2012.

[57] Jules Dupuis (Vaneigem), *A Cavalier History of Surrealism*, trans. Donald Nicholson-Smith. Available: http://www.cddc.vt.edu/sionline/postsi/cavalier05.html. Accessed: 14/7/2012.

[58] Cousin, 22. My translation.

[59] Cousin, personal correspondence, 24/7/2012.

The Beach

During a brainstorming session in Contrescarpe Cousin proposed the slogan '*Il y a de l'herbe sous les pavés*' [there is grass under the paving stones]. Killian rejected this however, thinking grass too naturalistic a symbol, and arguing it would be understood as referencing drugs. Cousin offered a revision, recalling students tearing up cobblestones in the clashes of Boulevard Saint-Michel: they had opened hydrants in order to counter the effects of teargas grenades and the result - the mingling of water and the sand used to bed the cobbles – created the impression of a beach. Killian accepted the revision and quickly took to spraying it on the walls around Contrescarpe and rue Bonaparte.[60] Cousin was happy to let him take it on, fearing reprisals from his professors should it be attributed to him. Thus it became associated with the 'pro-situ' Killian and so in turn became understood as a 'situationist' slogan.[61]

Cousin claims the slogan's initial incarnation derived from a childhood story, concerning a captive wolf looking mournfully at grass growing through the cracked pavement of its cage, longing for freedom. The metaphor is clear, and clearly Romantic, indeed Rousseauian. Nature - as embodied in the grass - represents a notion of liberty, authenticity and something originary that has been lost, awaiting rediscovery beneath the trappings of urban civilisation. This taps a classic mythological trope; it speaks of a garden of paradise lost, of another world beneath the mundane. Yet to equate this with the SI's ideas is inadequate, as I shall now elaborate.

Cousin states that he saw the slogan as a piece of 'maieutics'[62] - something that may seem to unite his professed Platonism, Killian's notion of 'Situationism' and advertising together - the 'giving birth' to ideas with which the mind and economic conditions are pregnant. Yet whereas for Cousin the beach continued his Romantic or Platonic idealist metaphor, evoking an underlying freedom and childhood authenticity, for the SI the beach had been subsumed into the leisure industry. Following the Second World War, the French economy had undergone a period of sustained growth that became known as 'The 30 Glorious Years' and by the 1960s the beach holiday came to symbolise an increasingly affluent consumer culture. The beach of the slogan would therefore suggest more than a return to some originary nature, importantly also bringing forth current contradictions evident in the false division of work and leisure.[63]

In fact, the beach is rarely addressed by the SI, although their hostility to tourism is frequently evident. 'The actions of Danish comrades [who] [...] re-

---

[60] Cousin, 31-4.
[61] Cousin, personal correspondence, 24/7/2012.
[62] Cousin, 34.
[63] Ibid.

sorted to incendiary bombs against the travel agencies that organize tourist voyages to Spain' is given as an example of 'acts that have our total approval'.[64] Tourism is labelled as 'violence', 'organized alienation' and 'comfortable boredom'.[65] Elsewhere Debord refers to tourism as 'that popular drug as repugnant as sports or buying on credit.'[66]

Yet one of the more interesting SI articulations of the beach comes in Bernstein's *Tous les chevaux des roi*. Here it is an ambivalent place where the boredom of bright sunlight is set against the adventures of a dark Parisian night. Yet it is also a site of play, a place for 'the invention of games of an essentially new type'.

Gilles and Geneviève, the autofiction surrogates for Debord and Bernstein, find the beach tiresome and alienating - 'a great place to sleep' claims Geneviève as they long to be back in Paris - 'I'm not such a beach person' she states.[67] Their companion however, the child-like Carole, is in her element - running, swimming, tanning and posing for invisible photographers. The beach, by implication is associated with Carole, the *jeune-fille* – that popular post-war cultural trope of a youthful, sexually available woman that so regularly adorns the pages of the SI's journal. It has been argued that for the SI this figure exemplifies capitalism's embodiment of commodification, the 'becoming-image of desire.'[68]

Just as the images of the *jeune-fille* that adorn the pages of *IS* all accompany articles addressing alienation, so the beach by extension is an analogue, of youth and subjectivation made image, alienated and spectated upon, in this case by the self-conscious characters Gilles and Geneviève. These characters are not only self-conscious as such, but also self-conscious of their status *as* characters - 'We're all characters in a novel, haven't you noticed?' Gilles says to Carole at one point.[69] This is a literary device that Bernstein uses, détourning the *roman à clef*, playing with its overlaying of fiction upon life, precisely to foreground the spectacular alienation she sees as characteristic of the *reality* of modern life. Fiction overlaying life becomes a *true* representation of modern life - that is the life of the spectacle. Carole and the beach, appearing in a novel, figure this reification.

As true representations, they sit and watch Carole play, for her part unaware of her condition as character. Like the beach, Carole self-consciously becomes, acts out, a commodified image - in her case of femininity, youth and desire. Her subjectivity expressed through reified categories, this subjectivity itself is reified, she becomes an image. She does so for them, but also for Bernstein, and by extension, for us the reader. Her subjectivity becomes a battleground that over the

---

[64] It should be noted that the context of Spanish fascism also motivates this declaration.

[65] Guy Debord, *The Situationists and the New Forms of Action in Politics or Art* (1963), trans. Thomas Y. Levin, in McDonough, 2004, 161-2.

[66] Debord, 1955, in Knabb 2006, 11.

[67] Bernstein, 61.

[68] Kelly Baum, 'The Sex of the Situationist International,' *October* 126, Fall 2008, 34.

[69] Bernstein, 80-1.

course of the novel they, Bernstein, and arguably we, work to détourn. When Carole invites them to participate in her games Gilles replies, 'it's easier watching you', 'too bad there aren't any photographers around' Geneviève adds.[70] They know they cannot indulge in this false participation; the beach is merely a representation, a site of boredom, they, and we, are spectators.

As Greil Marcus proposes, for the SI the contradictions of contemporary society manifested 'as much [through] leisure as work'.[71] Consequently, it was 'necessary to throw new forces into battle over leisure.'[72] This entailed the dialectical overcoming of both work and leisure, identified with the refusal of work, but likewise a refusal of leisure, and the invention of new games for the active, immanent creation of a post-work/post-leisure subjectivity. They can only refuse Carole's notion of play, inventing their own game - i.e. *détournement*. In this game Carole herself, the becoming-image of desire, must be détourned, being both the form and content of the game. This is the negative dialectical move of *détournement* expressed by Khayati when he states:

> Every critique of the old world has been made in the language of that world, yet directed against it and therefore automatically in a different language.[73]

This is exactly what they do to Carole from within, and what Bernstein does with her détourned *roman à clef* from without.

In the 1964 'Leisure is Working' the SI had claimed that with the development of leisure, the economy had become dependent upon 'pseudo-culture and pseudo-games' to function.[74] Tellingly, they implicate Club Med in this process. An earlier article had claimed 'the emptiness of leisure stems from the emptiness of life in present-day society', to be overcome by the 'supersession of leisure through the development of an activity of free creation-consumption'.[75] For the SI this would be achieved not in an existentialist sense, in a meeting of subjective transcendence and facticity, but only via the active praxis of the revolutionary proletariat - a proletariat generalised to include all those denied creation of their own time. Transcending the division of labour and play enables the possibility of realising oneself through the creation of the world, history or time - that is the immanent and necessarily revolutionary *détournement*, of oneself and one's environment. This demanded a qualitative not quantitative subjectivation, not

---

[70] Bernstein, 62.

[71] Greil Marcus, 'The Long Walk of the Situationist International' in McDonough, 2004, 3.

[72] Guy Debord (1957), in Knabb, 2006, 40.

[73] Mustapha Khayati, 'Captive Words (Preface for a Situationist Dictionary)', *Internationale Situationniste* 10 (1966), in Knabb, 2006, 222.

[74] 'Leisure is Working', *Internationale Situationniste* 9 (1964), trans. Thomas Y. Levin. Available: http://www.cddc.vt.edu/sionline/si/leisure.html. Accessed: 4/7/2012.

[75] 'The Use of Free Time', *Internationale Situationniste* 4 (1960), in Knabb, 2006, 75.

beyond alienation, but alienated only by time itself: 'the *necessary* alienation, the terrain where the subject realizes himself by losing himself.'[76] Liberated from the alienation of the spectacle, which is primarily the reification of time, the subject is thrown into creative motion - creating not commodities, but precisely its own time, thus abolishing the condition of its proletarianisation.

By the 1960s the spectacle had subsumed the beach. Like Gilles and Geneviève, one could only spectate upon the 'organized alienation' and 'pseudo-games' it offered, its status prior to, or beneath capital no longer accessible. In spectacular society desire had become transactional, via the general equivalent of the image.[77] As Debord would remark:

> Tourism - human circulation packaged for consumption, a by-product of the circulation of commodities ... The economic organization of travel to different places already guarantees their *equivalence*.[78]

For him, extending Marx's analysis of the commodity form to the image itself, economic organisation through image offers a false unity through general equivalence, whilst fostering a 'pseudo-community' of isolated individuals, separated from and by the *images* of their subjectivation, like workers from the commodity and from each other.[79] Like the separation of concrete labour and abstract labour, the reduction of the concrete act of living to the commensurable equivalence of the spectacle was not for them a division between some really existing authentic sphere and another false one - a real beach beneath the image of a beach - the spectacular *was* the real, a real abstraction.

The first landing on Mars will pass unnoticed on Blackpool beach

The obvious idealism of Cousin's slogan, if taken romantically, leads nowhere, being more akin to the Surrealism the SI sought to overcome. The slogan did not spark revolt, coming a full twelve days after 'The Night of the Barricades', rather it was maieutically given birth to, from ideas already in 'proletarian' minds. It resonated precisely because it expressed those contradictions between the productive forces and the form of social organisation prevalent in France at that moment – an 'estranged present', unable to give birth to its possible future.[80] Rather than speaking to an authentic imagination that would conjure beaches

---

[76] Ibid.
[77] Debord 2009, 41.
[78] Ibid., 114.
[79] Ibid.,116.
[80] Ibid.,110.

and demons yet was everywhere in chains beneath the bureaucratic drudgery of capital, it can be interpreted as exposing the *immanent* contradictions of the spectacle, which pledged historical self-production yet offered only cyclical self-consumption. It is not the authorship of this slogan but rather its resonances, which make it possible, only given the qualifications I have set out, to conceive it as situationist.

Some have placed the failure of the SI's project in the contradiction between their apprehension of the spectacle's 'real abstraction' and their affirmation of a proletarian identity, albeit newly conceived.[81] These critics understand such an affirmation as postulating a certain ineffable vitalism, arguing the SI somehow posit life as something exterior to capital - a beach beneath the cobblestones.[82] Rejecting the 'authentic', originary freedom proposed by Romanticism, they fall back upon an 'authentic' proletarian.

One could indeed interpret the SI's identification of a generalised proletariat as affirming vital labour power as the constituent ground of capital. By 1968 in France, capital had indeed extended its productive forces in a qualitatively different way - as Debord states: 'The spectacle is the stage at which the commodity has succeeded in totally colonizing social life'.[83] Arguably such an understanding might also be held to prefigure elements found in certain autonomist and ultra-left currents regarding the subsumption of social life into capitalist forms as affective and cognitive labour - the daydreams of advertisers and marketers becoming the spectacle's foot soldiers.

To concur with this admittedly plausible reading of the SI would be to postulate that the notion of 'a beach beneath' resonates because within their thought it represents a vital abundance to which capital stands as a subtractive restriction, siphoning off the creative potential surging up from below. Capital's role as a parasitic limitation encloses and redirects this power into its own valorising circuits, thus denying a generalised proletariat's ability to shape their own time and subjectivations in more autonomous ways.

Hence the 1968 crisis arose from a 'surplus of imagination', specifically in the minds, and hands, of labour - in reality, a surplus of labour power that capital could not contain and valorise. Unvalorised, this overproduction of imagination threatened to burst through, to be put into practice in incommensurable and concrete ways, escaping the equivalence of the spectacle, along with the separations it imposed. Marketers momentarily became revolutionaries.

Such a reading would propose that it was the emergent class composition itself - ideas *already* in proletarian minds - that dictated the form of struggle,

---

[81] See the work of *Théorie Communiste* and *Endnotes* in particular.

[82] Benjamin Noys, '"Avant-gardes have only one time": The SI, Communisation and Aesthetics' (conference paper at *Situationist Aesthetics: The SI, Now*, University of Sussex, 8/6/2012).

[83] Debord, 2009, 38.

and of capital's response. Capitalism reconfigured in order to save itself, further accelerating the development of forms of social organisation to contain those forces of imaginative labour that threatened to escape it. This would somewhat vindicate the SI's analysis that modern productive forces had outstripped a paternal, functionalist and bureaucratic *dirigisme*, and that an insurrectionary situation would result. Yet this situation did not produce communism, rather a new, more intensely exploitative affective capitalism in which the colonising of all social life was deepened - the slogans of marketers leading the charge.

Such a reading however, denies the positive reality of capitalist power, whilst continuing to base subjectivation on the centrality of a valorisation of vital labour power, as such making valid the critiques of the SI as problematically vitalist. Whilst this reading arguably appears to fairly reflect Vaneigem's thinking in terms of 'positivity of subjectivity', Debord saw the SI's avant-garde - and through the propaganda of desires, a *generalised* and thus *dissolved* proletariat - as an immanent dialectical negation of capitalist power and its reduction of subjectivation to equivalence via images. *Détournement* - of which the black mass is given as a telling example[84] - is fundamentally a negation, its practitioners are the 'bad side' of history. Instead of understanding the subjectivation derived from labour as a positive force to which capital is a restriction, he instead conceives of the proletariat as negation, seizing the era's 'superior technical means' *only* as the dialectical movement of its own, and thus capitalism's, abolition.[85]

Perhaps then, for all its attempted and often facetiously-caricatured theoretical rigour, it is the contradictions within the SI itself that make it vulnerable to a simplistic equation with poetic ambiguity. However, this need not be a weakness: one of many things we can learn from the SI would surely be to take both slogans and theory as tactical interventions rather than dogma, remembering that they are available for *détournement*, weapons to be fought over, not positions to be held. The cobbles are not as fixed as they might appear, and the beach, it seems, might still be realised.

References

Aragon, Louis, 'Fragments of a Lecture given in Madrid at the Residencia des Estuiantes' from *Révolution Surréaliste* 4 (1925) in Maurice Nadeau, *The History of Surrealism*, trans.Richard Howard, London: Plantin, 1987.

Ball, Edward, 'The Great Sideshow of the Situationist International', *Yale French Studies* 73, 1987, 21-37.

---

[84] Guy Debord and Gil Wolman, 'A User's Guide to Détournement' (1956) in Knabb, 2006, 17.

[85] Noys arrives at a similar interpretation of Debord's thought in Benjamin Noys, *The Persistence of the Negative*, Edinburgh: Edinburgh University Press, 2012.

Baum, Kelly, 'The Sex of the Situationist International', *October* 126, Fall 2008, 23-43.

Baynac Jacques, *Mai Retrouvé – Contribution à l'historie du movement révolutionnaire du 3 mai au 16 juin 1968*, Paris: Editions Robert Laffont, 1978.

Bernstein, Michèle, *All the King's Horses* (1960), trans. John Kelsey, Los Angeles, CA: Semiotext(e), 2007.

Boltanski, Luc and Chiapello, Ève, *The New Spirit of Capitalism*, London: Verso, 2005.

Bonnett, Alastair, 'Situationism, Geography and Poststructuralism', *Society and Space* 7, 1989, 131-146.

Breton, André, 'The Second Manifesto of Surrealism' (1929) in André Breton, *Manifestos of Surrealism*, trans. Richard Seaver and Helen R. Lane, Ann Arbor, MI: University of Michigan Press, 1972.

Constant (Nieuwenhuis), 'Unitary Urbanism' (1960), trans. Robyn de Jong-Dalziel in *The Situationists and the City*, edited by Tom McDonough, London: Verso, 2009, 112-122.

Cousin, Bernard, *Pourquoi j'ai écrit: sous les pavés la plage*, Paris: Rive Droite, 2008.

_____, 'Sous les pavés, la plage. Quarante ans après.' Available: http://users.skynet.be/ddz/mai68/temoignages/souslespaves.html. Accessed: 1/7/2012.

Culler, Jonathan, 'Baudelaire's "Satanic Verses"', *Diacritics* 28:3, Autumn, 1998, 86-100.

Dark Star, *Beneath the Paving Stones: Situationists and the Beach, May 1968*, Edinburgh and San Francisco, CA: AK Press/Dark Star, 2001.

Debord, Guy, *Comments on the Society of the Spectacle* (1988), trans. Malcolm Imrie, London and New York, NY: Verso, 1998.

_____, *Complete Cinematic Works*, trans. Ken Knabb, Edinburgh and Oakland, CA: AK Press, 2003.

_____, 'Communique from the SI concerning Vaneigem' (1970), trans. John McHale in *The real split in the International: theses on the Situationist International and its time* (1972), London: Pluto, 2003.

_____, 'Contribution to the Debate "Is Surrealism Dead or Alive?"' (1958), trans. Tom McDonough in *Guy Debord and the Situationist International: Texts and Documents*, edited by Tom McDonough, Cambridge, MA: MIT, 2004, 67-8.

_____, *The Situationists and the New Forms of Action in Politics or Art*, June 1963, trans. Thomas Y. Levin in *Guy Debord and the Situationist International: Texts and Documents*, edited by Tom McDonough, Cambridge, MA: MIT, 2004, 159-166.

———, *Panegyric*, trans. John McHale, London and New York, NY: Verso, 2004.

———, 'Introduction to a Critique of Urban Geography' in *Les Lèvres nues* 6, (September 1955), trans. Ken Knabb in *Situationist International Anthology*, edited by Ken Knabb, Berkeley, CA: Bureau of Public Secrets, 2006, 8-12.

———, 'Report on the Construction of Situations and on the International Situationist Tendency's Conditions for Organization and Action' (June 1957), trans. Ken Knabb in *Situationist International Anthology*, edited by Ken Knabb, Berkeley, CA: Bureau of Public Secrets, 2006, 25-43.

———, *Œuvres*, Paris: Gallimard, 2006.

———, *The Society of the Spectacle* (1967), trans. Ken Knabb, Eastbourne: Soul Bay Press, 2009.

Debord, Guy, Kotányi Attila, Vaneigem Raoul, 'Theses on the Paris Commune' (1962), trans. Ken Knabb in n *Situationist International Anthology*, edited by Ken Knabb, Berkeley, CA: Bureau of Public Secrets, 2006, 398-402.

Debord, Guy and Sanguinetti, Gianfranco, *Theses on the Situationist International and Its Time* (1972), trans. John McHale in *The real split in the International: theses on the Situationist International and its time* (1972), London: Pluto, 2003.

Debord, Guy and Wolman, Gil, 'A User's Guide to Détournement' *Les Lèvres nues* 8 (May 1956), trans. Ken Knabb in *Situationist International Anthology*, edited by Ken Knabb, Berkeley, CA: Bureau of Public Secrets, 2006, 14-21.

Engels, Friedrich, Introduction to, Karl Marx, *The Class Struggles in France, 1848-1850* (1895), Clemens Palme Dutt, ed., New York, NY: International Publishers, 1934, 14.

Ivain, Gilles (Ivan Chtcheglov), 'Formulary for a New Urbanism' (1953), *Internationale Situationnist* 1 (June 1958), trans. Ken Knabb in *Situationist International Anthology*, edited by Ken Knabb, Berkeley, CA: Bureau of Public Secrets, 2006, 1-8.

Jappe, Anselm, *Guy Debord*, Berkeley, CA: University of California Press, 1999.

Joffrin, Laurent, *Mai 68: Historie des Événements*, Paris: Éditions du Seuil, 1988.

Khayati, Mustapha, 'Captive Words (Preface for a Situationist Dictionary)', *Internationale Situationniste* 10 (March 1966), trans. Ken Knabb in *Situationist International Anthology*, edited by Ken Knabb, Berkeley, CA: Bureau of Public Secrets, 2006, 222-8.

Löwy, Michael, 'Consumed by Night's Fire - The Dark Romanticism of Guy Debord', trans. Marie Stewart, in Michael Löwy, *Morning Star*, Austin, TX: University of Texas Press, 2009, 97-104.

Marcus, Greil, 'The Long Walk of the Situationist International' in *Guy Debord and the Situationist International: Texts and Documents*, edited by Tom McDonough, Cambridge, MA: MIT, 2004, 1-20.

Mension, Jean-Michel, *The Tribe*, trans. Donald Nicholson-Smith, London: Verso, 2002.

'The Night of the Baricades,' *Le Monde*, 12-13 May 1968, trans. Mitchell Abidor. Available: http://www.marxists.org/history/france/may-1968/night-barricades.htm. Accessed: 12/7/2012.

'Now, the SI', *Internationale Situationiste* 9 (1964), trans. Ken Knabb in *Situationist International Anthology*, edited by Ken Knabb, Berkeley, CA: Bureau of Public Secrets, 2006, 174-8.

Noys, Benjamin, *The Persistance of the Negative – A Critique of Contemporary Continental Theory*, Edinburgh: Edinburgh University Press, 2012.

Passot, Odile, 'Portrait of Guy Debord as a Young Libertine' (1999), trans. Paul Lafarge, reproduced as the afterword to Michèle Bernstein, *All the King's Horses*, trans. John Kelsey, Los Angeles, CA: Semiotext(e), 2007, 113-143.

Pinder, David, '"Old Paris is no more" Geographies of Spectacle and Anti-spectacle' in *Antipode* 32:4, 2000, 357-86.

Plant, Sadie, *The Most Radical Gesture*, London: Routledge, 1992.

Rimbaud, Arthur, *Poems*, edited by Peter Washington, trans. Paul Schmitt, London: Everyman, 1994.

Ross, Kristin, 'Establishing Consensus: May '68 in France as Seen from the 1980s', *Critical Inquiry* 28:3, Spring 2002, 650-76.

Unsigned, 'Leisure is Working', *Internationale Situationniste* 9 (August 1964), trans. Thomas Y. Levin. Available: http://www.cddc.vt.edu/sionline/si/leisure.html. Accessed 4/7/2012.

_____, 'The Bad Days Will End' *Internationale Situationniste* 7 (April 1962), trans. Ken Knabb in *Situationist International Anthology*, edited by Ken Knabb, Berkeley, CA: Bureau of Public Secrets, 2006, 107-114.

_____, 'The Dark Turn Ahead', *Internationale Situationniste* 2 (Dec 1958), trans. Reuben Keehan. Available: http://www.cddc.vt.edu/sionline/si/darkturn.html. Accessed 14/4/2012.

_____, 'The Struggle for the Control of the New Techniques of Conditioning', *Internationale Situationniste* 1 (June 1958), trans. Reuben Keehan. Available: http://www.cddc.vt.edu/sionline/si/struggle.html. Accessed 14/4/2012.

_____, 'The Use of Free Time' *Internationale Situationniste* 4 (June 1960), trans. Ken Knabb in *Situationist International Anthology*, edited by Ken Knabb, Berkeley, CA: Bureau of Public Secrets, 2006, 74-6.

Vaneigem, Raoul (Jules Dupuis), *A Cavalier History of Surrealism* (1970), trans. Donald Nicholson-Smith. Available: http://www.cddc.vt.edu/sionline/postsi/cavalier05.html. Accessed 14/7/2012.

_____, 'Basic Banalities I', *Internationale Situationniste* 7 (April 1962), trans. Ken Knabb in *Situationist International Anthology*, edited by Ken Knabb, Berkeley, CA: Bureau of Public Secrets, 1981, 117-130.

Vaneigem, Raoul and Kotanyi Attilia, 'Basic Program of the Bureau of Unitary Urbanism', *Internationale Situationiste* 6 (Aug 1961), trans. Ken Knabb in *Situationist International Anthology*, edited by Ken Knabb, Berkeley, CA: Bureau of Public Secrets, 1981, 86-90.

Vidalie, Anne, 'Sous les pavés, les slogans', *L'Express*, 30 April 2008. Available: http://www.lexpress.fr/actualite/politique/sous-les-paves-les-slogans_458376.html. Accessed 4/7/2012.

Viénet, René, *Enragés et situationnistes dans le mouvement des occupations*, Paris: Gallimard, 1968.

Wark, McKenzie, *The Beach Beneath the Street: The Everyday Life and Glorious Times of the Situationist International*, London and New York, NY: Verso, 2011.

2.

DEVANT LA MER:
THRESHOLDS OF FICTION AND THEORY

Patrick ffrench

Il y a beaucoup de gens qui se promènent au bord de la mer, qui tournent vers la mer des visages printaniers, poétiques […] Les hommes s'embrassent sans se connaître, les jours de déclaration de guerre ; ils se sourient à chaque printemps. Un prêtre s'avance à pas lents, en lisant son bréviaire. Par instants il lève la tête et regarde la mer d'un air approbateur : la mer aussi est un bréviaire, elle parle de Dieu. Couleurs légères, légers parfums, âmes de printemps. « Il fait beau, la mer est verte, j'aime mieux ce froid sec que l'humidité. » Poètes ! […] Je leur tourne le dos, je m'appuie des deux mains à la balustrade. La vraie mer est froide et noire, pleine de bêtes ; elle rampe sous cette mince pellicule verte qui est faite pour tromper les gens. Les sylphes qui m'entourent s'y sont laissé prendre : ils ne voient que la mince pellicule, c'est elle qui prouve l'existence de Dieu. Moi je vois le dessous.[1]

Le développement de la publicité, de la grande presse, de la radio, de l'illustration, sans parler de la survivance d'une infinité de rites communicatifs (rites du paraître social) rend plus urgent que jamais la constitution d'une science sémiologique, Combien, dans une journée, de champs véritablement *insignifiants* parcourons-nous? Bien peu, parfois aucun. Je suis là, devant la mer : sans doute, elle ne porte aucun message. Mais sur la plage, quel matériel sémiologique ! Des drapeaux, des slogans, de panonceaux, des vêtements, une bruniture même, qui me sont autant de messages.[2]

---

[1] Jean-Paul Sartre, *La Nausée*, Paris: Gallimard, 1938, 175. 'There are many people strolling along the seafront, turning springtime, poetic faces toward the sea […] Strangers kiss each other on days when war is declared; when Spring arrives they smile at each other. A priest moves along, reading his breviary. Sometimes he raises his head and looks at the sea with an approving air: the sea is also a breviary; it speaks of God. Light colours, light scents, springtime souls. "It's fine weather, the sea is green, I prefer this crisp cold to humidity." What poets! […] I turn my back to them and lean against the balustrade with both hands. The true sea is cold and black, full of beasts: it crawls beneath this thin green film, there to fool people. The sylphs around me have been taken in: they only see the thin film; it's what proves the existence of God. I see what is underneath.' All translations are my own.

[2] Roland Barthes, *Mythologies*, Paris: Seuil, 1957, 97. 'The development of advertising, of the national Press, radio, graphics, not to mention the persistence of an infinity of rituals of communication (rituals of social appearance), makes the constitution of a semiological science more urgent than ever. In the space of a day, how many truly *non-signifying* fields do we encounter? Scarcely any; sometimes none at all. I am there, by the sea: doubtless it does not carry any message. But on the beach, what a wealth of signifying material! Flags, slogans, banners, clothes, even the different levels of tan,

> Si ces dispositions venaient à disparaître comme elles sont apparues, par quelque événement dont nous pouvons tout au plus pressentir la possibilité, mais dont nous ne connaissons pour l'instant encore ni la forme ni la promesse, elles basculaient, comme le fit au tournant du XVIIIe siècle le sol de la pensée classique, – alors on peut bien parier que l'homme s'effacerait, comme à la limite de la mer un visage de sable.[3]

> Nous n'avons pas libéré la sexualité, mais nous l'avions, exactement, portée à la limite : limite de notre conscience, de notre inconscience ; limite de la loi, puisqu'elle apparaît comme le seul contenu absolument universel de l'interdit ; limite de notre langage : elle dessine la ligne d'écume de ce qu'il peut tout juste atteindre sur le sable du silence.[4]

The four epigraphs cited above establish the beach or the shore as the site of a threshold at which a troubled negotiation takes place, between the material truth of existence and the comforting illusion of anthropocentric projection, between an apparent absence of meaning and a plenitude of signifiers, between language and silence. This threshold is also the site of a series of tensions between different epistemologies, corresponding to the broad movements of what would come to be called existentialism, or to be more precise an existentialist humanism, and structuralism. These tensions were to play themselves out in the chronological gap which opens between the first epigraph, from Sartre's novel *La Nausée*, published in 1938, and those from Barthes and Foucault, which date from 1957 to 1966, the 'high point' of the 'anti-humanist' moment of structuralism. The implications of these tensions and differences extend evidently far beyond what it is possible to convey within the space of this essay, and it is not my intention to propose absolutely clear-cut distinctions between different philosophical standpoints. However it is possible, I would suggest, to attend to the differences of viewpoint and structure which arise from an analysis of similar figures or metaphors; a micro-analysis of the poetics of theory can contribute to a more detailed and complex understanding of broader philosophical and intellectual positions. My intention in this article is thus to map the differences between these thresholds and the epistemologies that they imply. The extract from Sartre's *La Nausée* will function primarily as a counterpoint in order to

---

which are all messages for me.'

[3] Michel Foucault, *Les Mots et les choses*, Paris: Gallimard, 1966, 398. 'If these arrangements were to disappear as they arrived, through some event of which we may be able to sense the possibility, without knowing for the moment either what form it will take or what it will bring, if they were to be overturned, as was the ground of Classical thought at the turn of the 18th century, then one could wager that the figure of man would be effaced, like a face drawn in sand at the edge of the sea.'

[4] Michel Foucault, 'Préface à la transgression' in *Dits et écrits I*, Paris: Gallimard, 'Quarto', 2001, 261. 'We have not liberated sexuality, but we have, to be more precise, brought it to the limit, the limit of our consciousness, of our unconscious, the limit of the law, since it appears as the only absolutely universal matter of taboo; the limit of our language, it designates the line of foam of what it can barely reach on the sand of silence.'

bring into relief the later positions of Barthes and Foucault, and thus to indicate the broad chronological shift between Sartrean existentialism and the structuralist currents to which Barthes and Foucault may be provisionally attached. Elements of continuity may also be identified, however, particularly as concerns the status of metaphorical and literal language. The outline of the philosophical divergence between existentialism and structuralism, as well as the difference between the genre of fiction and of 'theory' becomes blurred as one begins to consider the tensions within language between metaphor and literality. The beach or shoreline as literal and/or as metaphor also becomes the site of threshold on which the lines between metaphor and literality are crossed and blurred, and this affords the opportunity for a closer look at the context of Barthes and Foucault's interventions, and the extent to which fictional, poetic, semiological and philosophical genres inform each other and position a distinctive intertextual network.

While mindful of the limitations of taking the extract from Sartre's *La Nausée* out of context, and of considering it as a straightforward expression of a philosophy, we can briefly indicate some of the basic parameters of the threshold it establishes. The intradiegetic narrator of *La Nausée*, Roquentin, draws a clear opposition between the image of the sea projected by the bourgeois inhabitants of Trouville and the supposed 'knowledge' of the 'true sea', which the narrator 'sees'. The contrast is starkly established between the stereotypical and 'poetic' image of the sea, which speaks reassurance back to those who seek reassurance in it, and the 'underneath' of the sea which is full of animal life. This contrast is counter-intuitive; despite his hatred of the 'poetry' of the social stereotype, Roquentin's description of it also relies on metaphors which convey a 'poetic' sensibility. If the sea is a 'bréviaire' [breviary] for the passing priest who Roquentin despises, his own account of it also endows it with a kind of menacing agency, 'elle rampe' [it crawls]. Literal language is also not certain, and is open to dispute; 'Il fait beau, la mer est verte' [It's fine weather, the sea is green] is directly opposed by 'La vraie mer est froide et noire' [The true sea is cold and black]. An opposition is established between the surface of the sea, 'la mince pellicule verte' [the thin green film] and what is underneath, 'le dessous'. A contrast between two different 'ways of seeing' is established – the first limited to the surface of things, but in Roquentin's eyes illusory, and repressive of truth and reality, the second a form of vision which knows the truth underneath. Both are equally projective, equally characterized by the capacity of the imagination to go beyond perception in grasping the object in its totality, through analogy.[5]

The position of the viewpoint here, Roquentin at the balustrade, allows the expression of a divergence of attitudes, one which remains within the limits of established discursive constructions, and another which claims to express a tru-

---

[5] See Jean-Paul Sartre's *L'Imaginaire* (1940) for his account of the analogical operation of the imagination.

er grasp of the real. The 'true' sea is proposed as divergent from the religious or aesthetic, humanizing meanings that are projected onto it. Roquentin's position is the anchoring point of a divergence between two distinct visions of the real, one which is attacked as hypocritically reassuring, and another which claims to see the truth, but is no less based in the imagination of an identifiable subject.

In a footnote to the essay 'Le Mythe aujourd'hui', appended to the entries on individual myths collected in *Mythologies*, Barthes also indicates the beach as the site of a threshold, here between meaning and non-meaning. While the beach offers a plethora of signifying fields, the sea itself is hesitantly ('sans doute') designated as not bearing any message. What is striking is the manner in which Barthes's text (unintentionally) reprises the viewpoint of Sartre's Roquentin while also situating it in a chronological context which one might suggest to be specific to the contemporary moment – the development of advertising, or what Kristin Ross has referred to as 'the colonization of everyday life' that took place in the 1950s in France.[6] But Barthes's footnote does not restrict his perspective to this context (thus within the limits of a sociology of publicity) since he also adds to the reference to contemporary developments a reference to the persistence of social rituals, 'rites du paraître social'. This allows us to connect Barthes's situation 'au bord de la mer' to Roquentin's position via another route, since the situation Barthes alludes to is not thereby restricted to the slogans, advertisments and verbal messages of contemporary consumption, but also to the clothing and tan of the beach's visitors, which communicates aspects of social class and belonging, and moreover, to the very fact of being 'au bord de la mer'.

'Se promener au bord de la mer' [to stroll beside the sea] and 'être au bord de la mer' [to be beside the sea] pertain in both cases to a social ritual, a 'myth' in Barthes's sense, whereby the evidence of the senses is overlaid by a second-order discursive construction perpetuating a static vision of the world fixed as 'natural'. What both Sartre and Barthes's accounts suggest is the myth of certain 'being beside the sea'-ness, to which Sartre opposes an almost hallucinatory vision of the sea's material and physical reality. Unlike Sartre, Barthes does not explicitly propose an 'antidote' to the myth, but hints at an outside to the semiological plenitude of the beach. The opposition is differently structured; whereas Roquentin's vision relies on a capacity to imagine freed from reified anthropocentric constructions, but no less centred in a subject, Barthes' footnote implies a spectrum of semiological density; the beach is full of semiological material, while the sea's capacity to offer meaning, to 'carry messages' is limited. There is a reversal of agency; in Sartre's phenomenologically framed account, the subject has a certain intentionality with respect to what s/he sees; the imagination is projective and intentional with regard to its object. For Barthes, at this point, the subject is the receiver of a message; Barthes explodes the subject-centred

---

[6] Kristin Ross, *Fast Cars, Clean Bodies: Decolonization and the Re-ordering of French Culture*, Minneapolis, MN: MIT, 1996.

world implied in Sartre's fictional account into a dispersed semiological field in which the subject is merely a point of arrival and of relay. So while both Barthes and Sartre seek to establish a critical distance with regard to the bourgeois stereotype of being beside the sea, the parameters have been shifted; if for Sartre's Roquentin this critical capacity is derived from a more mobile and less constrained imaginative subjectivity, Barthes's derives it more neutrally from the activity of semiological and mythological analysis. Barthes hesitates, however, between situating the shore as a threshold between meaning and an absence of meaning, and a view of the entire field as a multiplicity of signifying messages, in other words as text. This hesitation leaves the field open, as it were, for a less subjectively-anchored vision of the sea, which does not construe it as 'other' or as 'outside' to the firm ground of reason and certainty.

The two citations from Foucault establish a different position. The first is well known, and oft-cited as evidence of the attachment of Foucault's work of the 1960s to the current of anti-humanist thought, of which the major critical target is the existentialist humanism of Sartre. It is the final paragraph of Foucault's 1966 bestseller *Les Mots et les choses* and concludes the account of the discursive structures of the human sciences with this quasi-prophetic (and Nietzschean) announcement of the future 'death of Man'. It makes this announcement by way of a metaphor which situates the beach as the threshold at which 'man' as an epistemically determined discursive figure will be superseded. If the trope designates 'man' as a face drawn in the sand, it thus brings into play a number of associations: the very notion of a figure, a tracing, an inscription, the provisional and transient nature of such a mark, and the effacement affected by the waves. The metaphorical status of the image does not, however, allow one to determine precisely the epistemological structure Foucault postulates here. As befits the de-centering effect of Foucault's thought in the wider sense, the trope does not determine the agencies at play, either the agent of the figure's tracing nor of its dispersal; both are anonymised, and the nature of the 'event' which will induce this dissolution is also indeterminate. At first glance one might suppose that Foucault postulates that 'man' is a temporary construction that will be dispersed in the relentlessly transformative flux of nature, that Foucault thus conceives of nature as an 'outside' to discourse. The basis of the metaphor is evidently the effect of effacement - the concept of 'man' will be effaced as would a face drawn in sand at the edge of the sea. But whereas we know that what would cause such a figure to dissipate would be the waves encroaching on the sand, Foucault's metaphor leaves undetermined the agent of dispersal on the conceptual side of the simile.

The metaphor of effacement by the waves is, moreover, not an isolated occurrence in Foucault's text; it takes place within the context of an extended reflection on the contemporary moment as approaching the limit of an 'arrangement' [*ces dispositions*] of thought, in which a number of textual tropes prepare for this final word. The discussion revolves around the issue of the threshold [*seuil*], and suggests that while the threshold between classicism and modernity, or as Foucault qualifies this chronology - between our prehistory and that which is still contemporary to us - has been definitively crossed, another threshold may be on the horizon. The motif of the horizon places us again on the shoreline, as Foucault writes:

> Ce qui s'est passé à l'époque de Ricardo, de Cuvier, et de Bopp, cette forme de savoir qui s'est instaurée avec l'économie, la biologie et la philologie, la pensée de la finitude que la critique kantienne a prescrite comme tâche à la philosophie, tout ceci forme encore l'espace immédiat de notre réflexion. Nous pensons en ce lieu. Et pourtant l'impression d'achèvement et de fin, le sentiment sourd qui porte, anime notre pensée, l'endort peut-être ainsi de la facilité de ses promesses, et qui nous fait croire que quelque chose de nouveau est en train de commencer *dont on ne soupçonne qu'un trait léger de lumière au bas de l'horizon*, ce sentiment et cette impression ne sont peut-être pas mal fondés.[7]

Foucault's diagnosis of an 'impression' that something is drawing to the close and of the distant imminence of something else on the horizon follows a consideration of Mallarmé and Nietzsche, in which the closure of an epoch and the imminence of something else is framed as a question about language. If Nietzsche asks of philosophy the question 'who is speaking' [*qui parle*]?, seeking thus to interrogate not the meaning but the will embodied in words, Mallarmé, Foucault postulates, responds to this question with his own *effacement*, seeking thus to answer that what speaks is language itself:

> L'entreprise de Mallarmé pour enfermer tout discours possible dans la fragile épaisseur du mot, dans cette mince et matérielle ligne noire tracée par l'encre sur le papier, répond au fond à la question que Nietzsche prescrivait à la philosophie.[8]

The motifs of a 'fragile' tracing or inscription and of effacement appear here with specific reference to the figure of the author, a focus Foucault would pick up four years later in the essay 'Qu'est-ce qu'un auteur?' but more significantly perhaps in the figure of the subject who is effaced or dissolved in the process of writing,

---

[7] Foucault, *Les Mots et les choses*, 396. My emphasis. 'What happened at the time of Ricardo, Cuvier, and Bopp, the form of knowledge that was installed with economics, biology and philology, the thought of finitude which the Kantian critique had prescribed as the task of philosophy, all of this still forms the immediate space of our own reflections. We think in this place. And yet the impression of closure and of immanent ending, the unspoken feeling which carries and animates our thinking perhaps dupes it too with the ease of its promises, making us believe that something new is beginning, something of which we only just glimpse a slight sliver of light at the edge of the horizon; this feeling and this impression are perhaps not unfounded.'

[8] Ibid., 316. 'Mallarmé's endeavour to enclose all possible discourses in the fragile dimensions of the word, in the slim materiality of the black line traced by ink on paper, is at bottom a response to the question Nietzsche prescribed for philosophy.'

Mallarmé's famous 'disparition élocutoire du poète' [elocutory disappearance of the poet].[9] If Foucault then says that '[…] il se pourrait bien que toutes ces questions se posent aujourd'hui dans la distance jamais comblée entre la question de Nietzsche et la réponse que lui fit Mallarmé', it appears that Mallarmé's response indicates the edge or the threshold of the epoch of which Foucault senses the approaching end.[10] The threshold appears then not as between discourse and something outside it, far less as human culture vis-à-vis a 'nature' which will envelop and dissolve the figure of man. It appears rather as a threshold between an epoch which attempts to situate the finitude of thought in relation to a finite subject in the absence of God, the epoch of 'Kantian critique' as Foucault puts it, and an epoch in which this subject is dissolved in the infinite folds of language liberated from an 'author' or subject, and now dispersed in: 'cette région informe, muette, insignifiante où le langage peut se libérer.'[11]

This allows us to situate the threshold that is at stake here in the context of a more chronologically precise interrogation of what Foucault refers to as 'l'être du langage' (the being of language). We can suggest that the shoreline, the threshold, on which the figure of 'man' is beginning to be effaced, while it may cover the whole stretch from Mallarmé and Nietzsche to Foucault's contemporaneity, may also be construed as covering a more localised chronological period, arbitrarily located between Barthes' intimation of the non-signifying being of the sea, in the 1957 footnote to *Mythologies* discussed above, and Foucault's conclusion to *Les Mots et les choses* in 1966. Since the points of reference in relation to which Foucault maps out the trajectory of this interrogation of language are primarily literary (a recurrent litany of marginal or 'limit-texts' including Mallarmé, Artaud, Roussel, Surrealism, Kafka, Bataille and Blanchot) it makes

---

[9] Michel Foucault, 'Qu'est ce qu'un auteur' in *Dits et écrits I*, 817. The opening sentence of this article, 'Qu'importe qui parle?' [Why does it matter who is speaking?], which Foucault draws from Beckett, extends the question proposed in the final pages of *Les Mots et les choses*, but it also relates to an interrogation which underlies the period of the 1960s in general among a loose group of writers focused on the implications of literature and its 'space' for the central assumptions of a metaphysics of the subject. Some further punctual points of intersection can be indicated in order to suggest the (incomplete) span of this epistemic focus: Barthes opens his 1960 essay 'Ecrivains et écrivants' with the question 'Qui parle? Qui écrit?'; the same question, addressed to Balzac's novella *Sarrasine* opens his celebrated 'La Mort de l'auteur' ten years later; a special issue of the review *Cahiers confrontation* of 1989 collected responses from a number of prominent philosophical figures (including Gilles Deleuze, Jacques Derrida, and Jean-François Lyotard) to the question – or proposition 'Après le sujet, qui vient' which also featured Maurice Blanchot's more enigmatic re-phrasing of the question as 'Qui?' *Cahiers Confrontation* 20 (Winter 1989).

[10] Foucault, *Les Mots et les choses*, 317. 'It is possible that all of these questions being asked today exist in the always open distance that separates Nietzsche's question from the answer given by Mallarmé.'

[11] Ibid., 395. 'This unformed, mute and non-signifying region in which language can free itself.'

sense to look more closely at the literary context of this chronological bracket 1957 to 1966, as a restricted and focused context of the threshold which is at stake.

The distinction Barthes tendentiously draws between the semiotic plenitude of material on the beach, and the absence of signification of the sea might in the first instance be connected to his investigation in the early 1950s of 'le degré zéro de l'écriture' [zero degree of writing], a late tendency of literature towards its own destruction in 'l'absence de tout signe' [the absence of all signs].[12] This also finds a resonance in a series of critical essays on the novels of Alain Robbe-Grillet in the mid-1950s, in which he focuses on what he sees as an 'objective' or 'literal' practice of writing resistant to analogy and thereby restricted to the visual surface of things. Robbe-Grillet had emerged in the early 1950s as the pioneer of a practice of writing which resisted analogy and introspection in favour of an apparently 'flat' and objective mode of writing, an aspect of what became known as the movement of the *Nouveau Roman*, in which Robbe-Grillet was grouped with Nathalie Sarraute, Robert Pinget, Claude Simon and Samuel Beckett. It is in Robbe-Grillet's early novels, however (*Les Gommes*, 1953; *Le Voyeur*, 1955; *La Jalousie*, 1957) that this mode of 'objective' writing is most prominent. In 'Littérature objective' for example, Barthes writes that in *Les Gommes* the reduction of the object to its bare existence, its *être-là*, has as a consequence 'la mise entre parenthèses' [the bracketing] of interiority.[13] We can infer from this that Roquentin's vision of 'le dessous' would be refused by Robbe-Grillet and by his narrators, whose viewpoint would indeed be restricted to the visual 'pellicule' [film] of the sea's surface. However in 'Littérature litérale', written a year later, on *Le Voyeur*, Barthes proposes that there is nevertheless a fault-line [*une faille*] in this apparently purely objective vision, which intrudes through the fact of the repetition of certain objects, their *re*-presentation.[14] In this instance the objects cease to be simply there, and become there for some purpose: 'la répétition et la conjonction dépouillent [les objets] de leur *être-là*, pour leur revêtir d'un *être-pour-quelque-chose*'.[15] This 'quelque chose' implies the (hidden) presence of a consciousness *for* which the objects serve a purpose or express a pathology. Thus the psychology of the intentional subject seeps back into the text: 'L'irruption d'un retour, c'est la brèche par où tout un ordre psychologique, pathologique, anecdotique, va menacer d'investir le roman'.[16] We are potentially back with Roquentin at the balustrade. However, Barthes identi-

---

[12] Roland Barthes, *Le Degré zéro de l'écriture*, Paris: Seuil, 1953, 10.

[13] Roland Barthes, *Essais critiques*, Paris: Seuil, 1964, 36.

[14] Ibid., 66.

[15] Ibid., 66. 'Repetition and conjunction relieve objects of their "being there" to re-adorn them with a "being for something"'.

[16] Ibid., 'The irruption of a return is the breach through which a whole psychological, pathological and anecdotal order will threaten to invest the novel.'

fies an important distinction in the profile of repetition in Robbe-Grillet's text, through which the reference back to a grounding subject or consciousness is rendered more ambivalent. The absence of focalisation in Robbe-Grillet's texts [*l'absence de foyer*] constitutes re-iteration as an act and as a process, rather than as expression or symbolization of a pre-existent reality: 'les constellations d'objets ne sont pas expressive, mais créatrices [...] elles ont un rôle dynamique, non euristique'.[17] This offers a purchase for a view of Robbe-Grillet's work as a textual production rather than as psychological revelation, a perspective which will develop in Barthes' criticism throughout the next decade to coalesce in the concept of the Text.

In a slightly later moment of the early 1960s we see a parallel development in several articles by Foucault on literature, a focus relatively unique in his work, but crucial in its evolution. Prominent among these works is an essay from 1963 ostensibly on the enormously influential but at that time somewhat marginal writer Georges Bataille, in a collection subtitled 'Hommage à Georges Bataille' and from which our fourth and final epigraph, and the title of this volume, is taken. Foucault's aim here foreshadows his later critique, in the first volume of the *Histoire de la sexualité, La Volonté de savoir* (1976), of the 'repressive hypothesis', in the proposition that far from previously being withdrawn from open expression and now being brought into the light, in the pre-modern, and Christian, world of 'des corps déchus et du péché', sexuality was the object of an impressive 'bonheur d'expression'. Conversely, sexuality has now become the domain of the limit: the limit of the law, since it is around sexuality that the only fully universal taboo may be identified; the limit of our consciousness, since, moreover, it is - after psychoanalysis - the only possible content we may read in our unconscious; the limit of our language, and since it is in and around sexuality that the limit of what it is possible to say is drawn. The key distinction between the two epochs for Foucault resides in the fact that whereas in the Christian era the discourse on sexuality took place with reference to nature, within the limits of a reference to nature, in our time [*dans l'experience contemporaine*], it is 'denaturalised', and thus placed within an empty space, without reference to a grounded conception of nature or of morality. We see thus a similar displacement from the fixed vantage point of a rational (or pathological) subjectivity as outlined above. What is particularly striking here, however, is the apparent reversal of perspective embodied in the metaphor, relative to that proposed at the end of *Les Mots et les choses*, or by Barthes in *Mythologies*. Rather than constituting the threshold between discourse – the discursive construction of the figure of 'man', for example, and its other or outside in a world that is insignificant, or purely 'there', the metaphor proposes the waves of the sea as encroaching on the sand of silence. The metaphor does not allow us to situate a perspective or a viewpoint

---

[17] Ibid., 'The constellations of objects are not expressive, but creative; they have a dynamic not a heuristic role.'

from which the sea is construed as a monstrous or meaningless expanse, but construes the land on which it advances as bearing the limit of language.[18] If the focus of the metaphors – 'figure de sable' [face drawn in the sand], and 'ligne d'écume' [line of foam] are different, one privileging effacement, the other the trace of a limit, both suggest the sea and its waves as a discursivity minus subjectivity, a 'process without a subject'. Taken together they suggest a consistent metaphorical thread which underlies other propositions, both in the relatively restricted context of Foucault's writing on literature, but also in his wider and longer term conception of discourse as 'anonymous murmur'.[19]

This shift pertains to the position of the writer him or herself, no longer observing like Roquentin from the balustrade, nor like Barthes facing the sea as silent or insignificant other, but immersed in the waves, as part of their anonymous recurrence. This seems to resonate with the role Foucault ascribes to literature in these essays of the early 1960s - to withdraw language from the fixed structures of epistemically defined discourses and to allow, through a kind of interior doubling of language upon itself, the being of language to be revealed as an infinite, and as lacking a transcendent subject. In 'Le Langage à l'infini', for example, he writes of literature as 'une murmure qui se reprend et se raconte et se redouble sans fin', 'selon une multiplication et un épaississement fantastiques où se loge et se cache notre langage d'aujourd'hui'.[20] The recurrent motif here is the notion of an interior doubling, which philosopher Gilles Deleuze makes a

---

[18] Foucault hints at a quasi-phenomenological reading of the poetics of water in a short article of 1963 on 'L'Eau et la folie', in which he writes: 'La déraison, elle, a été aquatique depuis le fond des temps et jusqu'à un date assez rapprochée. Et plus précisément océanique : espace infini, incertain, figures mouvantes, aussitôt effacées, ne laissant derrière elles qu'un mince sillage et une écume ; tempêtes ou temps monotone: routes sans chemin', *Dits et écrits I*, 292 ['Unreason has itself been acquatic since the depths of time and up to a relatively recent date']. On the one hand this draws on the same kind of phenomological analysis practised by Barthes in *Mythologies* (in 'Le vin et le lait', for example) and, earlier, by Gaston Bachelard in such works as *La Poétique de l'espace* and *L'Eau et les rêves*, while extending its scope to point to the ways in which such 'poetic' associations are materialized in clinical or punitive practices exercised on the bodies of the insane, and disassociating the thematics of substances and elements from any natural, essential or phenomenological grounding. On the other hand, it points to a potential divergence within Foucault's writing, analytically attentive to the use and abuse of analogical associations in social discourse and practice on the one hand, yet employing such analogies himself. My point here is that while Foucault is very aware of the 'aquatic' and 'oceanic' metaphor for madness and seems thus to distance himself from it, he uses a similar trope to designate the unregulated discursivity which will one day erase the figure of man.

[19] The notion and the expression of the 'anonymous murmur' of discourses is recurrent in Foucault's work, especially around the period of *Les Mots et les choses*. See, for example, the interview with Raymond Bellour, 'Entretien: Michel Foucault, *Les Mots et les choses*', *Les Lettres françaises*, 1125 (March 31, 1966).

[20] Foucault, 'Le Langage à l'infini' in *Dits et écrits I*, 280. '(A) murmur that repeats itself and tells itself and doubles itself endlessly'; 'in a fantastic multiplication and thickening in which our own contemporary language resides and is hidden.'

prominent motif of his book *Foucault*, and which explains Foucault's interest in and frequent reference to the writer Raymond Roussel, whose apparently fantastic narratives were shadowed by a typographic double.[21] Foucault also emphasizes this point in an essay on the novels and poetry of the writers associated with the review *Tel Quel* when he remarks that while these works may be seen to fall under the shadow of the work of Robbe-Grillet, they give it a 'different articulation', no longer determined by the oppositional play of perception and imagination, but taking place as a doubling of perception and language at the point of origin, which he calls 'l'identité buissonnante du Même au point de sa bifurcation'.[22] This proposes a different epistemological and ontological structure to that of a subject vis-à-vis an other or outside, displacing the essentially dialectical dynamic of Same or self and Other with a notion of immanent and productive difference.[23] This is a space of folds, relays and intermediaries rather than a divided space between perception and dream, or perception and imagination.[24] The analogical association of the ocean with the 'anonymous murmur' of discourse, and the concomitant notion of subjectivity as a fold within the same, as opposed to a transcendent position which would perceive this dimension as other or outside, is, I would propose summarized and encapsulated in the enigmatic conclusion to Gilles Deleuze's monograph on Foucault of 1986, when he writes, 'dans toute son œuvre, Foucault semble poursuivi par le thème d'un dedans qui serait le pli du dehors, comme si le navire était un plissement de la mer'.[25]

These textual figures and debates suggest, in the wake of Mallarmé, a textuality free of an anchoring subjectivity, gesturing towards the utopian plurivocity, fluidity and open-endedness of 'le Texte' which Barthes would postulate slightly later in the decade. They thus dissolve the figure of man in the eternal return of the Same, as infinite text. There is nevertheless a point of resistance through which subjectivity seeps back into these very theorisations, establishing a fixed vantage point, from the shore, and this is *metaphor*. Metaphoricity may be suggested as the terrain on which this dynamic of inscription, effacement, and resistance takes place, since metaphor seems to imply an intentionality; to compare the dissolution of the concept of man to a face drawn in the sand

---

[21] Cf. Gilles Deleuze, *Foucault*, Paris: Minuit, 1986, and Foucault, *Raymond Roussel*, Paris: Gallimard, 1963.

[22] Foucault, 'Distance, aspect, origine' in *Dits et écrits I*, 302. '(T)he burgeoning identity of the Same at the point of its bifurcation.'

[23] Ibid., 303. Foucault also refers here to the novelist and philosopher Pierre Klossowski, whose work on Nietszche was particularly influential. On Klossowski, see Ian James, *Pierre Klossowski: The Persistence of a Name*, Oxford: Legenda, 2000.

[24] Ibid., 305.

[25] Deleuze, *Foucault*, 104. '(I)n all of his work, Foucault seems to be pursued by the theme of an interior which would be the fold of the outside, as if the boat were a fold of the sea.'

washed away by the waves is to imply a consciousness which would both intend this analogy and function as its ground. If Roquentin's vision strives to see the 'real' sea beneath its aestheticized surface, this vision relies as suggested above on imagination. Foucault's attempts to erase the grounded perspective of the transcendent subject in the infinite murmur of language, and Deleuze's reiteration of this pursuit depend no less on a metaphorical hinge, *comme* or *comme si*, which position the space of folds as an image.

In this light Barthes' hesitation, 'Je suis là, devant la mer: *sans doute*, elle ne porte aucun message' [I am here, beside the sea; doubtless it does not carry any message] suggests a resistance to the imagining or metaphorization of the sea *as* this or that, but also a refusal to posit the sea as an opaque limit of absolute literality, since, perhaps, even this postulation would be conditioned by the recourse to metaphor. Roquentin's vision may thus persist in the theoretical endeavours to overcome it, establishing within the discourse of theory the resistance of fiction and the projections of the imaginary. Foucault's attention to the language of literature, however, posits such fictions and projections not as anchored in or by a transcendent subject but as folds within language, part of the process.

References

'Après le sujet qui vient', *Cahiers Confrontation* 20, 1989.
Bachelard, Gaston, *L'Eau et les rêves*, Paris: José Corti, 1942.
_____, *La Poétique de l'espace*, Paris: PUF, 1957.
Barthes, Roland, *Le Degré zéro de l'écriture*, Paris : Seuil, 1953.
_____, *Mythologies*, Paris, Seuil. 1957.
_____, 'Littérature objective' in *Essais Critiques*, Paris: Gallimard, 1964, 32-43.
_____, 'Ecrivains et écrivants' in *Essais Critiques*, Paris: Gallimard, 1964, 152-159.
_____, 'La Mort de l'auteur' in *Le Bruissement de la langue: Essais Critiques IV*, Paris: Gallimard, 1984, 63-69.
Deleuze, Gilles, *Foucault*, Paris: Minuit, 1986.
Foucault, Michel, *Raymond Roussel*, Paris: Gallimard, 1963.
_____, *Les Mots et les choses*, Paris: Gallimard, 1966.
_____, 'Préface à la transgression' in *Dits et écrits 1. 1954-1975*, Paris: Gallimard, 'Quarto', 2001, 261-278.
_____, 'Le Langage à l'infini' in *Dits et écrits 1. 1954-1975*, Paris: Gallimard, 'Quarto', 2001, 278-289.
_____, 'Distance, aspect, origine' in *Dits et écrits 1. 1954-1975*, Paris: Gallimard, 'Quarto', 2001, 300-313.

———, 'Qu'est ce qu'un auteur' in *Dits et écrits 1. 1954-1975,* Paris: Gallimard, 'Quarto', 2001, 817-849.

Foucault, Michel and Bellour, Raymond, 'Entretien: Michel Foucault, *Les Mots et les choses*', *Les Lettres françaises* 1125, March 31, 1966.

Ross, Kristin, *Fast Cars, Clean Bodies: Decolonization and the Re-ordering of French Culture*, Minneapolis, MN: MIT, 1996.

Sartre, Jean-Paul, *La Nausée*, Paris: Gallimard, 1938.

———, *L'Imaginaire*, Paris: Gallimard, 1940.

3.

DEATH ON THE SAND: FROM TRAGIC HUMANISM TO DEPRESSIVE REALISM

Nicholas Gledhill

The terrible crime at the dark heart of Alain Robbe-Grillet's *Le Voyeur* (1955) is all the more affecting because of its ontological uncertainty. We never discover what really took place, or indeed if anything took place at all, and this lack of denouement is unsettling. Rather like a repressed trauma, the reader is unable ever to come to terms with what has happened, unable to achieve any kind of closure. Naturally we assume the worst, but the novel's lack of resolution – the impossibility of ever knowing with any certainty whether the rape and murder of a girl on a beach has in fact occurred in 'real life' or merely been played out in the protagonist's imagination – leaves us with a lasting feeling of unease. In a sense Robbe-Grillet reneges here on an unspoken pact with the reader; he breaks a kind of literary 'fourth wall', and in so doing draws our attention to the fact that what really lies at the centre of this mystery is an absence, a void. Just like Magritte's pipe that is not a pipe, the murder on the beach in *Le Voyeur* is of course always-already never a murder at all, and for Robbe-Grillet it was questions of representation – of what can and cannot be represented by literary fiction and how this must be done – which were his main concern as a writer.

Robbe-Grillet's choice of the beach as locus for his novel's central (non)event immediately gives rise to a concatenation of literary and cultural cross-references. The notion that the beach functions as a kind of signifier in the French literary imagination for a complex array of ideas is evidenced by its central presence in so many key works of fiction. From the iconic scenes of violence and existential crisis in Camus's *L'Étranger* and Sartre's *La Nausée*, through the fractured and opaque topologies of *nouveaux romanciers* like Robbe-Grillet and JMG Le Clèzio, to the washed out, depressive super-modernity depicted by contemporary writers like Michel Houellebecq, the beach as a site of dramatic tension in the modern and post-modern French novel seems so ubiquitous as to almost give the impression of an inside joke – of the beach-as-trope being a kind of self-conscious, self-reflexive device that principally serves to situate the work within a specific cultural tradition. There is a level on which it might be reasonable to argue that the symbolic power of the beach in French literature lies precisely in its power to allude to beaches already depicted elsewhere; that the beaches of *Le Voyeur* for example, or Le Clèzio's *Le Procès-verbal* or Houellebecq's *Extension du domaine de la lutte*, are in some sense echoes of Camus and Sartre's beaches, configured on an uncertain line between parody and *hommage*.

On a more conceptual level, the metaphorical power of the beach can also be understood in terms of its function as a kind of vanishing point between various pairs of binaries. As a liminal space between land and ocean, civilisation and wilderness, the beach can be figurative of both divergence and synthesis, presenting a grey area within which splits and collisions are constantly taking place. The sand itself operates as a palimpsest, the sea and the sky form and reform in constant motion to create a background of perpetual change while at the same time existing in an eternal stasis, a landscape essentially unaltered since pre-human times which at the same time is colonised, at once both tame and wild, *heimlich* and *unheimlich*. Absence and presence, metaphor and literality, imaginary and real: the beach is a conflicted allegorical zone of confrontations and doublings which serves on some level in all of these novels as the setting for transgressions, revelations and violent confrontations between the other and the self.

Further, the literary trope of the beach can serve as a conceptual thread along which to trace the development of the French novel from its era of high modernism to the present day, demonstrating transitions between differing artistic approaches and philosophical outlooks that are much further-reaching than the genre of the novel and that I propose can be understood as moving through three distinct stages. Beginning with the existentialism of Sartre and Camus and then transiting into the *nouveau roman* period, changes in approaches to literary fiction in post-war France mirrored the wider divergences taking place between humanism and structuralism, modernity and post-modernity. Finally, arriving in the present, I suggest that there is now emerging a new phase in this development, the representation of a specifically 'late-capitalist' or 'super-modern' set of attitudes in a distinct style that has recently begun to be referred to as 'depressive realism'.[1]

Throughout this evolution the beach continually returns, a symbolic Archimedean point that offers a unique angle of insight into these transitions, drawing attention to the convergences and divergences between a series of works that differ greatly but can nonetheless be seen as comprising an integrated dialogue spanning nearly a century of changing approaches. The beach is a signifier at once of both consistency and change.

---

[1] See Ben Jeffery, *Anti-Matter: Michel Houellebecq and Depressive Realism*, Winchester and Washington, DC: Zero Books, 2011.

To a great extent, the *nouveau roman* was a reaction against the spectre of naturalism that many younger writers felt was still haunting the modern novel in the 1950s and 60s. Robbe-Grillet's key work of theory, *Pour un nouveau roman* (1963) reads largely as a polemic against the literary giants of the preceding generation, in particular Sartre and Camus, and can be read in the context of the general movement from existentialism to structuralism that had been taking place in the wider milieu of French academia. In much the same spirit as Foucault's famous dismissal of Sartre as 'a man from the nineteenth century trying to think the twentieth',[2] Robbe-Grillet's main line of attack was that the existentialists, while presenting themselves as cutting edge both philosophically and in terms of literary fiction, in fact did little more than re-hash a tired Victorian approach to both of these, producing novels in a style that he pejoratively labelled 'tragic humanism'.[3]

At the core of tragic humanism is, on Robbe-Grillet's view, a formal tendency towards anthropomorphic metaphor which betrays a dated and essentially romantic conception of a human nature that in some sense extends outwards into and defines nature itself (as in the external, natural world). This rests on the presumption that the external world has a kind of 'inner meaning' beneath its surface which is in some sense *accessible* to the human subject (or at least to one who is sufficiently existentially aware), available to be revealed, understood and defined in human terms: 'the old myths of depth'.[4] For Robbe-Grillet, nature, and objective reality in general, is something radically external that can only be apprehended superficially, something of which we can only ever perceive the surface. In keeping with structuralism's transition to a less subject-oriented philosophy, Robbe-Grillet's novels convey the sense that (rather like the Lacanian Real) the true nature of objects is unknowable. The Real of nature, if there is such a thing, is not comprehensible to the human subject, the objective world is indifferent to and independent of human thought: 'Man looks at the world, and the world does not look back at him'.[5]

The existentialist protagonist seeks to master objects as a kind of prelude to mastering themselves. In *La Nausée* (1938) for example, Roquentin constantly 'sees beneath' the surface of things, sees signs in everything, perceives a hidden 'truer' reality that only he has access to. In one of several scenes of epiphany set on the beaches of the coastal town where Roquentin is living, Bouville, he has turned away in disgust from the crowds of people around him and is looking out over the water when suddenly he sees the sea *as it really is*:

---

[2] 'L'homme, est-il mort?: un entretien avec Michel Foucault,' *Arts et Loisirs* 38, 15 June, 1966, 8. (My translation).

[3] 'Nature, Humanism, Tragedy' in Alain Robbe-Grillet, *For a New Novel*, trans. Richard Howard, Evanston, IL: Northwestern University Press, 1989.

[4] Ibid., 49.

[5] Ibid., 58.

> The real sea is cold and black, full of animals; it crawls underneath this green film which is designed to deceive people. the sylphs all around me have been taken in: they see nothing but the thin film, that is what proves the existence of God. I see underneath![6]

As well as the sea, everything around Roquentin seems 'really' to exist only to the extent that it exists *for* him, everything is meaningful specifically in the sense that it is meaningful to *him*. He is empowered with a unique view into the true nature of objects, and what he sees never fails to be deeply affecting and personal. Fundamentally what Roquentin is doing is projecting his own subjectivity out into the external world and seeing himself reflected back in it. Looking at some tattered posters on a wall, he states that '[i]t is as if a restless criminal passion were trying to express itself through these mysterious signs'.[7] Commenting on the weather, we are told that 'these cold rays which the sun projects like a pitiless judgement on all creatures enter me through my eyes; *I am illuminated within by an impoverishing light*' (my emphasis).[8] Along with the obvious romanticism of Sartre's use of metaphor here, in the context of post-modernity the philosophical redundancy of what he is trying to convey, the sense in which it is 'nineteenth century', to echo Foucault's critique (although 'pre-war' might be fairer) is that Roquentin is still counting on the existence of a kind of binding meta-consciousness that can give meaning to the world, a master narrative that will explain the existence of things and his place amongst them. Despite his professed atheism, Sartre's position is essentially a religious one.

Grandiose prose styling and a tendency towards romantic sentiment were de rigueur in French 'philosophical novels' of the 1930s and 40s. In another memorable allegorising of the beach, we can read a scene similar on many levels to that of Roquentin's moment by the balustrade at Bouville in Maurice Blanchot's *Thomas l'Obscur* (1941), where Thomas has an experience of merging with or 'becoming' the sea in which he is swimming, a sea which is again configured as comprising two distinct and conflicting ontological presences, one 'ideal' and the other 'real': 'this ideal sea which he was becoming ever more intimately had in turn become the real sea, in which he was virtually drowned'.[9] The figurative doubling associated with the beach is again prominent here, the divergence and convergence of subject and object, interior and exterior, the blurring of the distinction between living and inert. Along with this is a sense of nature as imbued with a profound inner meaning that the subject in some sense has to 'de-code', to make sense of in order to themselves become existentially more 'complete'. Things are *significant* – the sea, the landscape, the world of objects; all possess

---

[6] Jean-Paul Sartre, *Nausea*, trans. Robert Baldick, London: Penguin, 1963, 179.

[7] Ibid., 42.

[8] Ibid., 28.

[9] Maurice Blanchot, *Thomas the Obscure*, trans. Robert Lamberton, New York, NY: Station Hill, 1988, 8.

secrets that will enlighten the subject, providing he (and it is always a he) can unlock them.

Similarly, in Camus's *L'Étranger* (1942) everything is *alive* for Mersault, everything is vivid; he is absorbed in the depth of things, emotionally immersed in an environment which appears laden with semiotic resonances intended solely for him. Also paralleling *La Nausée*, there is an unrestrained metaphorical exuberance throughout *L'Étranger* that gives the lie to the idea of Mersault as the detached, affectless character that Camus supposedly intended. The hyperbole reaches a kind of crescendo when Mersault is about to shoot the Arab on the beach: the sunlight reflecting off the Arab's knife is 'a dazzling spear', and not simply bright but *solid*, like a physical presence: 'a red hot blade gnawing at my eyelashes and gouging out my stinging eyes'. Meanwhile, in a jarring deployment of the pathetic fallacy, the sea has become truly apocalyptic: 'a great breath of fire', and the sky too is 'splitting from end to end and raining down sheets of fire'.[10] But despite the blinding sun, glinting blade and oppressive heat of Camus's beach it is still clear that it is Mersault, in his sovereign subjectivity, who remains central. The beach, the sun, the revolver in his hand (and of course the unfortunate Arab) are really nothing more than props through which to demonstrate his freedom.[11] He is free to shoot or not to shoot, just as he is free in Part II of the novel to play the game he is expected to play and be acquitted, or to be 'authentic' and face execution. Even in death, the existentialist subject is what *he* makes of *him*self. In fact, it is in facing death that Mersault feels most liberated: 'I laid myself open to the benign indifference of the world. And finding it so much like myself, in fact so fraternal, I realised that I'd been happy, and that I was still happy.'[12] Mersault finds the world 'fraternal' and 'so much like himself'. He looks at the world, and sees himself in it. He looks at the world and the world looks back at him.

For Robbe-Grillet the failure of Camus and Sartre as novelists was precisely this presumption to be able look into the objective world and see their own message within it. Further, a problem with this anthropocentric fallacy is that it entailed a loss of the possibility of understanding what phenomena actually are: 'drowned in the depth of things, man ultimately no longer even perceives them'.[13] The existentialist/humanist understanding of nature was therefore criticised as being not only belief in a myth, but also in one that (ironically) disrupted any possibility of actual freedom. In this sense Robbe-Grillet's critique of

---

[10] Albert Camus, *The Outsider*, trans. Joseph Laredo, London: Penguin, 1983, 60.

[11] Another obvious point here being that the primacy of both Mersault and Roquentin as subjects who are white, European, heterosexual and male is also problematic. As well as Mersault's very clear assumption of superiority over both Arabs and women in *L'Étranger*, Roquentin's reaction of disgust to the homosexual 'autodidact' in *La Nausée* should sit uncomfortably with the contemporary reader.

[12] Op. cit., 117.

[13] Robbe-Grillet, *For a New Novel*, 68.

Sartre and Camus is basically a reformulation of the famous quote of Goethe's – none are more hopelessly enslaved than those who falsely believe they are free:

> To reject our so-called 'nature' and the vocabulary which perpetuates its myth, to propose objects as purely external and superficial, is not – as has been claimed – to deny man; but it is to reject the 'pananthropic' notion contained in traditional humanism, and probably in all humanism. It is no more in the last analysis to lay claim, quite logically, to my freedom.[14]

It is more liberating to accept that certain things cannot be known than to create fictions which serve to entrench ignorance even more deeply. To accept the world as external and superficial is not to limit the human but to free him/her of his/her delusions. Philosophically, Robbe-Grillet's critique of Sartre is similar to that of Marcuse – that in spite of itself existentialism is deeply idealistic, and as such becomes part of the ideology it attacks: 'its radicalism is illusory'.[15] For Robbe-Grillet there would be nothing beneath the 'deceptive green film' of Sartre's sea, or at least if there was we would have no access to it. In its place there is instead a sense of absence, a kind of silence, an acceptance that the world is fundamentally enigmatic and ambiguous, and that unlike the existentialist hero we can never hope to impose ourselves on it and 'master' it.

In a formal context this new approach is expressed through the removal of omniscient narration and authorial intent, as well as the introduction of elements of narrative undecideability and a more sparse and ambivalent use of metaphor. Robbe-Grillet's beach differs markedly from Camus and Sartre's beaches in its lack of affect – it is neither a place of burning sun and blinding white light nor of dark turbulence and lurking depths of meaning. Instead it simply *is*, in something of a matter-of-fact way; there is a sense of coldness to it, of flatness, of unfathomable distance and limitless time: 'a pale sunbeam' illuminates the beach with 'a wan flat light', the 'lustreless white' of the 'motionless' gulls in the sky gives 'an impression of distance [that it is] impossible to estimate'.[16] Strewn along the empty beach is 'unidentifiable debris'.[17] The protagonist, Mathias, is detached from an environment that has no depth, he is unable ever to commune with it in the way that Mersault and Roquentin do. Robbe-Grillet's descriptions of the landscape generally draw attention to what remains unknown and unseen – the text raises far more questions than it answers.

Returning then to the initial point made at the opening of this chapter, it is the conveyance of exactly this sense of absence and mystery which lies at

---

[14] Ibid., 57.

[15] Herbert Marcuse, 'Sartre's Existentialism', trans. Joris De Bres, in *Studies in Critical Philosophy*, London: NLB, 1972, 161.

[16] Alain Robbe-Grillet, *The Voyeur*, trans. Richard Howard, London: Alma Classics, 2009, 91.

[17] Ibid., 23.

the heart of *Le Voyeur* and manifests above all in the absence of clarification about what did or didn't happen to the girl on the beach. Whatever we decide, as readers, amounts to the same: there is literally no truth to be found. All views are equally (in)valid. Further, by confronting us with the obvious absurdity of trying to assign different levels of truthfulness to equally fictional events, Robbe-Grillet implicitly forces us to reassess our relationship with the novel, perhaps to question what we expect from artistic representation generally. We know very well that Mathias is a creation, we know very well that whatever he has or hasn't done on the island is equally fictional too, but still we want to know what 'really happened'. We yearn for some unequivocal authority at some point to clear things up for us, to decide for us, to put our minds at rest. The truly disturbing thing about *Le Voyeur* is not the violation and murder of a young girl but the uncovering of our own false consciousness in the way we approach representations of reality. We find ourselves to be willing self-deceivers – we're happy to settle for a proscribed truth and semblance of objectivity even though we know that this truth is itself a fiction, and we're unsettled when we aren't able to do this. We find ourselves, in our approach to the text, in the same position as Slavoj Žižek's cynical ideologue: *Je sais bien, mais quand même* . . .[18]

Perhaps we can understand the world that the *nouveau roman* heralded as a world which was in some sense being *drained of meaning*, drained of the same sense of transcendent meaning to which the existentialists were trying desperately to cling – a remnant of religious faith, thinly veiled as faith in humanity or in Enlightenment rationalism. For Robbe-Grillet, any writer of fiction who feels that they have a clear message about what is or isn't meaningful, any writer with 'something to say', in the sense of an ulterior moral/political purpose to their writing outside the text itself, has lapsed into a redundant way of thinking:

> When a novelist has 'something to say', they mean a message. It has political connotations, or a religious message, or a moral prescription. It means 'commitment', as used by Sartre and other fellow-travellers. They are saying that the writer has a world view, a sort of truth that he wishes to communicate, and that his writing has an ulterior significance. I am against this. Flaubert described a whole world, but he had nothing to say, in the sense that he had no message to transmit, no remedy to offer for the human condition.[19]

The Sartrean term 'commitment' suggests a level of faith in the possibility of positive socio-political change through Art; the idea that the artist can 'speak truth to power'. Clearly this rests on the presumption that there is a 'truth' to be spoken, and that it is within the artist's power to realise it. When Robbe-Grillet states that he, alternatively, has 'no remedy to offer the human condition' what he

---

[18] See for example Slavoj Žižek, *The Sublime Object of Ideology*, London and New York, NY: Verso, 1989, 28-30.

[19] 'Alain Robbe-Grillet, The Art of Fiction No. 91' Interview by Shusha Guppy, *Paris Review* 99, Spring, 1986.

is expressing is precisely disbelief in this possibility. The emergence of such nihilism in terms of Art's socio-political effectiveness can be read as a kind of harbinger of post-modernity. If, like Frederic Jameson, we trace the origins of what came to be called postmodernism to 'some radical break or *coupure*, generally traced back to the end of the 1950s or the early 1960s',[20] then it follows that the theoretical break with the past that Robbe-Grillet had achieved by 1963 stands as an important marker not only of a radical change in approaches to literary praxis in France but also for this much wider shift in the history of ideas. The concepts that Jameson would term 'depthlessness',[21] and 'the extinction of the sacred',[22] in fact seem particularly apt in configuring a postmodernist reading of *Le Voyeur*. The new era that this text went in some way to inaugurating would be one in which concepts of authenticity and ultimate truth became meaningless, replaced by a confusion of conflicting discourses all of which shared equally incomplete status. Robbe-Grillet's approach as a writer can be understood as an attempt to articulate this new sense of uncertainty, and it is uncertainty about what has or hasn't happened and what the implications of this may or may not be that comprises the void at the centre of *Le Voyeur*. It is an approach, literally, that knows its limits. As Foucault put it:

> . . . with Robbe-Grillet the difference between what has happened and what has not happened, even though (and to the extent that) it is difficult to establish, remains at the centre of the text (at least in the form of a lack, a white page or a repetition): it is a limit and an enigma. . .[23]

Another novel of the same period that engages with concepts of limit and enigma and also offers another key representation of the beach is JMG Le Clèzio's *Le Procès-Verbal* (1963).[24] In it Adam, a young loner existing in a kind of amnesiac fugue state on the periphery of society, breaks into and inhabits an abandoned seaside villa where he proceeds gradually to lose his grip on reality. He also intermittently interacts with a girl, Michèle, whom at one point he takes onto the beach and 'rapes', although just as in *Le Voyeur* it is very unclear to what extent this act of violence has 'actually' happened due to a general blurring of fantasy and reality and questions over how the event was perceived by Michèle herself. As the literal and the figurative collide, Adam's relationship with his surroundings becomes increasingly dissonant, inchoate and fragmented until

---

[20] Frederic Jameson, *Postmodernism, or, The Cultural Logic of Late Capitalism*, London: Verso, 1991, 1.

[21] Ibid., 6.

[22] Ibid., 67.

[23] Michel Foucault, 'Distance, Aspect, Origin', trans. Patrick ffrench, in Patrich ffrench & Roland-François Lack (eds.) *The Tel Quel Reader*, London and New York, NY: Routledge, 1998, 101.

[24] First published in English translation in 1970 as *The Interrogation*.

it is as though reality itself is disintegrating into chaos. 'Hypnotised' by a terrifying, Bataillesque vision of the sun, he begins to 'reconstruct a world of childish terrors'. The beach transforms to resemble an alien or prehistoric landscape, nightmarish and surreal:

> He could feel the fossilized monsters coming to birth somewhere, prowling round the villa, the joints of their huge feet cracking . . . from the pools there rose an armoured nation of parasites or shrimps, of abrupt, mysterious crustaceans, hungering to tear off shreds of his flesh. the beaches were covered with strange creatures who had come there, accompanied by their young, to await no-one knew what. . .[25]

Le Clèzio's approach differs to Robbe-Grillet's – the fantasy world of horrors into which Adam is absorbed contrasts the pale, drained landscape that Mathias inhabits – but even so they can be read as expressing a similar central idea. What is fundamental to both is that neither character is seeing the world 'as it really is'; both are faced with an external reality that is incomprehensible and alienating, both texts have in common the mystery, incompleteness and narrative undecideability which comprise, formally, the radical departure from writers like Sartre and Camus.

On a more conceptual level, *Le Procès-Verbal* can be read as depicting a situation in which objective reality is in a sense *rebelling against the subject*, the protagonist is under attack from the phenomenal environment, being 'subjected' *to* it rather than using their own subjectivity to define it, as Roquentin does. Further, unlike Mersault, the protagonist is very clearly no longer 'free', instead attention is drawn to the enfeeblement of the human in the face of a powerful and indifferent natural world. An example of what I would argue is the same concept (albeit differently rendered) in *Le Voyeur* would be the obsessive attention given to the series of small, seemingly banal objects that in his paranoia Mathias is convinced might become evidence of his 'guilt' – cigarette butts, sweet wrappers – shreds of seemingly inconsequential matter that suddenly begin to loom terrifyingly large as they acquire the power to send him to the guillotine. The subject has now become the 'victim' of the objective world rather than its master; the illusion of control has been removed, anthropocentric humanism rejected. Essentially, the transition from the existentialist novel to the *nouveau roman* in terms of the depiction of the phenomenal world is from a world that is knowable, 'fraternal', deep and meaningful, to one that is unknowable, opaque, superficial and alienating. There is also a transition from the depiction of a human subject who is empowered, free and central to one who is weak and contingent, and who rather than defining reality has become lost in it, trapped in its web.

---

[25] JMG Le Clèzio, *The Interrogation*, trans. Daphne Woodward, London: Penguin, 1970, 13.

If we continue with this chain of thought, seeing the existentialists as 'masters' of objective reality, and the *nouveaux romanciers* as bearing witness to reality's figurative 'revolt' against the subject, it follows to understand depressive realism – the final stage in this three-stage process – as representing a situation where the human has now been completely 'defeated'; a form of literary fiction in which the subject is depicted as powerless in the face of a hostile objectivity.

In the pivotal moment of Michel Houellebecq's debut novel *Extension du domaine de la lutte* (1994)[26] the unnamed narrator hands his colleague Raphaël Tisserand a knife and encourages him to go down onto the beach and use it on a young couple. It is night, and other than the couple (who are unaware of the presence of the narrator and Tisserand) the beach is deserted. The air is pleasant, in fact 'abnormally pleasant', the moon is bright and two very beautiful young people are about to make love by the ocean, 'under the splendour of the stars'.[27] The scene would be romantic, or perhaps a Hollywood cliché, but Tisserand's instructions are to murder the boy and then rape and murder the girl. The motivation for this act of violence is simple, timeless even. Earlier that evening the girl spurned Tisserand's advances, and the narrator is egging him on to enact a bloody revenge.

In essence this could be a scene from a Greek tragedy or a Norse saga; Houellebecq is dealing with themes that are as old as literature itself: lust, jealousy, pride, envy, wrath. And while it might seem counter-intuitive to evoke antiquated texts like these when discussing Houellebecq – a writer who after all is known for his depictions of life in contemporary, late-capitalist culture – the comparison can actually be extended much further. There is a distinct element of atavism in the world Houellebecq depicts; there is a starkness, a raw, uncompromising brutality that has echoes of the pre-Enlightenment or even pre-Christian. This is because the world of Houellebecq's fiction is one where the old ideological certainties have entirely collapsed, and what's left behind is really little more than an 'every man for himself' state of nature, a nature red in tooth and claw. Beneath a veneer of modern culture and technology, Houellebecq's protagonists are living in what amounts to a form of neo-barbarism, a merciless Darwinian struggle that pits every individual against all others. Concomitant to this, and another aspect of Houellebecq's work that oddly echoes the likes of Homer, Sophocles and the *Íslendingasögur*, is the idea that the human subject is essentially powerless at the hands of fate.

'Fate' in Houellebecq's fiction is not determined by gods or other transcendent forces, but is something straightforward and entirely mundane in origin. It is the effect of biological, economic and socio-cultural structures which inevitably pre-determine and limit the human in a radically materialist representation

---

[26] First published in English in 1999 as *Whatever*.

[27] Michel Houellebecq, *Whatever*, trans. Paul Hammond, London: Serpent's Tail, 1999, 119.

of the world. In Houellebecq's novels a sense of helplessness and loss hangs over everything; all that remains of ideology is cynicism, and humanity has been reduced to an atomised mass of individuals in a constant state of petty, internecine struggle. Life is alienating and capricious, devoid of any kind of goal other than the drive to satisfy hedonistic desires – a drive that can only ever end in frustration due to the inevitable onset of physical decrepitude and death. It is the representation of a world where the human subject is neither empowered and central, nor has the option to define itself according to wider social collectivities and shared systems of belief. As a result, in an oddly regressive way, 'fate', or perhaps more accurately *luck*, suddenly begins to seem very important.

Tisserand's fate, the destiny that has led him to his moment of reckoning on the beach, is simply to have been born physically ugly in a culture that despises physical ugliness. There is nothing he can do about this – no romantic notions about overcoming adversity or the triumph of the will are ever going to make Tisserand more handsome or the society he lives in less superficial. Fate, basically, has been unkind, and the idea of kicking against it, of attempting to master it, is futile. Tisserand must simply accept the fact that he's been dealt a bum hand in the relentlessly vicious, miserable contest that is the Houellebecqian vision of life, and succumb either to destructive rage, suicidal despair or simply acquiesce in a kind of numbed acceptance. Barred from ever consummating the kinds of acts he has been conditioned to desire, Tisserand has never been able to find a sexual partner, let alone 'love'. The result is a sad, lonely existence of frustration, exclusion, self-loathing and a constant sense of loss. It is a predicament Houellebecq darkly outlines in his narrator's blunt assessment of the situation:

> It's been hopeless for a long time, from the very beginning. You will never represent, Raphaël, a young girl's erotic dream. You have to resign yourself to the inevitable; such things are not for you. It's already too late, in any case. The sexual failure you've known since your adolescence, Raphaël, the frustration that has followed you since the age of thirteen, will leave their indelible mark. Even supposing that you might have women in the future – which in all frankness I doubt – this will not be enough; nothing will ever be enough. You will always be an orphan to those adolescent loves you never knew. In you the wound is already deep; it will get deeper and deeper. An atrocious, unremitting bitterness will end up gripping your heart. For you there will be neither redemption nor deliverance. That's how it is.[28]

Philosophically this amounts to what we might call 'dark determinism', a view that you have no real choice in how your life will unfold and that, ultimately, things are going to go badly.

In terms of a literary genre, depressive realism is an articulation of exactly this general outlook, offering a representation of contemporary society as a kind

---

[28] Ibid., 116.

of already-existing-dystopia.[29] Houellebecq's fatalism is understood through concepts that are scientific (essentially a combination of socio- and bio-determinism) but in terms of its impact on individuals it effectively differs very little from what would be a more archaic understanding of fate as mystic or divine will, an irony of which Houellebecq seems to be aware. His choice of words in the quotation above ('redemption', 'deliverance') hint at this faux-religious element in his thought, as do recurring themes in his work – the quack religions and faddish new age cults in *Les Particules élémentaires* and *La Possibilité d'une île* for example.[30] One of the typical sources of alienation for protagonists in Houellebecq's novels is that while secondary characters are often seen making efforts to empower themselves by searching for some kind of transcendent meaning to their lives, the protagonist will recognise such efforts as pointless. Perhaps it would be apposite to understand the core message of depressive realism as basically reiterating, in a contemporary context, King Lear's great howl of despair: 'As flies to wanton boys are we to the Gods; / They kill us for their sport'.[31]

The beach scene in *Extension du domaine de la lutte* is one in which Tisserand is forced to confront himself, to come to terms with the reality of his position, but in so doing he remains disempowered (he cannot go through with the violent act, instead masturbating, returning the unused knife and then dying soon afterwards in a suicidal car crash). In this sense Houellebecq's rendering of the beach scene is interesting in the context of the literary beaches that have preceded his. Two things that stand out immediately are that the scene takes place at night, and that the 'act' doesn't happen. In a sense, this is almost a direct inversion of Camus's beach, its darkness and inactivity are like a photographic negative of the bright light and decisive action on the beach in *L'Étranger*. Also, unlike Mersault's, Tisserand's confrontation on the beach is neither violent nor profound, instead it is merely banal, pathetic, expressing a sense of impotence and the worthlessness of trying to take any kind of action. Rather than having his freedom affirmed, Tisserand leaves the beach in the full knowledge of his inability to do anything effective other than end his life.

As with Robbe-Grillet, the sparseness and lack of affect in Houellebecq's figurative language also stands as a point of contrast with the existentialists. While on Camus's beach the sun is 'crashing down into the sand and shattering into little pieces';[32] the sea 'unbearable';[33] the sand 'so hot it seemed to have turned

---

[29] As well as Houellebecq, Jeffery suggests David Foster-Wallace and Margaret Atwood as examples of depressive realists. I would tentatively add to this list the British novelist Tom McCarthy.

[30] Published in English as *Atomised* (1998) and *The Possibility of an Island* (2005).

[31] Act IV. Scene 1.

[32] Camus, *The Outsider*, 56.

[33] Ibid., 54.

red',[34] for Houellebecq the weather is simply 'pleasant', the moon 'bright'. However, Houellebecq's beach differs significantly from Robbe-Grillet's in its absence of mystery; there is no 'void' at the centre of any of Houellebecq's novels, no undecideability. There is no hidden 'depth' to things, but neither is there the disturbing sense of our being unable to perceive such depths. There is neither the feeling of profundity nor of a profound lack of it, just a generalised sense of hopelessness. For Ben Jeffery this is expressive of a contemporary double-bind he terms 'flattening':

> Modern materialism has this strange kind of double effect on self-perception. On the one hand, it isolates the individual by (seemingly) dispelling various illusions of communion (the decline of religion being the paradigm example). On the other, progress in social sciences, psychology and neurology encourages us to think about ourselves in various external fashions: as the product of genetic resources, social and economic starting position, and so on. These modes of thought are uncomfortable because they imply that our view of things 'from the inside' is illusory or distorted, and that what we experience as central or singular in our personal day-to-day lives are actually nothing more than instances of general truths about human behaviour.[35]

On the one hand, contemporary life isolates us from one another, destroying a sense of communion and causing us to focus inwards and see the world subjectively. On the other, it causes us to see ourselves as nothing more than a product of various structures that are external to us. As a result, the subject is paralysed, offered no recourse either to external answers (such as religious faith, or faith in social progress for example) or any kind of internal self-actualization (as with the existentialists). So what is there that can fill this vacuum?

Although Houellebecq engages with a range of themes, those expressed in *Extension du domaine de la lutte* have remained central to all his subsequent novels, reiterated most recently in *La carte et le territoire* (2010).[36] A recurring idea is that the idealistic social revolutions of the 1960s drastically failed, and that the 'freedoms' they instigated have perversely led to everything in contemporary western society being subsumed into the relentlessly competitive, totalitarian logic of the market, the titular '*domaine de la lutte*' (domain of struggle). As a result nothing has meaning in any terms other than instrumentality within capitalist paradigms of value, and historically, for Houellebecq, we're subsequently at a kind of dead end: 'we're at a point where success in market terms justifies and validates anything, replacing all the theories. No one is capable of seeing further, absolutely no one'.[37] This marketisation transcends the ideolog-

---

[34] Ibid., 55.
[35] Jeffery, *Anti-Matter*, 35-6.
[36] Published in English as *The Map and the Territory* (2011).
[37] Michel Houellebecq, *The Map and the Territory*, trans. Gavin Bowd, London: Vintage, 2011, 135.

ical and economic, encompassing the biological and natural as well. People's bodies have value only in terms of being sexually desirable, and the reduction of objects to their function as commodities has been extended to the very landscape itself, which becomes meaningful only in its utility for consumer driven recreation. The beach is the most commonly recurring trope in these terms, as a resort and site for sex tourism, most notably in *Platforme* (2001),[38] although in *La carte et le territoire* this landscape-as-commodity idea is extended to the entire territory of rural France.

To a great extent then, it is the 'invisible hand' of the market that has filled the vacuum left behind by the collapse of belief in both transcendent external forces and individual will. It is capitalism, basically, that provides the faux-mystical determinist force underpinning Houellebecq's neo-fatalist vision. It is the market which is now in control. Houellebecq's alignment with the longstanding idea of capitalism-as-religion is expressed very explicitly in *La carte et le territoire*: Bill Gates, 'the sincere capitalist' is described as 'a creature of faith' and 'the evangelist of capital'.[39] Capitalism operates in Houellebecq's fiction like an implacable new God, an irresistible spectral force that brings both subject and object entirely under its sway. It is as though, curiously, the West's cultural development has come full-circle: the great progressive systems of belief that reached a kind of apotheosis during the Enlightenment having failed, we are figuratively returned to the caves – to cowering supplication before a new and unfathomable god.

The significance of the transition from tragic humanism to depressive realism is most clear in the polar difference between representations of the human subject's predicament offered by Sartre and Houellebecq. From radical freedom and political commitment: 'man is nothing but what he makes of himself . . . [and] In fashioning myself I fashion man',[40] to helpless fatalism: 'we too are products . . . we too will become obsolete'.[41] Standing as a kind of liminal space between these two extremes is the *nouveau roman*, a transitional phase in which formal and conceptual certainties break down. If the central feature of Robbe-Grillet's work is the articulation of a void, then it is the implications of this void that are, a generation later, the concern of writers like Houellebecq.

Further, as the numbing reality of life under neoliberal capitalism is the most ostensible thematic concern of Houellebecq's novels, it is interesting that capitalism itself, as an ideology, is often viewed by its critics as a kind of void or lack, as being rather than a system of values as such, more what manifests in the absence of such a system. The concept of 'reflexive passivity' that Mark Fisher

---

[38] Published in English as *Platform* (2003).

[39] Houellebecq, *The Map and the Territory*, 124.

[40] Jean-Paul Sartre, *Existentialism and Humanism*, trans. Philip Mairet, London: Methuen, 1997, 28-30.

[41] Houellebecq, *The Map and the Territory*, 110-11.

deploys, for example, in reference to late-capitalism's effect on culture parallels the concept of 'flattening' that Jeffery deploys in reference to the depressive realist novel.[42] According to Fisher, subjects in contemporary western culture are caught in a negative feedback loop, a 'self fulfilling prophecy' in which the feeling of inability to take any positive action to improve their state of affairs itself serves to create the state of affairs they are in, an analysis that could aptly be applied to any of Houellebecq's protagonists. Similarly Fisher's 'depressive hedonia', denoting feelings of helplessness and depression that manifest in obsessive, nihilistic pleasure seeking,[43] is echoed in recurring Houellebecqian tropes: nightclubs, orgies, the hedonistic resorts of Thailand and Club Med.

Which brings us back, finally, to the beach: a figurative point of reference through which to trace the divergences between these three different literary approaches. As the positivity of the existentialists gives way to the uncertain void of the *nouveau roman* and then finally the absolute nihilism of Houellebecq, the trope of the beach persists. If the binary function of the beach is its most fundamental allegorical power, then it might be best to understand its metaphorical significance in this context as above all figuring a dialectic of absence/presence. In all of these novels the beach is a site for and signifier of the seminal event, the moment of transgression around which the rest of the plot revolves, the moment of meaning. However it also serves, ironically, as a means symbolically to draw attention to how the assumption of 'meaningfulness' in any human activity has been to a great extent undermined. Its deployment by these writers follows a line from positivity to negativity, from presence to absence, a disintegration of the affirmative – 'Camus: something happens on the beach; Robbe-Grillet: something *might* have happened on the beach; Houellebecq: nothing happens on the beach.

References

Blanchot, Maurice, *Thomas the Obscure*, trans. Robert Lamberton, New York, NY: Station Hill, 1988.
Camus, Albert, *The Outsider*, trans. Joseph Laredo, London: Penguin, 1983.
Le Clèzio, JMG, *The Interrogation*, trans. Daphne Woodward, London: Penguin, 1970.
Fisher, Mark, *Capitalist Realism: Is There No Alternative?*, Winchester & Washington, DC: Zero Books, 2009.
Foucault, Michel, 'L'homme, est-il mort?: un entretien avec Michel Foucault,' *Arts et Loisirs* 38, 15 June, 1966, 8-9.

---

[42] Mark Fisher, *Capitalist Realism: Is There No Alternative?*, Winchester & Washington, DC: Zero Books, 2009, 21.
[43] Ibid.

———, 'Distance, Aspect, Origin', trans. Patrick ffrench, in Patrich ffrench & Roland-François Lack (eds.) *The Tel Quel Reader*, London and New York, NY: Routledge, 1998, 97-108.

Houellebecq, Michel, *Whatever*, trans. Paul Hammond, London: Serpent's Tail, 1999.

———, *The Map and the Territory*, trans. Gavin Bowd, London: Vintage, 2011.

Jameson, Frederic, *Postmodernism, or, The Cultural Logic of Late Capitalism*, London: Verso, 1991.

Jeffrey, Ben, *Anti-Matter: Michel Houellebecq and Depressive Realism*, Winchester and Washington, DC: Zero Books, 2011.

Marcuse, Herbert, *Studies in Critical Philosophy*, London: NLB, 1972.

Robbe-Grillet, Alain, 'Alain Robbe-Grillet, The Art of Fiction No. 91' Interview by Shusha Guppy, *Paris Review* 99, Spring, 1986.

———, *For a New Novel*, trans. Richard Howard, Evanston, IL: Northwestern University Press, 1989.

———, *The Voyeur*, trans. Richard Howard, London: Alma Classics, 2009.

Sartre, Jean-Paul, *Nausea*, trans. Robert Baldick, London: Penguin, 1963.

———, *Existentialism and Humanism*, trans. Philip Mairet, London: Methuen, 1997.

Žižek, Slavoj, *The Sublime Object of Ideology*, London and New York, NY: Verso, 1989.

II. Framing the Beach

4.

PROUST AND THE BEACH AS *ÉCRAN*

Áine Larkin

Introduction: beach and screen

In Marcel Proust's *À la recherche du temps perdu* (1913-1927), the Balbec seashore functions as the liminal space where water, with all its connotations of life-giving power, meets the constraints of land, with its intricate social hierarchies and interactions. The painter Elstir instructs the young protagonist in his way of regarding this seashore, which leads ultimately to a blurring of the defining line between land and sea for the artist keen to convey his personal vision. The protagonist takes full advantage of this education and later confirms its value when, on the point of kissing Albertine for the first time, he observes that in so doing, he hopes to 'embrasser toute la plage de Balbec' [be kissing the whole Balbec sea-shore] (Proust: II, 658; III, 361).[1] This conflation of girl and beach is developed carefully throughout the Proustian narrative, and will be traced in this paper. It will explore the ways in which the beach serves as both screen and frame for the protagonist's experience of desire and love, and is framed by literary and painterly practices, even as it enacts a process of framing itself. Film and television adaptations of Proust's work, and allusions to it where the beach is represented, will also be considered. Notable in such works is the reversal occasioned by the need visually to represent Proust's written account of the beach as his protagonist perceives it. As a network of real and imagined spaces, the beach simultaneously eliminates and affirms boundaries of class and gender, played out most notably in the protagonist's relationship with Albertine Simonet. It may be argued that the ambiguous, permanently changeable mingling of land and seawater at Balbec functions as a metaphor for the necessarily confused and unhappy, but also idiosyncratic and enriching experience the protagonist must acquire in order to realise his creative literary ambitions. The beach serves as a site where anxieties about class erasure are triggered, potential

---

[1] All French references to Proust's work are taken from the Pléiade edition in four volumes, published 1987-89 under the editorship of Jean-Yves Tadié. The English edition consulted is the 2002-2003 Penguin Classics translation produced under Christopher Prendergast's general editorship.

sexual transgressions are imagined but fail to materialise, and the official narrative of the beach as a site of vitality and good health is juxtaposed with that of a space of social and physical transgression.

The predominance of the visual as source of imagery and metaphor in the Proustian narrative has long been affirmed.[2] Looking and seeing, enframing and recollecting felt experience in visual terms are all central concerns of *À la recherche du temps perdu*, both figuratively and thematically.[3] The spaces in which the narrative unfolds — Paris, Venice, Combray, Balbec — make up a narrative world where the real and the imaginary co-exist peaceably, and where a site as mundane as Balbec beach can constitute an important multi-layered network of such concrete and invented places. Jean-Didier Urbain notes that with the development of a summertime beach leisure culture throughout the nineteenth century, in which bodies were gradually exposed to the sea and to each other, the beach was transformed from a space of work for fishermen to 'un vaste *living theatre*: un théâtre où s'abolira la frontière entre public et comédiens' [a vast 'living theater' in which the boundary between audience and actors was abolished].[4] The jetty or sea-wall is a modern man-made structure which was a key structural element for re-zoning the space of the beach, acting as a screen between the reduced, marginalised working environment of the Ancient Mariner and the leisure society's pleasure beach. The jetty was usually built out into the water to divide the spaces of both shore and water into separate sections, and it cut off working fishermen and their activities physically from other beach-goers.[5] This was done deliberately for social, aesthetic, and economic reasons. As such, the sea-wall both masks different environments from each other, and enables the projection of preconceived prejudices onto those environments and their inhabitants. For the bourgeoisie, the maritime community is 'un au-

---

[2] A few scholarly examples spanning the last fifty years include Nathalie Aubert, ed., *Proust and the Visual*, Cardiff: University of Wales Press, 2013; Marion Schmid and Marion Beugnet, *Proust at the Movies*, Aldershot: Ashgate, 2004; Mieke Bal, *The Mottled Screen: Reading Proust Visually*, Stanford, CA: Stanford University Press, 1997; Victor E. Graham, *The Imagery of Proust*, Oxford: Basil Blackwell, 1966; Howard Moss, *The Magic Lantern of Marcel Proust*, London: Faber & Faber, 1963.

[3] A chapter of Howard Moss's *The Magic Lantern of Marcel Proust* studies the sexual connotations of windows in the novel; the first chapter of Roxane Hanney's *The Invisible Middle Term in Proust's 'A la recherche du temps perdu'*, New York, NY: Edwin Mellen Press, 1990, examines the shift from looking in to looking out of windows; Pedro Kadivar's *Marcel Proust ou l'esthétique de l'entre-deux: poétique de la représentation dans 'A la recherche du temps perdu'*, Paris: L'Harmattan, 2004, contains a section entitled 'Poétique de la fenêtre'.

[4] Jean-Didier Urbain, *Sur la plage: mœurs et coutumes balnéaires (XIXe-XXe siècles)*, Paris: Petite Bibliothèque Payot, 2002, 122. The English translation is *At the Beach*, London and Minneapolis, MN: University of Minnesota Press, 2003, trans. by Catherine Porter, 69. All future page references will give the French page reference first, followed by the English one.

[5] Ibid., 86-91; 46-49.

tre monde, [...] un monde exotique' [a different world [...] an exotic one].⁶ *À la recherche du temps perdu* privileges the concept of the beach as 'le théâtre d'une agitation [...] mondaine et de loisir' [a very different sort of agitation, leisure-based and worldly].⁷ Nevertheless, the world of work, whether of fishing or painting, makes its presence felt there too.

Figure 1. *Little Miss Sunshine* (2006). DVD. Twentieth Century Fox Home Entertainment (2007). [Screenshot 16:18:25]

Proust's representation of the modern beach as *écran* continues to have a wide, ongoing cultural influence: Jonathan Dayton and Valerie Faris's American comedy drama *Little Miss Sunshine* (2006) pays homage to the significance of the sea and beach to the Proustian narrative during a pivotal scene involving two of the characters. One is Frank, the former 'number one Proust scholar' in the United States, who has recently attempted suicide; the other, Dwayne, is his troubled teenage nephew with a penchant for Nietzschean existentialism.⁸ The following conversation takes place at a beach to which they have briefly escaped from the children's pageant in which Dwayne's younger sister Olive is competing:

> DWAYNE: I wish I could just sleep until I was eighteen and skip all this crap — high school and everything — just skip it.
>
> FRANK: Do you know who Marcel Proust is?

---

⁶ Ibid., 90; 49.

⁷ Ibid., 78; 41.

⁸ Nietzsche's affirmation of the importance of creativity and the responsibility of the artist to his creative self could also be seen as relevant to Proust's aims in *À la recherche du temps perdu*, itself the story of how a man becomes a writer. Dwayne dreams of becoming a pilot and escaping his present life, an aspiration which chimes with Proust's eloquent reflections on the vertiginous collapsing of space and time brought about by air travel (III, 417 and III, 612-13; IV, 423 and V, 92-3).

DWAYNE: He's the guy you teach.

FRANK: Yeah. French writer. Total loser. Never had a real job. Unrequited love affairs. Gay. Spent twenty years writing a book almost no one reads. But he's also probably the greatest writer since Shakespeare. Anyway, he uh… he gets down to the end of his life, and he looks back and decides that all those years he suffered, those were the best years of his life, 'cause they made him who he was. All those years he was happy? You know, total waste. Didn't learn a thing. So, if you sleep until you're eighteen… Ah, think of the suffering you're gonna miss. I mean high school? High school — those are your prime suffering years. You don't get better suffering than that.

Figure 2. *Little Miss Sunshine* (2006). DVD. Twentieth Century Fox Home Entertainment (2007). [Screenshot 16:18:29]

Frank explains Proust's ideas about suffering (IV, 480-85; VI, 210-215) while he and Dwayne are standing at the end of a wooden jetty overlooking a beach and the waters of the Pacific Ocean (Figure 1). This choice on the part of the directors may be regarded as a tribute to the importance of Balbec beach and the relationships which the protagonist begins there in *À la recherche du temps perdu* as the source of both the suffering and learning which he needs in order to become the writer he wishes to be. It also flags up the decisive lessons he learns there on his quest for a creative vocation. Dwayne's conversation with his uncle in the scene on the jetty helps him to resolve to become a pilot despite being colour-blind; Balbec beach informs the development of the protagonist's identity as writer. This identity is at the time of his Balbec holidays merely an idle fantasy, constantly deferred by procrastination. The holiday resort with its distinct spaces of water, sand, sea-wall, esplanade, and hotel, its many and diverse visitors, and its uncertain social networks attracts his attention as an object of sociological interest; such a space does not fit with his ideas of the kind of space(s) inhabited by creative writers and artists, repeatedly imagined in the novel as remote from the bustle and business of the social and professional world, akin to the camera obscura of the Renaissance artist/scientist. Social stratification is unclear in this new, temporary society where many benefit from 'ce changement des proportions sociales, caractéristique de la vie de bains de mer' [the alteration in social proportions which is characteristic of holiday life at the seaside] (II, 154; II, 376). The protagonist notes astutely that Balbec beach and the Grand Hôtel's motley crew of visitors reflect the rapid social and economic changes of the Belle Epoque, which saw luxury hotels transformed into obtainable leisure destinations for the bourgeoisie alongside aristocratic regulars of long standing.[9] Balbec beach serves as a space which both levels and reaffirms class, gender and generational hierarchies. At the same time the young protagonist's initial inability to consider it as conducive to creative art production underlines his acceptance of the prevailing medical idea, affirmed by his naturistic grandmother, of the beach as a space reserved solely for the body at rest, its health and animal pleasures.

The painter Elstir shows the young protagonist how mistaken his perception of the beach is when he admits him to his studio at Balbec. For Jack Murray, 'it is highly significant that the artists flourish only when away from the bustle of Paris', particularly Elstir at Balbec and Vinteuil at Combray.[10] Certainly Elstir is prolific and focused in his work at the large studio which is the reason he has taken the suburban house where the protagonist visits him. There, in his many seascapes, some of which depict fishermen at work, the protagonist recognises the painter's ability to represent nature as the senses confusedly perceive it before the intelligence corrects the initial erroneous impression. He appreciates Elstir's art for its depiction of sea and sky: 'une de ses métaphores les plus fréquentes dans les marines qu'il avait près de lui en ce moment était justement celle qui comparant la terre à la mer, supprimait entre elles toute démarcation' [One of the metaphors which recurred most often in the sea-pictures which surrounded him then was one which compares the land to the sea, blurring all distinction between them] (II, 192; II, 415). This important lesson in the poetic representation of the world may be seen as having shifted from Elstir's paintings to the Narrator's representation of the *jeunes filles*, most particularly Albertine. Indeed, a few pages before the protagonist visits Elstir for the first time, the Narrator reinforces the connection already established in the narrative between Albertine and the sea, when recalling his earliest memory of her on the sea-wall among the other girls:

---

[9] Cynthia Gamble, 'From Belle Epoque to First World War: the social panorama', in *The Cambridge Companion to Proust*, ed. by Richard Bales, Cambridge: Cambridge University Press, 2001, 7-24. Mme de Villeparisis with her entourage and personal effects is an example of the latter.

[10] Jack Murray, 'Proust's Beloved Enemy', *Yale French Studies* 32, 1964, 116.

> C'est ainsi, faisant halte, les yeux brillants sous son 'polo' que je la revois encore maintenant, silhouettée sur l'écran que lui fait, au fond, la mer, et séparée de moi par un espace transparent et azuré, le temps écoulé depuis lors, première image, toute mince dans mon souvenir, désirée, poursuivie, puis oubliée, puis retrouvée [...] (II, 186)

> [That is how I see her to this day: standing there, her eyes shining under her toque, silhouetted against the backdrop of the sea, and separated from me by the transparent sky-blue stretch of time elapsed since that moment, the first glimpse of her in my memory, a very slight image of a face first desired and pursued, then forgotten, then found again [...] (II, 409)

Together with the vision-based vocabulary in this passage, the mention of the sea as 'écran' i.e. screen or backdrop for his primeval image of Albertine establishes a connection between his memories of her, and visual technologies, whether those of photography or cinema. The implication is that his memory functions in a manner akin to a darkroom in which disparate, discontinuous images are projected, mislaid, searched for, and rediscovered.[11] The fact that she is '*silhouettée*' against this screen is suggestive of silhouette portraiture, a pre-photographic system of visual representation by which the outline of a person's face or body in profile was traced on black paper, with the result that the details of their appearance are effaced. Here Albertine's '*yeux brillants*' are the only facial feature not overcome by either the sea-screen beyond her, or the spatialized time stretching out, '*transparent et azuré*', between the present moment and the recollected image. Her bright eyes at that first sighting see him from a great distance and show only indifference, reinforcing her individuality and inaccessible secret life (II, 151-53; II, 374-76). The protagonist senses differences in social class between himself and the *petite bande*, initially wondering if they might be the young mistresses of professional cyclists because of their lack of decorum (II, 151; II, 374). Thus we find that the specificity of Albertine is already somewhat overwhelmed by the context in which the protagonist first encountered her. In this '*première image*', the sea could almost be regarded as absorbing her, eroding her distinctive characteristics, and threatening to engulf her absolutely, even as it separates her from her spatio-temporal location. Here the beach may be seen as both a screen and a stage, in the theatrical sense of a place of performance, where Albertine has 'posed' in passing to enable the protagonist to fix this image of her in his memory. It is an image divorced from any stable markers of social class or moral standing; it records an object of pure desire. The idea of the beach as liminal space where the real and the imagined intersect is here posited in relation to Albertine before being confirmed by Elstir.

Elstir's troubling of the dividing line between sky and sea continues into his depictions of the frontier between sea and land. In his *Port de Carquethuit* paint-

---

[11] Áine Larkin, *Proust Writing Photography: Fixing the Fugitive in 'À la recherche du temps perdu'*, Oxford: Legenda, 2011, 119-28.

ing, which the protagonist examines and considers at some length, this results in a curious intermingling of land- and water-based activities:

> Dans le premier plan de la plage, le peintre avait su habituer les yeux à ne pas reconnaître de frontière fixe, de démarcation absolue, entre la terre et l'océan. Des hommes qui poussaient des bateaux à la mer couraient aussi bien dans les flots que sur le sable, lequel, mouillé, réfléchissait déjà les coques comme s'il avait été de l'eau. (II, 193)

> [On the beach in the foreground, the painter had accustomed the eye to distinguish no clear frontier, no line of demarcation, between the land and the ocean. Men pushing boats out moved in the tide as on the sand, which being wet reflected the hulls as though it was water.] (II, 416)

In this pictorial blurring of the boundary between land and sea Elstir acknowledges the absence of a clear demarcation between these two ostensibly diverse realms. The metaphor he repeatedly employs in his seascapes and in the *Port de Carquethuit* painting conveys an important message to the protagonist on a number of levels: about the difficult working lives still lived and deemed worthy of artistic representation by Elstir at what is for the protagonist and the bourgeoisie a place newly devoted to leisure; about the realities of social life, not only at Balbec, but everywhere that seemingly hermetically sealed and inaccessible worlds are in fact open to connections or relationships with people from outside; and about the power of art to challenge received wisdom about the world, even in a scene as unremarkable as a small sea port where boats are shoving off. His seascapes empty of human figures situate Elstir's paintings in a modern trend for a '*désertification symbolique du littoral*' [symbolic desertification of seaports, beaches [...] and their surroundings], and his fishermen inhabit the port rather than the beach, a fact also in line with the tendency of late nineteenth and early twentieth century French painters to ignore working men or eliminate them from their representation of the shore.[12]

I. Space/Time as real/imagined

Physical suffering is the reason why the protagonist of *À la recherche du temps perdu* finds himself by the sea; as a young man, he is brought by his devoted grandmother to stay by Balbec beach because of his poor health. Immediately therefore we find the sea, the beach, and their environs associated with a sanitary and fortifying lifestyle, one his grandmother, known for her love of walking in the rain at Combray (I, 11; I, 15), is keen for her grandson to experience as much as possible. Her desire to expose him constantly to the health-giving properties of the sea leads to comical scenes, such as when she surreptitious-

---

[12] Urbain, op. cit., 81-2; 43.

ly opens a window in the dining room of the Grand Hôtel, admitting the stiff breeze which sends menus and newspapers flying, and ruffles both the hairstyles and tempers of the *'touristes méprisants, dépeignés et furieux'* [guests [united] against us in contempt, outrage and dishevelment] around her, while she remains determinedly unaware of the chaos (II, 35; II, 253). During the course of the nineteenth century, 'la pratique du bain et la sociabilité de plage s'organisent [...] autour de la maladie' [the practices of bathing and beach sociability were organized definitively around illness].[13] In keeping with the figure of the sickly male protagonist in French literary culture, such as Jean Des Esseintes in Huysmans' *A rebours* (1884), Proust's protagonist is an invalid, a would-be writer who never picks up a pen. This rejection of the conventional healthy male hero situates him in the Decadent literary tradition which itself emerged from a Romantic concern with passive or morbid characters, Benjamin Constant's Adolphe, the eponymous hero of the 1816 novel, being one pertinent example.[14] An ironic reversal is established whereby it is the aged grandmother who exults in the fresh air and liberation from social ties offered by the beach, while the young male protagonist mopes, unable to devote himself to any productive activity, least of all creative.

For Anne-Lise Amadou the journey to Balbec 'involves a confrontation with the living springs of existence' in the form of seawater and the human culture which exists around the beach.[15] Her comment implies the importance of the symbolism of the sea with regard to fecundity, and its primordial importance as source of human life, a symbolism reinforced by the French homophones 'la mer' and 'la mère'; however, no creative impulse stimulates the young protagonist into literary action at Balbec beach, and he is never described as entering the water at all. Edward J. Hughes notes 'the plural uses and significances of social spaces and practices' in Proust's novel, and the spaces that the protagonist inhabits in the Proustian narrative are repeatedly represented as a complex interplay between the real and the imagined.[16] The novel opens with a lengthy description of the difficulty of deciphering one's location in space and time on waking (I, 3-8; I, 7-12); the beach is no different as regards the intricate nexus of reality and imagination or memory which constitutes the protagonist's world. In common with many nineteenth and early twentieth century holiday-makers, the protagonist does not bathe in the sea: there is no plunging into or embracing of the violent physical sensations open to him here, but instead the gentler

---

[13] Urbain, op. cit., 133; 76.

[14] In her nuanced study, Marion Schmid shows how important the Decadent aesthetic movement was to the development of Proust's style: *Proust dans la décadence*, Paris: Honoré Champion, 2008.

[15] Anne-Lise Amadou, 'The Theme of Water in *A la recherche du temps perdu*', Modern Language Review, 72.2, April 1977, 317.

[16] Edward J. Hughes, 'Proust and Social Spaces', in *The Cambridge Companion to Proust*, ed. by Richard Bales, Cambridge: Cambridge University Press, 2001, 151-167.

baths 'de sable, d'air ou de vent, de soleil ou de lumière' [in sand, air, wind, sun, or light] prescribed for the treatment of all kinds of illnesses, and adopted by many fearful or even disgusted by the idea of physical contact with the sea.[17] As everywhere, the protagonist hovers on the edge of life and action.

The protagonist's ideas of what he will find at Balbec have already been stimulated and informed by conversations in his family and with M. Legrandin, a snobbish neighbour at Combray who waxes lyrical about the beauty of the sunsets over the beach of a 'petite baie d'une douceur charmante' [little bay, charmingly gentle] (I, 128; I, 131) at Balbec. Several classical allusions feature in his description of this bay, where 'les plages d'or semblent plus douces encore pour être attachées comme de blondes Andromèdes à ces terribles rochers des côtes voisines, à ce rivage funèbre, fameux par tant de naufrages' [the golden beaches seem gentler still because they are chained like blonde Andromedas to those terrible rocks of the nearby coast, to that gloomy shore, famed for the number of its wrecks] (I, 129; I, 131-2). This mention of the myth of Andromeda, the defenceless daughter forced to wait for death at the jaws of a sea-monster until rescued by Perseus, will later contrast amusingly with the powerful young girls the protagonist, an acknowledged weakling, actually encounters on the sands — a point to which I will return. It also underlines the way in which the beach constitutes an imagined space for the protagonist, attracting his interest through the superimposition of centuries-old images of mythical beasts and maidens onto the banal screen of the strip of sand in front of the Grand Hôtel. The beach is not the only place at Balbec to undergo this juxtaposition of real and imagined spaces; the same dynamic underpins the protagonist's apprehension of the church at Balbec, which Swann's admiring descriptions have filled with an exoticism and poetry which are disappointed when the protagonist sees it for himself (II, 19-21; II, 237-239). While the church leaves the protagonist unimpressed due to the significance he attaches to such edifices as repositories of Gothic art and history, the beach, as evinced by the reference to the Andromeda myth, is imbued with altogether earthier physical and sexual associations which are later borne out in the protagonist's interest in the *jeunes filles*.

Space as a significant frame for identity formation thus emerges as a recurrent motif in the Proustian narrative. Returning to the concerns of the opening pages of *À la recherche du temps perdu*, the protagonist's relationship with Balbec is first articulated through his adjustment to his Grand Hôtel bedroom. As elsewhere in the novel, his bedroom is a significant focus of anxiety. On arrival, he is disconcerted by how very unfamiliar it is; the furniture, the layout of the room and the loudly ticking clock all make him conscious of his strangeness in this environment, and he struggles to accept the fact of a future life in which he will appreciate this bedroom as much as he has done his previous one. However, the next morning brings a change in his attitude towards the space he will

---

[17] Urbain, op. cit., 142; 82.

inhabit while at Balbec:

> Mais le lendemain matin! […] quelle joie, pensant déjà au plaisir du déjeuner et de la promenade, de voir dans la fenêtre et dans toutes les vitrines des bibliothèques, comme dans les hublots d'une cabine de navire, la mer nue, sans ombrages et pourtant à l'ombre sur une moitié de son étendue que délimitait une ligne mince et mobile, et de suivre des yeux les flots qui s'élançaient l'un après l'autre comme des sauteurs sur un tremplin! (II, 33)

> [But what a delight there was the following morning! […] how exhilarating it was, amid pleasant prospects of breakfast and a walk, to see not only the window but all the glass doors of the bookcases, as though they were the portholes of a ship's cabin, filled by the open sea, which showed no dark designs towards me (though half of its expanse was actually darkened by a shadow, marked off from the rest of it by a thin shifting frontier), and to gaze at the long rollers which came plunging in, one after the other, like divers from a board!] (II, 251)

The images of the sea reflected in the screens formed by his bedroom window and glass bookcases indicate the insistent visual invasion of the private space of intimacy, reverie, and illness. The outside world moves emphatically indoors in this scene, suggesting the fluidity of several kinds of boundaries in the seaside town, whether spatial, social, or psychological. Anne-Lise Amadou observes that for the protagonist, going to Balbec 'is an experience that takes place before life comes to mean petrifaction. Balbec is the place that opens up to the sea, that dissolves the very boundaries between land and sea'.[18] Certainly, the simile in this passage of '*les hublots d'une cabine de navire*' transforms the Grand Hôtel into a great ship breasting the waves, another image suggestive of constant movement and change, but exciting now rather than threatening as on his arrival the previous evening. The proximity of the sea and the beach along which the ritual of the '*promenade*' takes place stimulates the protagonist, and it is the light reflecting off the water and the sand that transfers '*la mer nue*', with all its ambiguous promise, into his bedroom, with the happy result that it propels him out of it. The simile of the waves as divers jumping on a springboard indicates the protagonist's acceptance of the energy- and health-giving properties attributed to the sea, and the springboard itself implies a kind of frivolity and exuberant fun which are seldom part of his life. The sea reflected in the screen of the glass obscures the books in the three cases in his bedroom, suggesting the possibility that life here will involve less stillness, reading, introspection and imagining, and more looking, moving, and living of his own.

---

[18] Anne-Lise Amadou, op. cit., 317.

II. Body and Space

But how does Marcel actually interact with the beach? In spite of his initial enthusiasm as expressed in the quotation above, his solitude and physical frailty mean that, far from playing tennis or horse-riding daily like some of the young people staying at the hotel who appear to him to be 'statues équestres de demi-dieux' [equestrian statues of demi-gods], he has no exciting pastimes, and sees himself in comparison with them as a 'pauvre garçon […] qui ne quittait la salle à manger de l'hôtel que pour aller s'asseoir sur le sable' [paltry person, who had nothing to do other than exchange a seat in the hotel dining-room for a seat on the sands] (II, 43; II, 261-2). Here the sand functions less as a neutral meeting-place which dissolves social barriers, thereby facilitating and allowing friendships between people from different socio-economic backgrounds who would not interact anywhere else, than as a blank wasteland divorced from the teeming social potentialities of the hotel itself. In his isolation the protagonist on the sand lacks any framework which might enable him to meet and interact with those around him. Thus we see the beach as maintaining social boundaries and conventions, in spite of its apparent openness and liminality as a space. Furthermore, the protagonist receives no help from his meagre existing social network, since 'ma grand'mère […] trouvait qu'aux bains de mer il faut être du matin au soir sur la plage à humer le sel et qu'on n'y doit connaître personne, parce que les visites, les promenades sont autant de pris sur l'air marin' [my grandmother […] believed that when staying at a seaside resort one should be on the beach from morning to evening inhaling the salt and that one ought not to know anyone thereabouts because visits and excursions were only so much time taken from the sea air] (I, 128; I, 131).

Though forming or renewing social contacts are the least of his grandmother's priorities at Balbec (II, 45-6; II, 264-5), they are the protagonist's dearest wish, and so his interactions with this seaside space are, as in Paris, shaped by the relationships he cultivates there. The physical space of the beach with its screening sea-wall serves, like other places in the Proustian narrative, as the frame within which those relationships first develop, as Georges Poulet observes in *L'Espace proustien*, where he states that:

> Immanquablement donc, chez Proust, dans la réalité comme dans le songe, lieux et personnes s'unissent. L'imagination proustienne ne saurait concevoir les êtres autrement qu'en les posant contre un fond local qui les fait apparaître en leur servant de tain de miroir. Evoquer un être human, cet acte si simple, qui est l'acte premier du romancier composant son œuvre, revient, chez Proust, à rendre visible une forme en la plaçant dans un cadre.[19]

---

[19] Georges Poulet, *L'Espace proustien*, Paris: Gallimard, 1963, 41-42.

[Infallibly, then, with Proust, in reality as in dream, persons and places are united. The Proustian imagination would not know how to conceive beings otherwise than in placing them against a local background that plays for them the part of foil and mirror. To evoke a human being, this act so simple, which is the first act of the novelist composing his work, is tantamount with Proust to rendering a form visible and putting it in a framework.][20]

The beach's potential dissolution of social barriers is an important characteristic which distinguishes it from many other sites in *À la recherche du temps perdu*, even if initially this does not appear to be happening for the young protagonist.[21] The late nineteenth century saw a rapid acceleration in the pace of economic development in France, with the result that many were lifted from petit bourgeois to upper-middle class status, and this alteration in the social landscape is reflected in Proust's novel where, as Malcolm Bowie observes, 'the narrator serves a long apprenticeship in the discrimination between classes, and addresses his reader as one eager learner to another'.[22] Walter Benjamin noted 'the explosive power of Proust's critique of society', with the family, the bourgeoisie, and the aristocracy all fair game. The bourgeoisie's codes of rigid social classification and sharply defined castes play out on the beach where the protagonist may gaze upon but not speak to or play with those around him.[23]

Watching young people passing on the sea-wall, he is aware of how being at a seaside resort alters the links between himself and them: 'je les regardais avec une curiosité passionnée, dans cet éclairage aveuglant de la plage où les proportions sociales sont changées' [I sat gazing at them with passionate curiosity, as they dawdled in that seaside dazzle which alters social dimensions] (II, 35; II, 253). He is acute in his observation of a broad range of other hotel residents from a variety of socio-cultural backgrounds, and almost a hundred pages are devoted to his accounts of their movements and conversations before his own social life begins to develop. Far from being independent of his background in bourgeois Paris, however, his introduction to the aristocratic Robert de Saint-Loup comes about as a direct consequence of his grandmother's long friendship with Saint-Loup's relative Mme de Villeparisis, a friendship renewed in spite of his grandmother's efforts to ignore the latter, when the two ladies meet in a hotel doorway (II, 54; II, 272-3). This friendship and his pre-existing acquaintance with Bloch, also resident at Balbec, are the exception to the circumstances surrounding the most important links the protagonist establishes with others by

---

[20] Georges Poulet, *Proustian Space*, trans. by Elliott Coleman, Baltimore, MD and London: The Johns Hopkins University Press, 1977, 27.

[21] Jupien's male brothel in Paris during the First World War is another such space where socially imposed boundaries are suspended in deference to the demands of desire (IV, 388-412).

[22] Malcolm Bowie, *Proust among the Stars*, London and New York, NY: Columbia University Press, 1998, 127.

[23] Walter Benjamin, 'The Image of Proust', *Illuminations*, London: Pimlico, 1999, 202.

the beach, and they serve to affirm that in spite of its seeming promise of freedom from social convention, the beach is never really isolated from the other social spaces the protagonist inhabits. It does however permit a certain degree of erosion of social boundaries, as evinced by the fact that it is through the protagonist that the very modern, middle-class Jewish character Bloch becomes acquainted with Saint-Loup who is the embodiment of timeless French aristocratic virtues. In spite of Bloch's keen interest in Saint-Loup, however, the latter declines to deepen the acquaintance. The beach may facilitate some seepage between diverse social groups, but ultimately the established modes of exclusion prevail.

The most significant relationships the protagonist forms at Balbec are his friendships with the painter Elstir and the *petite bande* of young girls in bloom after whom the second volume of the novel is named. In uncharacteristically proactive style, he begins his acquaintance with Elstir by writing him a letter at the restaurant where they are both dining (II, 182-84; II, 406); and it is this acquaintance which leads to his introduction to Albertine, for him the most significant member of the *petite bande* (II, 224-29; II, 448-52). This introduction is the culmination of many hours spent on the beach contemplating the girls, who will, as Amadou states, become Balbec for him.[24] When he sees the *jeunes filles* for the first time, they are represented as distinct from other residents of the town, and even from humanity:

> [...] presque encore à l'extrémité de la digue où elles faisaient mouvoir une tache singulière, je vis s'avancer cinq ou six fillettes, aussi différentes, par l'aspect et par les façons, de toutes les personnes auxquelles on était accoutumé à Balbec, qu'aurait pu l'être, débarquée on ne sait d'où, une bande de mouettes qui exécute à pas comptés sur la plage — les retardataires rattrapant les autres en voletant — une promenade dont le but semble aussi obscur aux baigneurs qu'elles ne paraissent pas voir, que clairement déterminé pour leur esprit d'oiseaux. (II, 146)

> [[...] still far away along the esplanade, where they made a strange mass of moving colours, I saw five or six young girls, as different in their appearance and ways from all the other people one was used to seeing in Balbec as the odd gaggle of seagulls which turns up out of the blue to strut along the beach, the stragglers flapping their wings to catch up with the leaders, in a procession which seems as obscure in its purpose to the bathers, whom they seem not to see, as it is clear to their bird-minds.](II, 369)

Here we find the beach serving as a screen for the projection of the wishful protagonist's desires and dreams of the young girls who are described as beings apart, both literally, given their spatial position on the sea-wall, and figuratively, in the analogy established between their synchronised movements and a flock of seagulls. This avian analogy implies their suitability for their environment, while also pointing up the crowd mentality hinted at in the lack of differentia-

---

[24] Op. cit., 315.

tion between them in this description. The association of Albertine with birds will be a recurrent feature of the protagonist's representation of her, and may be traced in part to the fact that he first saw her on the Balbec sea-wall, and partly to the aptness of such a metaphor for a girl who remains fundamentally elusive throughout her relationship with the protagonist, and even after her death. For Randi Marie Birn, 'Proust consciously and successfully structured Albertine around an idea of intangibility. If she is the most difficult character in the novel to get to know, it is because Proust intended her to be so'.[25] The beach functions now as a space which opens up all the potentialities the protagonist requires for his imaginative perception of the passing girls; yet it will be through the exploitation of existing social structures and hierarchies that he will gain admittance into the girls' world, thanks to their mutual acquaintance with Elstir.

The choice of the seagull ties together both the elusive freedom of all flying birds, and the marine environment where Albertine and Marcel first met: Victor Graham notes that 'the sea gull itself is a bird of ill omen, and it is aesthetically fitting that Albertine, who causes Marcel so much grief, should be primarily associated with that bird'.[26] The fact that the girls wear sports clothes and carry golf clubs, as one pushes her bicycle, further indicates their vigorous engagement with all those recreational possibilities of the seaside which the protagonist cannot enjoy; their 'tenue spéciale' [accoutrements] (II, 146; II, 369) marks them out as modern sportswomen, and their confidence of gesture, 'que donne un parfait assouplissement de son propre corps et un mépris sincère du reste de l'humanité' [which comes from the perfect mastery of a supple body and sincere contempt for the rest of humanity] (II, 147; II, 370), reinforces their difference from the puny protagonist who is so interested in all those around him. Just as the protagonist's vigorous grandmother contrasts to comic effect with her ailing grandson, these girls overturn the established gender distinctions firmly in place in the late nineteenth century with regard to their admirer. For him, they are models of human beauty 'que je voyais là, devant la mer, comme des statues exposées au soleil sur un rivage de la Grèce' [that met my eye, against the sea, like statues in the sun along a shore in Greece] (II, 149; II, 371); they move along the sea-wall 'comme une lumineuse comète' [like a shining comet] (II, 149; II, 371). Using the Classical simile of Greek statues together with that of a comet in the sky shows both the temporal and spatial separation he sees as existing between him and the girls on the Balbec beach: they are beyond his reach in every sense. The sea-wall protects the land from the encroachment of the sea; it also carves up the shoreline, like the jetty designed to separate fishermen from holidaymakers. The bird-girls walking along it imply their ease in multiple territories — i.e. in the worlds on either side of the sea-wall: land, air, and water

---

[25] Randi Marie Birn, 'Love and Communication: An Interpretation of Proust's Albertine', *The French Review* 40.2, November 1966, 221.

[26] Graham, *The Imagery of Proust*, 65.

— and so their elusiveness for the inhibited protagonist. Once again we see here an exploitation of the beach as a site of potentiality where he may project his desire for the unattainable without considering the possibility of actual contact between him and his object.

III. The Beach and Albertine

The protagonist's own belief that the goddess-like *jeunes filles* on the sea-wall are inaccessible is of course overturned thanks to his acquaintance with Elstir, who knows them and facilitates Marcel's introduction at his studio to a demure Albertine (II, 226-28; II, 449-52). Soon after this first meeting, it is she who approaches Marcel on the sea-wall and addresses him in an abrupt, familiar tone which contrasts strongly with her previous decorum:

> 'Vous ne faites rien ici? On ne vous voit jamais au golf, aux bals du Casino; vous ne montez pas à cheval non plus. Comme vous devez vous raser! Vous ne trouvez pas qu'on se bêtifie à rester tout le temps sur la plage? Ah! Vous aimez à faire le lézard?' (II, 231)

> [Don't you do anything here? You're never to be seen at the golf-course or the dances in the Casino, and you're never out riding a horse either. You must find it all a great bore. You don't think that people who just stay on the beach are a bit silly? Oh, I see, you like just lazing about.] (II, 454)

As well as making her dynamism, love of sport, and attitude to the protagonist's idleness clear, Albertine's questions imply that, contrary to his idea that she and the rest of the *petite bande* were beings apart, aloof and unapproachable, she had previously noticed him on the beach and wondered at his absence from the seaside amusements available to the young people at Balbec. He has been part of her inner world, just as she has become part of his. Marcel is thrilled at this discovery, and his rapid introduction to the other *jeunes filles* gives him access not only to Albertine, but to all of the young girls. Infatuated with them all, his imagination runs away with him with regard to the silent Gisèle when she smiles at him on being introduced:

> Sans doute m'avait-elle remarqué sur la plage même quand je ne la connaissais pas encore et pensait-elle à moi depuis; peut-être était-ce pour se faire admirer de moi qu'elle s'était moquée du vieux monsieur et parce qu'elle ne parvenait pas à me connaître qu'elle avait eu les jours suivants l'air morose. De l'hôtel, je l'avais souvent aperçue le soir se promenant sur la plage. C'était probablement avec l'espoir de me rencontrer. (II, 241-42)

> [She must have noticed me down on the beach, at a time when I had no knowledge of her, and must have been thinking about me ever since — perhaps her reason for laughing at the old gentleman had been so that I should admire her,

perhaps her reason for going about, the following days, with such an unhappy look, was her displeasure at not being able to get to know me! Sitting in the hotel, I had often noticed her taking an evening stroll down by the beach. She must have been hoping to meet me!] (II, 465)

The protagonist moves swiftly from one extreme to another – from a sense of his own absolute non-existence for the *jeunes filles* (II, 151-153; II, 374-6) to this comical conviction ('sans doute', 'c'était probablement') that his own attractiveness explains Gisèle's behaviour both with the *petite bande* on the seawall, and when she is alone on the beach. The idea of separate, enclosed social worlds at Balbec has thus been superseded by that of a community populated by curious individuals communicating silently their mutual fascination through their interlocking gazes and smiles — or by jumping over an old man in his deckchair (II, 149-50; II, 372-73). So the beach as social space is central to the development of the protagonist's evolving understanding of the nature of perception and communication, and of the fundamental importance of time as an element of both processes. Here we find the protagonist deftly juxtaposing an imagined future for Gisèle within his own remembered past: real and imagined combine to encouraging effect for him as regards his proximity to an object of erotic desire. Similarly, an old photograph of the *jeunes filles* as small children tells the Narrator a good deal about the girls' past (II, 180-81; II, 403), while their future is also clear to him as they play together on the beach:

> Comme sur un plant où les fleurs mûrissent à des époques différentes, je les avais vues, en de vieilles dames, sur cette plage de Balbec, ces dures graines, ces mous tubercules, que mes amies seraient un jour. Mais qu'importait? En ce moment, c'était la saison des fleurs. (II, 246)

> [As though on a seedling whose blossoms ripen at different times, I had seen in old ladies, on that beach at Balbec, the dried-up seeds and sagging tubers that my girl-friends would become. But, now that it was the time for buds to blossom, what did that matter?] (II, 469)

The beach is here represented as the stage upon which the girls' organic lives will be played out, and upon which they will ultimately wither from beautiful girls in bloom to tough old ladies, 'ces graines dures, ces mous tubercules'. The simile connecting the beach and a seedling or nursery plantation ('un plant') is significant in that it underlines the importance of the beach as a space of potentiality now conducive to health, fertile growth, and longevity; Andrée, as well as the protagonist, is at Balbec in pursuit of strength and well-being (II, 247; II, 470). Far from the sterile empty space it was when he first arrived, the beach is transformed by his social inclusion into what he perceives as lush soil, nourishing his indiscriminate love for all the girls before his attention becomes fixed on Albertine. Less sand and lonely liminality, it is the fruitful means by which his relationship with the *petite bande* grows and develops.

In Paris, many pages later, after Albertine's flight from the controlling, jealous protagonist and her death in a horse-riding accident, the beach is central to the protagonist's description of his emotional state when he finds himself tormented by jealousy about her possible homosexual affairs at Balbec: 'Je me voyais perdu dans la vie comme sur une plage illimitée où j'étais seul et où, dans quelque sens que j'allasse, je ne la [Albertine] rencontrerais jamais' [I saw myself lost in life as if I were alone, on a boundless shore where, whichever direction I took, I would never meet her] (IV, 101; V, 486). This simile expresses internal emotional upheaval in purely spatial terms, themselves so broad ('illimitée') as to be completely disorienting. The loss of Albertine, and his uncertainty about her identity and sexual preferences, leaves the protagonist without a focal point around which to make sense of his life. This desire for the woman he loves to play the role of anchor (to extend the maritime metaphor) has already been made explicit with regard to Albertine when he describes her as 'une pierre autour de laquelle il a neigé, [...] le centre générateur d'une immense construction qui passait par le plan de mon cœur' [a stone covered in snow, [...] no more than the core of an immense construction elaborated by my heart] (IV, 22; V, 406). The beach is central to his construction of her identity and appearance, resulting in this evocation of his frightening isolation in a space which, when divorced from the society and culture surrounding Balbec, leaves him floundering. A limitless beach suggests an environment hostile to individual human life, and stripped of meaningful contact with either the sea or the land; the protagonist is effectively suspended in a sandy no man's land. He wonders about the sexual encounters Albertine may have had with other girls among the dunes, once more underlining how rich in potential for transgression the beach is, for the imagined lives of the *jeunes filles*, if not for his real one.

IV. Proust's beach in film and on TV

Given the significance of the visual in *À la recherche du temps perdu*, as outlined early in this chapter, the ways in which Proust's novel has influenced the work of film and television-makers who have adapted parts or all of it, or simply been inspired by it, seemed a pertinent question, specifically in relation to the beach motif. This is due also to the fact that the scope of Proust's novel, as it explores a life lived in the late nineteenth and early twentieth centuries, has secured it a place in the literary canon which continues to affect the work of writers and creative artists working in a variety of media.[27] As such, Proust's work may func-

---

[27] In recent years, there have been popular comic book adaptations by Stéphane Heuet; Véronique Aubouy has developed an art project around the challenge of video-recording people reading Proust aloud http://www.aubouy.fr/proust-lu.html. Harold Pinter adapted Proust for a screenplay in 1972.

tion both as an inspiration and a foil against which to articulate new ways of thinking about French society and culture. The beach is a space which is used in diverse ways by those, like Jonathan Dayton and Valerie Faris, working with or referencing Proust's novel. Directors such as Nina Companeez, Chantal Akerman, and Raoul Ruiz have in diverse ways made compelling use of the beach in their cinematic and televisual adaptations of Proust's work. Akerman's film *La Captive* (2000), inspired by Proust's work rather than a direct adaptation, opens with the protagonist Simon watching a home video of a group of girls playing among the waves on a Normandy beach, and ends with the death by drowning of the Albertine character, named Ariane in this film. As Martine Beugnet and Marion Schmid point out in *Proust at the Movies*, Proust had originally intended to have Albertine die by drowning in the sea, an act she threatens to carry out at one point in *Sodome et Gomorrhe* during an argument with the protagonist.[28] In fact, however, Albertine dies as a result of a horse-riding accident; her association with speed and sport from her earliest appearance at Balbec with her bicycle and golf clubs continues in the manner of her death. Akerman's film thus returns Albertine to the sea by which the protagonist first encounters her, in a neat dovetailing with the opening scenes.

In *Le Temps retrouvé* (1999), Raoul Ruiz privileges the beach to such an extent that it dominates the film poster, forming a background screen against which the back of the aged protagonist, in evening dress, is silhouetted. Nina Companeez's television adaptation of *À la recherche du temps perdu* in two 110-minute episodes was shown on French television (France 2) on the 1st and 2nd February 2011.[29] Like Akerman and Ruiz, Companeez places the beach at the centre of Balbec life during the chapter devoted to *À l'ombre des jeunes filles en fleurs*, overlaying the calls of sea birds on the scene of the protagonist and his grandmother's arrival at the Grand Hôtel, and providing a shot outwards from the hotel reception area, through the revolving door, to the sunny seascape (I: 5mins 34s). His grandmother's enthusiasm for the sea and fresh air is narrated over a sequence depicting her joy at being on the beach, raising her arms in exultation at having avoided her old friend Mme de Villeparisis (I: 11mins 13-14s). The sea-wall, beach, and seascape are the backdrop to many sequences: that of the protagonist's developing friendship with Saint-Loup, of their meeting with Bloch, of the representation of Bloch's seductive sisters who as part of the Jewish community at Balbec are considered a society apart, neither acknowledged by nor acknowledging any of the other people at the seaside (II, 98; II,

---

[28] Beugnet and Schmid, *Proust at the Movies*, 174-5.

[29] In a review quoted in *La Croix*, Jean-Yves Tadié questions the wisdom of condensing Proust's novel into only four hours of television, and suggests that English television, which he sees as having greater respect for literary culture, would have made a twelve-hour adaptation. Available: http://www.la-croix.com/Culture-Loisirs/Culture/Actualite/Nina-Companeez-sous-le-charme-de-Proust-_NG_-2011-01-28-562651. Accessed 30 October 2012.

318-9) — the Jewish community at Balbec is the only social world which appears to remain truly shut off from the rest of society. (This is of course not really the case, as Albertine's silent communication with two Jewish lesbian girls via a mirror in the Casino makes plain in *Sodome et Gomorrhe* (III, 198; IV, 203).) The protagonist's first sighting of the *petite bande* likewise takes place along the promenade, ending with the girls shot from the back leaning against the seawall and looking out over the beach to the sea. Companeez's adaptation, though necessarily truncated in many respects because of its brevity, is careful to underline the importance of the beach, the sea, and the seawall, with many scenes and conversations not explicitly taking place on the beach being filmed there.

Conclusion

On his second stay at Balbec, two years after his first, the protagonist is very aware of the importance of his meeting with Elstir as regards the development of his own ability to see the world around him. The sea and beach prove this to him:

> Comme la première année, les mers, d'un jour à l'autre, étaient rarement les mêmes. Mais d'ailleurs elles ne ressemblaient guère à celles de cette première année, soit parce que maintenant c'était le printemps avec ses orages, soit parce que, même si j'étais venu à la même date que la première fois, des temps différents, plus changeants, auraient pu déconseiller cette côte à certaines mers indolentes, vaporeuses et fragiles que j'avais vues pendant des jours ardents dormir sur la plage en soulevant imperceptiblement leur sein bleuâtre d'une molle palpitation, soit surtout que mes yeux instruits par Elstir à retenir précisément les éléments que j'écartais volontairement jadis, contemplaient longuement ce que la première année ils ne savaient pas voir. (III, 179)

> [As in that first year, the seas were rarely the same from one day to the next. But they scarcely resembled those of that first year, on the other hand, either because now it was spring, with its storms, or because, even if I had come on the same date as the first occasion, the different, more changeable weather might not have recommended this coast to certain indolent, vaporous and fragile seas that I had seen on days of burning heat sleeping on the beach, lifting their blue bosom imperceptibly with a soft palpitation, or above all because my eyes, educated by Elstir to retain precisely those elements that I had once wilfully discarded, dwelt at length on what that first year they had not known how to see.] (IV, 185)

Thanks to his time at Balbec, Marcel has learned to see many things he had not previously been able to make out, and the beach has been instrumental in his education, both as the place where he saw and came to know the jeunes filles whose beauty and grace, together with the invisible social codes he has learned, made them appear initially so distant and unassailable, and as the space represented in Elstir's paintings which conveyed a key message about the power of art. The power of art in framing the beach is mirrored in the power of the beach to frame social and amorous experiences which later come to demand literary representation, in the form we have just read thanks to the dual narratological structure of the Proustian narrative, which looks simultaneously forward and back in time. In his essay 'The Parergon', Jacques Derrida notes that 'a frame is in essence constructed and therefore fragile, this is the essence or truth of the frame. If such a thing exists'.[30] For the protagonist, both Elstir's paintings and the beach itself serve as frames facilitating his apprehension of previously unsuspected truths about the way society and perception are constructed, socially and individually. These truths about perception, memory, and time will go on to frame the literary narrative the protagonist feels compelled to write. The beach itself actively frames the protagonist's encounters with other people and their social, sexual, and cultural idiosyncrasies. In his nuanced representation of the French beach in the late nineteenth and early twentieth centuries, Proust successfully articulates and uses its multiple layers of meaning and function. It serves as an elemental site which is subjected to different framing processes (physical, social, painterly, and imaginative) but can also be seen to enact a process of framing itself in actively shaping the protagonist's interaction with his surroundings.

Some of the relationships begun on the sands and in the cliffs by the beach will prove central to his developing knowledge of the mysteries of human behaviour and the obsessive nature of sexual jealousy. They will make him very unhappy, while also leading him to appreciate all the more the wonder of fleeting intimacy and the fugitive joy of love. When he believes he may kiss all of Balbec beach on Albertine's cheeks (II, 658; II, 361), because of 'les impressions d'une série maritime qui m'était particulièrement chère' [the impressions of a series of sea-scapes that were particularly dear to me] (II, 658; II, 361) which surround the figure of this girl, he acknowledges how her very inaccessibility has nourished his desire for her. Pleasure and pain thus crystallize in the image of Albertine 'profilée sur la mer' [silhouetted against the sea] (II, 658; II, 361), never to be truly possessed or even remembered. The elusive girl and the ever-changing sea and shoreline at Balbec beach are inscribed together inextricably in the protagonist's mind: quixotic, powerful, and playful by turns, each proves to be an invaluable and inexhaustible source to be sounded and marvelled over as he struggles to realise his vocation as writer.

---

[30] Jacques Derrida and Craig Owens, 'The Parergon', *October* 9, Summer, 1979, 33.

References

Amadou, Anne-Lise, 'The Theme of Water in *A la recherche du temps perdu*', *Modern Language Review*, 72.2, April 1977, 310-21.

Aubert, Nathalie, ed., *Proust and the Visual*, Cardiff: University of Wales Press, 2013.

Bal, Mieke, *The Mottled Screen: Reading Proust Visually*, Stanford, CA: Stanford University Press, 1997.

Benjamin, Walter, *Illuminations*, London: Pimlico, 1999.

Beugnet, Martine and Schmid, Marion, *Proust at the Movies*, Aldershot: Ashgate, 2004.

Birn, Randi Marie, 'Love and Communication: An Interpretation of Proust's Albertine', *The French Review* 40.2, November 1966, 221-8.

Bowie, Malcolm, *Proust among the Stars*, London and New York, NY: Columbia University Press, 1998.

Derrida, Jacques and Craig Owens, Craig, 'The Parergon', *October* 9, Summer, 1979, 3-41.

Gamble, Cynthia, 'From Belle Epoque to First World War: the social panorama', in *The Cambridge Companion to Proust*, ed. by Richard Bales, Cambridge: Cambridge University Press, 2001, 7-24.

Graham, Victor, E., *The Imagery of Proust*, Oxford: Basil Blackwell, 1966.

Hanney, Roxane, *The Invisible Middle Term in Proust's 'A la recherche du temps perdu'*, New York, NY: Edwin Mellen Press, 1990.

Hughes, Edward J., 'Proust and Social Spaces', in *The Cambridge Companion to Proust*, ed. by Richard Bales, Cambridge: Cambridge University Press, 2001, 151-167.

Áine Larkin, *Proust Writing Photography: Fixing the Fugitive in 'A la recherche du temps perdu'*, Oxford: Legenda, 2011.

Kadivar, Pedro, *Marcel Proust ou l'esthétique de l'entre-deux: poétique de la représentation dans 'A la recherche du temps perdu'*, Paris: L'Harmattan, 2004.

Murray, Jack, 'Proust's Beloved Enemy', *Yale French Studies* 32, 1964, 112-17.

Moss, Howard, *The Magic Lantern of Marcel Proust*, London: Faber & Faber, 1963.

Poulet, George, *L'Espace proustien*, Paris: Gallimard, 1963. Translated as *Proustian Space*, trans. by Elliott Coleman, Baltimore, MD and London: The Johns Hopkins University Press, 1977.

Proust, Marcel, *À la recherche du temps perdu*, ed. Jean-Yves Tadié, 4 vols, Paris: La Pléiade, 1987-89.

_____ , *In Search of Lost Time*, ed. Christopher Prendergast, 6 vols, London: Penguin, 2003.

Schmid, Marion, *Proust dans la décadence*, Paris: Honoré Champion, 2008.

Urbain, Jean-Dider, *Sur la plage: mœurs et coutumes balnéaires (XIXe-XXe siècles)*, Paris: Petite Bibliothèque Payot, 2002. Translated as *At the Beach*, trans. by Catherine Porter, London and Minneapolis, MN: University of Minnesota Press, 2003.

Filmography

Little Miss Sunshine, directed by Jonathan Dayton and Valerie Faris, DVD, Twentieth Century Fox Home Entertainment, 2007 [2006].

5.
VACANCE: VACANCY AND VACATION IN THE FILMS OF JACQUES ROZIER

Gilles Chamerois

The story of the beach in French cinema begins on 28 December 1895, the date generally accepted, at least in France, as marking the birth of cinema. Indeed the final film to be shown as part of the first ever paid public screening by Auguste and Louis Lumière in the Grand Café in Paris was 'La baignade en mer,' [*Bathing in the Sea*]. Yet films such as 'Workers Leaving the Lumière Factory' or 'The Arrival of a Train at La Ciotat Station'[1] are more immediately associated with the beginnings of cinema than this view of what the tourists actually did once they had disembarked from the train in the seaside resort of La Ciotat. Shot during the family's regular holiday in the resort, the *Baignade* had been shown before, on 21 September 1895. It was included in the screening the brothers held at the end of the vacation, at the family manor house, Le Clos des Plages, in La Ciotat. The audience comprised a total of 150 viewers compared to 35 at the December screening in Paris.[2] But as the paid screening in Paris has laid its claim to posterity over the free holiday screening far away from the capital, so the images associated with work and technology have taken precedence over those of the beach in the Golfe d'Amour during summer.

Still, there is a mysterious affinity between the new medium and the relentless movement of the white line of the waves, together with the children's playful repetitive act of walking to the end of the jetty, jumping into the water and splashing about. Furthermore, the issue of the cinematographer's role in creating this fugitive moment of play by dint of his presence on the beach remains an open question.

---

[1] Ironically the latter was not actually shown during this first screening. Deac Rossell, *A Chronology of Cinema, 1889-1896*, special issue of *Film History* 7.2, Summer 1995, 136.

[2] Jacques Rittaud-Hutinet, *Les frères Lumière: inventeurs du cinéma*, Paris: Flammarion, 1993, 373. Rittaud-Hutinet gives the date as 22 September but seems here to be mistaken, as the invitation card shown in the La Ciotat Museum attests. See http://www.museeciotaden.org/cinema/cinematographe.htm. Accessed 15/05/2015. The name given for the film shown in La Ciotat, *Baignade sur la plage*, is slightly different from the one given to that shown in Paris, but the film seems to be the same, as there is no *Baignade sur la plage* in the Lumière catalogue.

This chapter considers the importance of the beach and holidays for a director whose cinema 'is so spare and devoid of sophistication that it brings us back to the original purity of the Lumières' first films.'[3] With the exception of his first short film, *Rentrée des Classes*, and his last, unreleased feature film, *Fifi Martingale*, all Rozier's films give a prominent place to the beach. In all four of his released feature films he has brought his camera and his characters away from Paris and back to the very beach that saw the birth of cinema, at least long enough for an eerie vacation.[4] I will first delineate how Rozier's career takes stock of the evolution of the vacation in French society, and of the way increased emphasis on freedom provided less and less space in which to exercise and enjoy such freedom. Then, using the paradoxical template of Rozier's only beachless film, *Rentrée des classes*, I will suggest that the beach is not only the exemplary locus of the gradual commodification of vacations, but can transcend such commodification for several reasons. In Rozier's films, it is precisely because the beach constitutes a liminal place, associated with a liminal time, that of the end of the vacation, that it can enable encounters with strangers and welcome the unexpected through the vacancy of its space.

Vacation

Rozier's short filmography draws a portrait of the evolution of French society's relationship with vacations over a thirty-year period. In the short film *Blue Jeans* (1958), the two *dragueurs*, or pick-up artists, drifting on the Croisette in Cannes hopefully ask their would-be conquests if they are from Paris. Only a few years later, the sixties are already in full swing in Rozier's first feature film *Adieu Philippine* (1962). When Michel, who works in television in Paris, has to decide on his final holiday before being drafted into the army and fighting in Algeria, Cannes has ceased to be a destination of choice. He first goes to the Club Méditerranée village in Calvi, Corsica, at that time a laboratory for the supposed abolition of hierarchies in a network of equal individuals.[5] The film offers a sequence worthy of Jean Rouch on the budding consumer society invading once pristine places[6] as well as the free time of the vacation, and even

---

[3] Jean de Baroncelli, review of *Du côté d'Orouët*, *Le Monde*, September 28, 1973. Unless otherwise indicated, all translations from sources referenced in French are mine.

[4] As is so neatly encapsulated in the title of his last released film, *Maine Océan*, named after the train departing from Paris Montparnasse Station, on Avenue du Maine, to the Atlantic coast.

[5] See Alain Ehrenberg, 'Le Club Méditerranée: 1935-1960,' in *Les vacances : un rêve, un produit, un miroir*, ed. Brigitte Ouvry-Vial, René Louis and Jean-Bernard Pouy, *Autrement* 111, January 1990, 117-129.

[6] On the link between the two filmmakers, see Maxime Scheinfeigel, *Les âges du cinéma: trois parcours dans l'évolution des représentations filmiques*, Paris: L'Harmattan,

the psyche in regressive and infantile games and so-called primitive dances. The general movement of colonization of the beach, whereby Club Med villages supposed to emulate the savages' huts and presumed sexual freedom begin to encroach on the landscape, is fast destroying the 'authenticity' that is supposed to be their main asset, and Michel and his two girlfriends have trouble finding secluded beaches.

This presumably is not possible at all a few years later, at the time of *Du côté d'Orouët* (shot in 1969), and the Club Méditerranée village in fashion then is still further away, in Sicily. Even that destination is marked as somewhat *passé*, since it is proposed by Gilbert, the obtrusive and dorky boss trying at his own peril to gatecrash the holiday one of his employees is sharing with her two female companions. As Jacques Mandelbaum has argued, *Du côté d'Orouët* 'settles the score, four years before [Jean Eustache's] *La Maman et la Putain* (1973), with the sexual revolution in the wake of May 68, exposing it as a more efficient obstacle than the social and moral barriers it supposedly abolished.'[7] In order to keep up the pretence of freedom and authenticity, the civilisation of leisure has had to find 'authentic' places further and further away before having inexorably to move on in the search for ever 'freer' experiences. By the time of Rozier's next film, *Les naufragés de l'île de la Tortue* (1976), the quest for exoticism has shifted to the Caribbean, and even there Jean-Arthur Bonaventure cannot find a real desert island for his Robinson-like holiday concept.[8] The film relates his blundering location survey, and Mandelbaum notes that with it Rozier goes even further in his denunciation of a society that has managed to turn dreams into a commodity. Finally, the train controller of *Maine Océan* (1986) will at the end of a surreal, alcohol-infused weekend in Île d'Yeu briefly dream of becoming a star in New York thanks to a South-American impresario, offering 'another occasion for Rozier to expose the myth of success in what was arguably the vainest decade of all, the eighties.'[9] In each film, the myth that the space and time of the vacation is at the very least a reprieve from hierarchical relations is undermined. Indeed, the beach offers the perfect locus for an incisive probing of these hierarchical relations shaping society at large:

2002, 83-90, and Gilles Mouëllic, *Improviser le cinéma*, Crisnée: Yellow Now, 2011, 68-69.

[7] Jacques Mandelbaum, 'Le présent lui appartient,' in *Jacques Rozier: le funambule*, ed. Emmanuel Burdeau, Paris: Cahiers du cinéma/Centre Pompidou, 2001, 14.

[8] The two catchphrases mentioned in the film are self-explanatory: '3000 francs, rien compris'—'3000 francs, nothing included'—and 'Robinson, démerde-toi !'—'Robinson, you're up shit creek, without a paddle.' On this film as a 'counter hippie manifesto,' see Michel Marie 'L'aventure, c'est parfois l'aventure, parfois la galère,' in *Aventure et cinéma*, ed. Jacques Aumont, Paris: Cinémathèque française, 2001, 106.

[9] Mandelbaum, 'Le présent lui appartient,' 14.

> The contemporary beach is the theater of an 'oblique' society, one that deceives its world in that it does not inscribe itself definitely either in an extension of external society or in a total break with that society.[10] It is less the exotic scene of a total inversion than the scene of a tribal inflection of values and models of sociability that are transported to the seaside and installed there.[11]

All the films, accordingly, offer a vision of social hierarchies distorted by the looking-glass of the beach or by their anamorphic presence in the background. Despite riding Vespas, Francis and René, the pick-up artists in *Blue Jeans*, cannot compete with those who have expensive cars. In *Adieu Philippine* Michel will have to leave for the war in Algeria, and cannot please two girls at the same time. The boss in *Du côté d'Orouët*, gatecrashing the seaside family house on the coast of Vendée, cannot get his employee to forget who he is, and suffers uninterruptedly at the hand of her two friends. Jean-Arthur Bonaventure is nothing if not a bossy Robinson when he is out of the office. And while positions of power in *Maine Océan* shift according to the space in which the characters are placed, these positions will never completely disappear.[12] However, in each of these films, hierarchical relations have not only been identified. They have been allowed some play, something has happened. Not much, to be sure, and certainly far less than the deluded characters want to believe, or than society would have us believe. However, my purpose here is to try and approach the elusive nature of this 'something' in order to show how it is linked to the space of the beach and the time of the vacation. Subsequently, I will also show the potential affinities these have with the space of cinema and the time of film.

Rentrée des classes

It may seem counterintuitive to begin this approach with the only film directed by Jacques Rozier which does not feature any beaches. However, Rozier's first short film *Rentrée des classes* (1956), about a young child playing truant on his first day of school, neatly encapsulates the director's aims and methods, and we will see that they afford a definition of the beach in all its essentials. Thus the beach is already the perfect setting for Rozier, *in presentia* in most of his films, *in abstentia* in *Rentrée des classes*, quite befittingly, as the beach is the symbolic, temporal and spatial antithesis of *la rentrée des classes*. Interestingly enough,

---

[10] The French word *plagiaire*, 'plagiarist,' which comes from *plage*, 'beach,' according to the 1973 *Petit Robert Dictionary*, is thought to derive from the Greek root *plagios*, meaning 'oblique, deceitful' (Urbain's footnote).

[11] Jean-Didier Urbain, *At the Beach*, trans. Catherine Porter, Minneapolis, MN: University of Minnesota Press, 2003 [1994], 206.

[12] The controller is, for example, master in his train but nowhere else. See Éric Derobert, '*Maine Océan* : la dérive maritime du contrôleur Le Garrec,' review of *Maine Océan*, *Positif* 303, May 1986, 68-69.

there is no English noun for this pillar of French civilisation, the *Rentrée des classes*. The French for 'playing truant' is *faire l'école buissonière* [the school of the bush], after the bushes the children can—or rather could—hide and play in. The phrase is in keeping with the rural roots of the French collective imagination, but *l'école de la plage* would nicely encapsulate the antithesis between the open space of the beach and the enclosed classroom, as well as the span of time – *plage de temps* – during which the child playing truant prolongs or brings back the summer of the beach through the long autumn of school.

The young truant in *Rentrée des classes* spends most of the film swimming or rather drifting down a river, fully clad, as he tries to catch the schoolbag he has thrown away. When he finally gets to school, he frightens the whole class with the water snake he has brought back from his adventure. The first point to make is that, although there is no beach in *Rentrée des classes*, there is land and water, and the film is the story of the passage from one to the other, and back again. This pattern will be repeated on the beach in all of Rozier's other films. Let us also note the importance of liminal places: the film starts on a bridge, from which the child throws his schoolbag into the river, and the etymological link between *rive* [river bank], *dériver* [to drift] and *arriver* [to arrive/to happen], as elaborated upon by Jacques Derrida in *Parages*, is taken literally here, and is paramount in all of Rozier's films.[13] Rozier is also interested in liminal times, here this consists of the day school begins and the holidays come to an end. All his films end on the precise day when holidays end, a moment which the film and the characters alike often try to extend out of all proportion, knowing full well that the return cannot be avoided, just as Michel knows in *Adieu Philippine* that he will have to go to war in Algeria.

One of the reasons why Rozier is interested in these liminal places and times is that they are the perfect stage for imaginary transgressions that tell much about the phantasms of a given society, and its capacity to lie to itself. They are also the locus of real if minor transgressions, at the very least in the etymological sense, a stepping across, sometimes a false step [*faux pas*] contravening the 'must not' [*faut pas*] of the interdiction.[14] Having characters cross a physical limit allows them to be placed in a new environment and the boy in *Rentrée des classes* spends most of the film immersed in water. This is an experience in itself, an experience which is at the very same time anecdotal and important, possibly life-changing, albeit in ways that remain mysterious and elusive. But something can be brought back from this new environment, for example the water snake in *Rentrée des classes*. This 'catch', however, is radically different from the souvenir that can be brought back from holidays to take its place on the mantelpiece after the daily routine of work has seamlessly taken over from the 'time out' of the

---

[13] Jacques Derrida, 'Pas', in *Parages*, Paris: Galilée, 1986, 23-25 and 65 for *dériver*, passim for *arriver*.

[14] Ibid., 50.

holidays. This catch should lead to a disruption of established order, as indeed it does in the film with the irruption of the water snake in the classroom. This disruption, political in its modest scope, is the essential element of the film taken as an *ars poetica*. If the catch of the child is a metaphor for what the artistic process can hope to achieve, it means that the 'time out' of the film should be as disruptive as the water snake for the spectator, and that it should not only be a cultural souvenir consumed before returning to the *status quo*. It should lead to the 'reframing of material and symbolic space' through which 'art bears upon politics' according to Jacques Rancière.[15] 'What is operative, here,' writes Rancière elsewhere, 'is a vacancy [*vacance*].'[16] What the word means in this context is that time has to be reclaimed, removed from what the power structure had allocated as 'time out,' so as to become something else or something more than the plural term *vacances*, the holidays. Rancière takes the example of a carpenter in 1848 relating the time he took to admire the vista from his employer's window.[17] Likewise, the child in *Rentrée des classes* has his true *vacance* when he decides to extend his *vacances* beyond their normal span. *Vacance* for Rancière also means that art begins when an object has been taken out of its place within the power structure and is as such vacant of the meaning it had within that structure, allowing for other meanings to be reassigned to it. And a place for art is found when a place is taken out of its normal use, becomes vacant and thus available for a new use. For Rancière, these operations are at the heart of art, and equally of politics. The first step in our analysis of the beach *in presentia* in Rozier's film will be to delineate the different forms this 'reframing of material and symbolic space' can take, before turning our attention to time and then to the displacement that is central to the experience of the beach, concluding with the notion of the catch.

A liminal space

Perhaps it is best to approach the beach by boat, as is indeed a recurrent occurrence in Rozier's films. Sometimes with great awkwardness, to get to the beach non-sailors repeatedly imitate sailors, those 'zanies who approach the coast the wrong way around and feel they are at the end of everything when they touch ground.'[18] Rozier pays utmost attention to these moments, as is obvious in the

---

[15] Jacques Rancière, *Aesthetics and its Discontents*, trans. Steven Corcoran, Cambridge: Polity Press, 2009 [2004], 24.
[16] Jacques Rancière, *Le spectateur émancipé*, Paris: La Fabrique, 2008, 69.
[17] Ibid., 68-69.
[18] Jean-Bernard Pouy, 'Des symboles à la dérive,' in *Les vacances: un rêve, un produit, un miroir*, ed. Brigitte Ouvry-Vial, René Louis and Jean-Bernard Pouy, *Autrement* 111, January 1990, 106.

memorable end of *Maine Océan*, or in Pierre Richard's arrival on the *Île de la Tortue*. The actors remarks on the shooting of the scene are illuminating:

> We had sailed five hours to get to the islet. It was impossible to land directly, so all the gear had to be transported to the beach. Jacques filmed us with just the sea behind us. And what about the reverse shot? No reverse shot. So, we could have shot the scene back in front of the hotel! To which Rozier answered, 'In your eyes, it would not have been the same.'[19]

The boat is the best way to approach the beach because it shares some of its characteristics, and to some extent encapsulates them. It is a piece of land on the sea, and it is a closed environment for the filmic experience, and an image of this very experiment, where the experience of the actors and that of the characters merge, and the fiction film becomes a documentary about its own making. This is unmistakably felt in the unfeigned hectic first-time sailing sequence in *Du côté d'Orouët*,[20] but is always at the core of Rozier's most memorable scenes, and the villa in the same film was a boat of sorts for the crew.[21] Pierre Richard notes of *Les naufragés*, 'if there had been a making-of, it would have been extraordinary, but in any case the film has kept the trace of this non-standard shooting.'[22] This is doubly true of the extraordinary sequence in the boat, which precedes the arrival on the island. Emmanuel Burdeau remarks:

> At the beginning of the seventies, Rozier had a project named *Winch*, the story of a cruise which, obviously, ends badly. A boat would have been at one and the same time the studio, a setting for the story and lodging for the crew. An editing room would have even been installed in the cabin. *Winch* would have been the absolute movie, the perfect alliance between the two islands: the island of fiction, where everything settles directly on the water or on the sand, and the island of the shooting, where everything settles directly on the celluloid.[23]

The island is of course a fitting image, and a number of the beaches in Rozier's films are located on islands. Alain Bergala sees the island as the symbol of modernity in cinema, because it is 'the ideal filmic setting for a tabula rasa,' and because the crew will have to 'live together during the whole shoot, and have no

---

[19] Pierre Richard, 'La bonne aventure,' interview by Jean-Philippe Tessé, *Cahiers du cinéma* 592, July-August 2004, 39.

[20] See Mouëllic, *Improviser le cinéma*, 86-90. Apparently Rozier, who shot from the same dinghy as the girls, and then from another, also nearly fell overboard with the camera.

[21] Rozier remembers how Bernard Menez used, and vented, his real frustration at the three girls' constant nagging on and off set in the scene when he throws a fit. Rozier, 'Inventaire I,' 42.

[22] Richard, 'La bonne aventure,' 38.

[23] Emmanuel Burdeau, 'Rozier à son rythme,' in *Jacques Rozier: le funambule*, ed. Emmanuel Burdeau, Paris: Cahiers du cinéma/Centre Pompidou, 2001, 152.

other choice but to stay "in the film."[24] But even when not located on an island, each beach is insular in nature, and in itself epitomizes the notion of limit.[25]

Rozier's second short film, *Blue Jeans*, which so deeply impressed Godard,[26] offers the perfect image of the liminal character of the beach. The two heroes spend the movie trying mostly unsuccessfully to chat up girls on the coast in and around Cannes. They quickly abandon the city streets, where 'the girls are too snobbish' [*c'est toutes des bêcheuses*] and drift alongside the beach. One of the shots presents in succession the street, where the two boys crawl along on their Vespa, then the sidewalk, where their prey are likely to be found, then below this elevated sidewalk, the beach proper, then the line of foam and the sea, and finally the horizon and the sky [figure 1]. The beach is in-between spaces, between the sea and something else which is no longer the beach. The limit can be quite clear-cut, as in the case of the downtown beach at Cannes due to the difference in levels between the beach and the sidewalk, or later in the film due to the cliffs surrounding the cove where the boys bring their would-be conquests. There are several ways in which Rozier draws our attention to the limit. Early in *Blue Jeans*, René has his Vespa climb onto the sidewalk of the Croisette, and later lies on the road, his head still on the pavement, in the mock suicide attempt of a desperate lover. A limit is never more visible than when it is transgressed, as indeed 'a limit could not exist if it were absolutely uncrossable and, reciprocally, transgression would be pointless if it merely crossed a limit composed of illusions and shadows.'[27]

The lines on the screen can also make limits tangible. When René, one of the boys, first chats up his would-be conquest on the secluded beach, they are sitting on the edge of the water. Separating the dark grey of the sea from the light grey of the pebble, a double diagonal crosses the frame behind the actors, the white line of the foam doubled by the black line of the pebble of a darker hue where it

---

[24] Alain Bergala, *Monika de Ingmar Berman*, Crisnée: Yellow Now, 2005, 15. See the whole chapter 'Un film insulaire', 15-39. Bergala mentions for example the island in Godard's *Pierrot le fou*, 'a flamboyant remake' of *Monika*, 15.

[25] The image of Robinson pervades Jean-Didier Urbain's comprehensive study of the beach, for example.

[26] He found the film was 'fresh, young and beautiful like the twenty-year-old bodies sung by Arthur Rimbaud,' Jean-Luc Godard, 'Chacun son Tours,' in *Godard par Godard: Les années Cahiers, 1950-1959*, ed. Alain Bergala, Paris: Flammarion, 1989, 190.

[27] Michel Foucault, 'A Preface to Transgression,' in *Language, Counter-memory, Practice: Selected Essays and Interviews*, ed. Donald F. Bouchard, trans. Donald F. Bouchard and Sherry Simon, Ithaca, NY: Cornell University Press, 1977 [1963], 34. Both Foucault and Derrida at some point use the image of the wave to approach the relation between transgression and limit: see for example 'transgression incessantly crosses and recrosses a line which closes up behind it in a wave of extremely short duration,' Ibid. See also Derrida's remarks on *déferlement* [surging] in *Le monolinguisme de l'autre, ou la prothèse d'origine*, Paris: Galilée, 1996, 57-59.

has been dampened by the waves [figure 2]. There will be some light petting on the beach, but the line of water is also symbolic of the line the boys are unable to cross in *Blue Jeans*. The beach is the place where the sea meets the land, and where boys meet girls in summer, and in *Adieu Philippine* the association is obvious, as for example when Liliane and Juliette, immersed in water, talk with the boys on the sand at the Club Méditerranée [figure 3]. The overriding question concerns how to approach, to accost - *aborder* in French being also the word used more specifically for 'chatting up' or 'coming on to.' It might prove useful to recall some of Derrida's remarks on the word *aborder*:

> It is always on the edge [*bord*] that everything happens, or is on the brink of happening. [...] Approaching [*aborder*] entails a strange slow movement, between gestures and words, which still does not attain its aim, its end, here the coast, a movement which has not happened yet, has not arrived. As *pas*, so as movement, as pace, as step or as absence thereof, it fails to touch the edge, and the edge itself only stays an edge inasmuch as it has not been attained, or inasmuch as contiguity does not abolish distance.[28]

Figure 1. Screenshot from *Blue Jeans*, dir. Jacques Rozier, Films du Colisée, 1958. DVD Potemkine/agnès b., 2008.

The shot is representative of Rozier's cinema. Despite the fact that nothing happens, precisely because nothing happens, and in spite and because of the levity of tone, in the pure vacancy of nothing happening, it places itself relentlessly at the edge, and probes the incommensurable distance to be found in proximity,

---

[28] Derrida, 'Pas,' 95-96. My translation does not attempt to do justice to the proliferating polysemy of the terms, except for '*pas*.'

and most especially in the proclaimed proximity of the contemporary.

The beach is itself a limit, but it also has limits. We can recall the two different words which merged into the modern '*plage*.' One comes from the Italian *piaggia* but ultimately from the Greek *ta plagia* [sides] and thus from the idea of limit, and the other comes from the Latin *plaga* [region, zone] and thus from the idea of something which itself has limits.[29] Crossing these limits is part of the experience, is indeed the initiation, the beginning of the experience. Witness the arrival of the three girls on the beach that will be the main setting of *Du côté d'Orouët*. First, strangely enough, they arrive by way of the sea, as they took a fisherman's boat to avoid the long walk along the isthmus. Then, they painfully climb the sand dune that marks the limit between the estuary and the beach. They giggle all the way, as they will do throughout most of the film, and in the exertion one loses the button holding up her trousers. The loss is symbolic of an initiation into a new space, and a transgression at least in the etymological sense of a crossing of borders.

Figure 2. Screenshot from *Blue Jeans*, dir. Jacques Rozier, Films du Colisée, 1958. DVD Potemkine/agnès b., 2008.

In *Adieu Philippine*, the whole episode in Corsica is indeed the result of a double transgression. Michel, who is about to be drafted into the army to fight in Algeria, is working as a television cableman and accidentally steps into the frame of the camera. He is scolded for that blunder after work, but tells his boss off.

---

[29] All etymological notations are taken from Alain Rey, ed. *Dictionnaire historique de la langue française*, Paris: Robert, 1992.

When his friend asks him why, he answers that in a fortnight he will be in the army and won't be able to tell anybody off anymore, so he may as well do it while he can, and anyway he wants time off before joining the army. There is no beach in this sequence, no more than there is in *Rentrée des classes*, but the scene nevertheless sums up what in my view the beach is about for Rozier, in two ways at least. The first is the parallel that can be made between the space of the frame and the space of the beach. The frame is like the beach, both a limit and a space, a space that, if it is to hold any interest, must be ready to accept the unexpected, unlike what happens when Michel crosses the frame of the telefilm. As Rozier's film leaves the television studio and finally Paris, it will be to locate in the beach a space in which to wait and prepare for the unexpected. This is at the heart of the symbolic power of the beach, even when it is demeaned by the bogus transgressions and encounters faked by Club Med. The second point to be made is the more obvious parallel between the space of the beach and the time of the holiday. As the beach is a place set apart, being neither completely land nor sea, by telling his boss off Michel has given himself a time that is set apart, between his work and his conscription.

Figure 3. Screenshot from *Adieu Philippine*, dir. Jacques Rozier, Alpha Productions/Euro International Films/Rome Paris Films, 1961, released in 1963. DVD Potemkine/agnès b., 2008.

A liminal time

The holiday is limited in time as the beach is limited in space, and of utmost importance in Rozier's films is the question of the temporal end to the holiday. Again, *Rentrée des classes* is paradigmatic, as the very aim of the boy is to extend the limit of the holidays, first by playing truant, then by bringing something back from his holiday, the water snake, to disrupt the order of non-holiday time, to bring something of the experience of the holiday into 'normal' time. But the most harrowing scene in the whole opus is the long farewell sequence in *Adieu Philippine*, during which the two girls wave as Michel departs in the boat that leads him back to the continent, from where he will join the war in Algeria.[30] The sequence is extremely long, as is controller Le Garrec's very long return to the continent in *Maine Océan*, to catch the 10:26 train where he is to resume work after his alcohol-induced dreams of becoming a singer in New York have vanished.[31] The very length of the sequence, as Le Garrec first hops into ever-smaller boats before wading to shore and walking on the sand, makes this a reversed homage to Truffaut's ending to *The 400 Blows*. The disillusionment is marked by a point-by-point opposition between the characters and the situations in the two films. In 1959 Truffaut filmed a young boy facing the sea and his uncertain future, in 1986 Rozier follows an older if slightly immature man going back to his routine, trying to make sure the water does not get into his waders and ruin his work trousers. However, the mysterious beauty of the sequence has in part the same basis as that of Truffaut's ending as analysed by Jacques Doniol-Valcroze:

> The secret of these last shots is inexpressible. It is possible to understand but not really to penetrate their mechanism. First there is 'length': Antoine runs interminably, followed in a single tracking shot, he really gets out of breath, really becomes exhausted, really starts to slow down.[32]

And the length in time of the shots showing Le Garrec's difficult way across sea and land, as well as the length of the shots showing Juliette and Liliane waving at the boat leading Michel to Marseilles and waving so obviously at us, is a way of reaching across to us and of drawing attention to a fundamental limit, that between the space of the story and the space of the cinema. It is impossible not to wonder at some stage, accompanied for some spectators with a quick glance at their watches in the dark, as to the real time spent showing and thus watching the scene.

This sending back of the spectator to his own time thus achieves in time what another characteristic gesture of the New Wave achieves in space, namely the direct look into the camera. In *The 400 Blows*, Antoine Doinel turned towards us and looked straight into our eyes as he reached the end of his journey. In the

---

[30] Censure actually forbade showing a ship directly sending soldiers to Algeria. Jacques Rozier, *Supplément au voyage en terre « Philippine »: extraits, photos de travail, musiques du film* Adieu Philippine, DVD bonus to *Adieu Philippine*, Potemkine, 2008.

[31] On this sequence see Fabrice Revault d'Allones, 'L'art du pataugage' [the art of wading], in *Jacques Rozier: le funambule*, ed. Emmanuel Burdeau, Paris: Cahiers du cinéma/Centre Pompidou, 2001, 98-99.

[32] Jacques Doniol-Valcroze, review of *The 400 Blows*, *Cahiers du cinéma* 96, June 1959, 41-42.

dancing scene in the beach bar in *Adieu Philippine*, in front of an immense black space with the white line of an advancing wave from time to time marking the pulse of the sea, Rozier has Liliane give the camera one long, memorable look, which again plays on its duration.[33] What is important here is to arrive at a time when the spectator feels vacant, and the actor too. Pierre Richard recalls the shooting of *Les naufragés de l'île de la Tortue*:

> Jacques always finished the camera magazines, and at the end of each take, as we didn't hear anybody say 'cut,' we had to fill the gaps, we had to manage these moments of unease. Rozier uses all this. He is not interested in the line, but in what is in between the lines, the gaps, all that we let out, that escapes our control. [...] He likes suspension points.[34]

In drawing out the time of the characters, the actors and the spectator,[35] what Rozier relentlessly tries to do in all his films is to use the beach, insistently, to bring together three times, that of the holiday for the characters, that of the shooting for the actors, and that of the viewing for the spectators. To achieve this, he uses the beach first and foremost as a place of vacancy.

As Marc Augé, the anthropologist of *non-lieux*, points out, the beach is the occasion 'to feel time pass, to feel how long a minute can be, and how short an hour. Time suddenly becomes concrete. This is the miracle of good weather: it gives substance to time.'[36] Jean-Didier Urbain insists on the importance of time as he draws parallels between the beach and the deep sea: 'This is the "bottom" the beach aims toward, even if it does not quite get there. The beach universe, as if it has sunk to the bottom of a dream of unity, of primariness, is itself apneic. It is a slowed-down, frozen, suspended world.'[37]

The wave and the *estran*

In *Du côté d'Orouët*, the emptiness that all spectators feel at some stage, and those more attuned to a stronger narrative thread might find unbearable, is bound up in this link between the stretching out of time and the pervasive pres-

---

[33] In his presentation in Cannes, Godard proclaimed, 'Anyone who hasn't seen Yveline Céry dancing with her eyes to the camera must no longer talk about cinema on the Croisette,' quoted in Jacques Rozier, *Supplément au voyage en terre « Philippine »*. See also Charlotte Garson, *Adieu Philippine de Jacques Rozier*, teaching documents, *Lycéens et apprentis au cinéma*, Paris: CNC/Cahiers du Cinéma, 2010, 16. The model is also, perhaps mainly, Monika's look to camera in Bergman's eponymous film.

[34] Pierre Richard, 'La bonne aventure,' 39.

[35] This is sometimes marked by devices such as the dissolves in the kissing scene on the beach in *Blue Jeans*, or by the titles indicating the days in *Du côté d'Orouët*.

[36] Marc Augé, 'Un ethnologue à la Baule,' in *L'impossible voyage: le tourisme et ses images*, Paris: Payot/Rivages, 1997, 40.

[37] Urbain, *At the Beach*, 278.

ence of the sea, visible even in the sequences shot in the villa. Outside the windows is the beach, outside, below, but it appears and disappears in the different sequences, to the rhythm of the tide, as the waves engulf the beach and seem to lick the villa's walls. Water invades the house, in the form of spilled bowls or, in one hilarious sequence, spilled eels which to the amused terror of the girls flood the floor.[38] But what both sustains and disquiets this hilarity is the same seductive power that gave Alain Corbin the incentive to write his book on *The Lure of the Sea*:

> Thus the fascination of the sea-shore and of zones of contact gradually developed which was to give me the idea for this book. Maleficent, pestilential breezes crept in through the interstices and the gap created by the contact between the elements. Through them all the intrusions and the threats that solicit the imagination wormed their way in, while dejections and discharges poured out. The interpenetrations that were to ensure the intense sexualisation of the strand became possible.[39]

This pervasive sexualisation becomes more explicit on occasions. When two of the girls experience their first sailing trip with an instructor, the soundtrack is filled with sexual innuendoes as the girls threaten to fall overboard and change elements each time they change course. In a similar vein, Kareen at one stage stands in the sea and utters a little cry each time a wave hits her. It is by adopting the male gaze, positing women on the beach in terms of territory to be conquered, that Rozier relentlessly questions this very gaze, and probes its relation to changing socio-cultural parameters.

The image of bodies in the waves is also to be found in *Blue Jeans* and *Adieu Philippine*. In the wave, the darkness of the water turns to white, and so does the grey sand, and we approach the essence of cinema, and the Lumières,[40] as the beach is also the place where white meets black. This is most obvious in *Adieu Philippine* when Michel tries to find refuge in the foam from the wasps invading the beach, as his two girlfriends watch from the beach, backlit by the sun, which makes the sea glitter and the foam glare before the sand turns to dark grey as the wave recedes [figure 4].

---

[38] See Sylvain Coumoul, 'La mer monstre,' in *Jacques Rozier: le funambule*, ed. Emmanuel Burdeau, Paris: Cahiers du cinéma/Centre Pompidou, 2001, 87-91.

[39] Alain Corbin, *The Lure of the Sea: The Discovery of the Seaside in the Western World 1750-1840*, trans. Jocelyn Phelps, Berkeley, CA: University of California Press, 1994 [1988], 168.

[40] Or Jean Vigo as, in *À propos de Nice*, a reiterated shot shows a patch of sand invaded by the wide foam. The shot seems to confront the relentless and inescapable work and rhythm of nature, and the force of cinema, to the ludicrous social order exposed in the film. The influence of Vigo is pervasive in Rozier's films, starting most obviously with *Rentrée des classes*, and in 1964 he directed a documentary on Vigo for the series *Cinéastes de notre temps*.

But if the sea and the waves are associated with the body and with life-affirming sexuality, their engulfing rhythm can also be attuned to a more melancholy mood, embodied by departure and the end of the holidays:

> Doesn't a wave of melancholy begin to swell inside us? A storm even, sometimes? After dreaming comes mourning—mourning for a death which did not take place, the death of time and of 'all the rest.' It is the end of the vertigo. The gods of the beach have become mortal again, and so have their loves.[41]

Water, the whole sea it seems, even seeps into the corner of Caroline's eyes as Gilbert leaves and she reflects, 'Holidays are over now.' This is immediately followed by a notably striking shot. After Gilbert and Kareen have left, the two remaining girls, Joëlle and Caroline, are eating in their room at dusk, wrapped in their blankets, symmetrically placed on each side of the window, whose space is filled with the sea [figure 5]. Nothing happens, except every few moments a wave in the background appears, visible only as an advancing darker line on the dark blue surface of the sea. One of the girls says, 'What emptiness' [*C'est vide, hein?*].

Figure 4. Screenshot from *Adieu Philippine*, dir. Jacques Rozier, Alpha Productions/Euro International Films/Rome Paris Films, 1961, released in 1963. DVD: Potemkine/agnès b. DVD, 2008.

Analysing the expression 'Nouvelle Vague,' Hervé Joubert-Laurencin comments on the importance of the image of Antoine Doinel at the end of *The 400 Blows*:

---

[41] Urbain, *At the beach*, 280, my translation. This melancholy mood is to be found in some measure in the numerous party scenes in Rozier's films, see the very long party in *Maine Océan*.

I would say that this deservedly famous shot became a true icon for the New Wave precisely because, with a paradoxical evidence, it proudly displays its uncertainty (feet in the waves and head in the vague [*les pieds dans les vagues et la tête dans le vague*]), and I would add that in the wave, I am interested in the trough more than anything else, in the emptiness necessary to the structure, which gives it shape and reality, and also in the image of endless repetition.[42]

Also in the wave the elements which the beach is supposed to separate are in fact mixing, and as the emptiness of the beach creates the break, and thus the emptiness of the wave, 'there are three interfaces, sea-air, sea-ground and ground-air.' These interfaces lead to the formation of foam, and to the sound of the wave, associated in part to the breaking up of its bubbles.[43] Thus the event of the wave, the crashing of the wave and the release of its energy is intimately linked to vacuity.[44]

Figure 5. Screenshot from *Du côté d'Orouët*, dir. Jacques Rozier, V.M. Productions/ Antinéa Production, 1969, released in 1973. DVD: Potemkine/agnès b. DVD, 2008.

On a wider scale, a specific area of the beach has particular affinities with the mixing of elements, and thus to allowing events to happen. The strand is the

---

[42] Hervé Joubert-Laurencin, 'La Nouvelle Vague comme vague nouvelle,' in *Nouvelle vague, nouveaux rivages: permanence du récit au cinéma, 1950-1970*, ed. Jean Cléder and Gilles Mouëllic, Rennes: Presses universitaires de Rennes, 2001, 202.

[43] Jérôme Brossard, 'Zoom sur interfaces,' in *Vagues : hommages et digressions*, exhibition catalogue, Paris: Somogy, 2004, 23.

[44] The French word *vague* has three etymologically unrelated meaning: 'wave,' 'indeterminate' as in 'vague,' and 'empty' as in *terrain vague* [waste land].

place where the stranger can be met, as the French word intimates, the *estran*, 'in between the familiar and the strange,'[45] even though *estran* is not in fact etymologically linked to *étranger* ['stranger' or 'foreigner'] or to *étrange* [strange], but to *été* [summer]. Both words find their root in Indo-European °*aidh* [burn]. Summer is the hot season, of course, and *estran* is related to the same root through the swell's evocation of boiling water. The *estran*, the place that is sea at high tide and land at low tide, is at one and the same time neither sea nor land and both together, the cauldron where water changes states. Thus placing yourself on the *estran* is opening yourself up to the risk of change, to the encounter with the stranger and to the estrangement from what you once were.

Three shrimps and a *sardine*

Another French word for the strand is the *laisses*, because on this in-between space the sea leaves [*laisser*] stuff to be found at low tide. In Le parti des choses, Rozier's short film about the making of Le Mépris, the inaugural shot shows Brigitte Bardot walking behind Godard, on a cliff overlooking the sea. Godard exits frame, Bardot picks up a piece of paper from the ground and shows it to Michel Piccoli. The film amounts to an *ars poetica*, Rozier's as much as Godard's, and this first shot encapsulates its meaning. It foregrounds the obvious and famous personae in order to better frame the setting, and to insist that this setting is important only inasmuch as it allows the capture of things so elusive as to necessarily run the risk of evading attention, or comprehension. As Rozier later reflects in his commentary, 'the camera is an apparatus to take pictures,' and this can be as modest as having your eyes open and picking up a piece of paper lying on the ground.[46] At the bottom of the cliff lies a secluded beach which is the setting for an unedited scene from Godard's film. The cliff is impressive, the technicians have to rope out their gear at the end of the day, and actors have to be brought in by rowboats. The beach's very existence is in this case ephemeral, it is the space between the waves and the cliff, and indeed the sequence will be abandoned because this space will prove to be reduced to nought at high tide, and because Godard, in Rozier's view as expressed in the commentary, refuses to force nature. The cove is presented as the first and main element in the long,

---

[45] Pierre-Yves Pétillon, 'De la mer en Amérique,' in La mer: terreur et fascination, ed. Alain Corbin and Hélène Richard, Paris: Bibliothèque nationale de France/Seuil, 2004, 111.

[46] On the set of Le mépris, Rozier also shot *Paparazzi*, stealing images of the paparazzi trying to steal images of Bardot. The same shot of Bardot and Godard is also to be found in *Paparazzi*, minus the moment Bardot picks up the paper, which vindicates the view that in Le parti des choses this particular instant was felt to be important, and important enough to open the film, before the beginning of the commentary.

Prévert-like, heteroclite list of elements needed to film the sequence,[47] and as somehow symbolic of the efforts, chance and readiness necessary to exercise this peculiar art. Filmed directly from above, from the top of the cliff, the dolly tracks, Brigitte Bardot and the improbable crew stuck between the cliff on one side of the shot and the advancing waves on the other seem at once slightly ludicrous and beautifully tragic. Rozier comments:

> Godard's ideal is to capture what he needs at once. At once means by chance, and it also means definitive. What he wants is the definitive by chance. [...] Why didn't he force things ? [...] Well the beauty of *The Odyssey* lies precisely in the belief in reality as it is, and which is what it is, take it or leave it. Take it or leave it. The camera is an apparatus to *take* pictures, and directing is, modestly, to take the side of things.

The beach is, like the frame, a space where the definitive can by chance occur. Chance comprises what is ordinarily understood as good or bad luck. In *Blue Jeans* the two drifters find a secluded cove to bring their girls to precisely because they have run out of petrol for their Vespas and have no money with which to buy more. The trio in *Adieu Philippine* meet an unlikely Italian-singing scuba diver because their car happens to break down in front of the beach where the diver's boat has broken down too. In the same way the filmmaker trusts bad luck to turn into something good. Sometimes he has to force bad luck, and these necessary *faux pas* have to be helped along. In *Adieu Philippine*, Rozier chose the beach where Michel is attacked by wasps because he and his wife had been attacked by a swarm there, but 'on the day of the shooting the wasps did not come, and one assistant had to go into the bushes with a jam pot' to attract them.[48]

It is only on the beach that we can meet strangers from another element, it is only on the beach that these things happen, which is to say that it is only on the beach that anything happens that escapes the expected, and so it is only on the beach that anything happens at all.

I would like to conclude with two final images, as modest as Brigitte Bardot picking up a piece of paper, but as exemplary of Rozier's *ars poetica* as the one he chose to open *Le parti des choses*. In *Du côté d'Orouët*, a very long travelling shot shows the three girls, at low tide, fishing for shrimps with large shrimping nets. Finally each girl catches a single shrimp. This is no doubt quite a failure for a fishing party, but the giggles of the girls each time one of them tries to catch the shrimp at the bottom of the net make up for it. The grace of the sequence soon brings to mind the idea that Rozier's ludicrous but magnificent aim has

---

[47] The list begins thus: 'Cinema's mysterious reasons: A secluded cove has been found, material has been off-loaded, four starlets have been made up, [...]'

[48] Jacques Rozier, 'Inventaire I,' in *Jacques Rozier: le funambule*, ed. Emmanuel Burdeau, Paris: Cahiers du cinéma/Centre Pompidou, 2001, 33.

been nothing more but also nothing less than to catch three 'shrimps' unaware, and to be able to have something to show for it. The scene will find its equivalent for Gilbert as the girls leave the house at the end of the film, at the end of the holidays. One finds a tent peg, in French a *sardine*, and, in memory of Gilbert and his tent, leaves it in front of the house in the horn of a small plaster statue. The trite sexual meaning and the mythological one are not mutually exclusive here. The statue represents Triton, half man, half fish, who by blowing in his horn controls the action of the waves. 'In Greek literature, every boundary zone is a dangerous area in which the activities of deities, human beings, and animals, living in confused, dangerous proximity, threaten to interfere with one another.'[49]

Ever since he followed the two inveterate '*dragueurs*' in *Blue Jeans*, Rozier drags, relentlessly using his frame as a '*drague*,' a dragnet. In fact, the Latin 'plaga' was originally also the name of a large hunting net, whose common meaning with the modern sense was 'something that is spread.' Thus, throughout Rozier's career, the beach has worked as a frame, and the frame as a beach. The beach has been the frame which has allowed him to scrutinize how the relationship between the French and their free-time has evolved, thanks to the angles of the frame, 'where things work and play and give,'[50] thanks to the peculiar angle of Rozier's point of view, and mainly thanks to the oblique angle of the anamorphic glass offered by the beach as it magnifies the details of discreet social hierarchies. The assessment has not been tender, rather cutting, as the beach and the vacation have mainly shown us the spectacle of society's illusions about itself. But the frame has also been a beach. The beach is where the stranger can be approached, and the frame has striven to attain a state of vacancy which is paramount for welcoming the unexpected. Not only to catch it in its net, but to allow oneself to be changed by it, as the wave needs vacuum to mix the elements the beach has both separated and brought into contact. The beach and the frame are the nets to catch the elusive grace and frailty of life, a grace that is gratuitous and free, a little flotsam which might escape the colonization of holidays, and might change us if we allow ourselves to be changed by it.

References

Augé, Marc, 'Un ethnologue à la Baule,' in *L'impossible voyage: le tourisme et ses images*, Paris: Payot/Rivages, 1997, 35-50.
Bergala, Alain, *Monika de Ingmar Berman*, Crisnée: Yellow Now, 2005.

---

[49] Corbin, *The Lure of the Sea*, 14.

[50] Jacques Derrida, *The Truth in Painting*, trans. Geoff Bennington and Ian McLeod, Chicago, IL: The University of Chicago Press, 1987 [1978], 81.

Burdeau, Emmanuel, 'Rozier à son rythme,' in *Jacques Rozier: le funambule*, edited by Emmanuel Burdeau, Paris: Cahiers du cinéma/Centre Pompidou, 2001, 143-152.

Brossard, Jérôme, 'Zoom sur interfaces,' in *Vagues: hommages et digressions*, exhibition catalogue, Paris: Somogy, 2004, 23-24.

Corbin, Alain, *The Lure of the Sea: The Discovery of the Seaside in the Western World 1750-1840*, translated by Jocelyn Phelps, Berkeley, CA: University of California Press, 1994 [1988].

Coumoul, Sylvain, 'La mer monstre,' in *Jacques Rozier: le funambule*, edited by Emmanuel Burdeau, Paris: Cahiers du cinéma/Centre Pompidou, 2001, 87-91.

de Baroncelli, Jean, Review of *Du côté d'Orouët*, *Le Monde*, September 28, 1973.

Derobert, Éric, '*Maine Océan*: la dérive maritime du contrôleur Le Garrec,' Review of *Maine Océan*, *Positif* 303, May 1986, 68-69.

Derrida, Jacques, *The Truth in Painting*, translated by Geoff Bennington and Ian McLeod, Chicago, IL: The University of Chicago Press, 1987 [1978].

_____, Pas,' in *Parages*, Paris: Galilée, 1986, 19-116.

_____, *Le monolinguisme de l'autre, ou la prothèse d'origine*, Paris: Galilée, 1996.

Doniol-Valcroze, Jacques, Review of *The 400 Blows*, *Cahiers du cinéma* 96, June 1959, 41-42.

Ehrenberg, Alain, 'Le Club Méditerranée: 1935-1960,' in *Les vacances: un rêve, un produit, un miroir*, edited by Brigitte Ouvry-Vial, René Louis and Jean-Bernard Pouy, *Autrement* 111, January 1990, 117-129.

Foucault, Michel, 'A Preface to Transgression,' in *Language, Counter-memory, Practice: Selected Essays and Interviews*, edited by Donald F. Bouchard, translated by Donald F. Bouchard and Sherry Simon, Ithaca, NY: Cornell University Press, 1977 [1963], 29-52.

Garson, Charlotte, *Adieu Philippine de Jacques Rozier*, Teaching documents. *Lycéens et apprentis au cinéma*, Paris: CNC/Cahiers du Cinéma, 2010.

Godard, Jean-Luc, 'Chacun son Tours,' in *Godard par Godard: Les années Cahiers , 1950-1959*, edited by Alain Bergala, Paris: Flammarion, 1989, 178-192.

Joubert-Laurencin, Hervé, 'La Nouvelle Vague comme vague nouvelle,' in *Nouvelle vague, nouveaux rivages: permanence du récit au cinema, 1950-1970*, edited by Jean Cléder and Gilles Mouëllic, Rennes: Presses universitaires de Rennes, 2001, 201-211.

Mandelbaum, Jacques, 'Le présent lui appartient,' in *Jacques Rozier: le funambule*, edited by Emmanuel Burdeau, Paris: Cahiers du cinéma/Centre Pompidou, 2001, 10-19.

Marie, Michel, 'L'aventure, c'est parfois l'aventure, parfois la galère,' in *Aventure et cinéma*, edited by Jacques Aumont, Paris: Cinémathèque française, 2001, 99-108.

Mouëllic, Gilles, *Improviser le cinéma*, Crisnée: Yellow Now, 2011.

Pétillon, Pierre-Yves, 'De la mer en Amérique,' in *La mer: terreur et fascination*, edited by Alain Corbin and Hélène Richard, Paris: Bibliothèque nationale de France/Seuil, 2004, 110-11.

Pouy, Jean-Bernard, 'Des symboles à la dérive,' in *Les vacances: un rêve, un produit, un miroir*, edited by Brigitte Ouvry-Vial, René Louis and Jean-Bernard Pouy, *Autrement* 111, January 1990, 106-110.

Rancière, Jacques, *Aesthetics and its Discontents*, translated by Steven Corcoran, Cambridge: Polity Press, 2009 [2004].

_____ , *Le Spectateur émancipé*, Paris: La Fabrique, 2008.

Revault d'Allones, Fabrice, 'L'art du pataugage,' in *Jacques Rozier: le funambule*, edited by Emmanuel Burdeau, Paris: Cahiers du cinéma/Centre Pompidou, 2001, 98-99.

Rey, Alain, ed., *Dictionnaire historique de la langue française*, Paris: Robert, 1992.

Richard, Pierre, 'La bonne aventure,' interview by Jean-Philippe Tessé, *Cahiers du cinéma* 592, July-August 2004, 39.

Rittaud-Hutinet, Jacques, *Les frères Lumière: inventeurs du cinéma*, Paris: Flammarion, 1993.

Rossell, Deac, *A Chronology of Cinema, 1889-1896*, Special issue of *Film History* 7.2, Summer 1995.

Rozier, Jacques, dir., *Rentrée des classes*, Dovidis/Films du Colisée, 1955.

_____ , dir., *Blue Jeans*, Films du Colisée, 1958.

_____ , *Adieu Philippine*, Alpha Productions/Euro International Films/Rome Paris Films, 1961, released in 1963.

_____ , dir., *Le parti des choses*, Films du Colisée, 1963.

_____ , dir., *Paparazzi*, Films du Colisée, 1963.

_____ , dir., *Jean Vigo (Cinéastes de notre temps)*, ORTF, 1964.

_____ , dir., *Du côté d'Orouët*, V.M. Productions/Antinéa Production, 1969, released in 1973.

_____ , dir., *Les naufragés de l'île de la Tortue*, Callipix Productions, 1976.

_____ , dir., *Maine Océan*, Les Films du Passage/French Line/France 3 cinéma, 1985.

_____ , dir., *Fifi Martingale*, Antinéa Production, 2001, not released commercially.

_____ , 'Inventaire I,' in *Jacques Rozier: le funambule*, edited by Emmanuel Burdeau, Paris: Cahiers du cinéma/Centre Pompidou, 2001, 22-49.

_____ , *Supplément au voyage en terre « Philippine »: extraits, photos de travail, musiques du film* Adieu Philippine, DVD bonus to *Adieu Philippine*, Potemkine, 2008.

Scheinfeigel, Maxime, *Les âges du cinéma: trois parcours dans l'évolution des représentations filmiques*, Paris: L'Harmattan, 2002.

Urbain, Jean-Didier, *At the Beach*, translated by Catherine Porter, Minneapolis, MN: University of Minnesota Press, 2003 [1994].

III. War Zones

6.

BODIES ON THE SAND: CORPOREALITY AND THE BEACH IN THE FILMS OF CATHERINE BREILLAT AND FRANÇOIS OZON

Fiona Handyside

Introduction

Contemporary French cinema has seen a recent wave of directors who have made films that aim to deal frankly and graphically with the body. In his survey of this *cinéma du corps*, Tim Palmer names directors such as Olivier Asseyas, Claire Denis, Marina de Van, Gasper Noé, Damien Odoul and Philippe Grandieux as involved in this combative project. He singles out two directors as of particular significance: Catherine Breillat is described as a 'seminal presence' whose work has explored themes of female sexual desire since the 1970s, albeit with much greater critical and commercial support from the 2000s onwards; and François Ozon is labelled as a 'global celebrity' with works poised between 'farce and horror' as he explores homo and heterosexual desire.[1] Palmer argues that while the provocative content of this *cinéma du corps* has attracted a great deal of critical interest, few commentators have paid much attention to its 'collective ambitions for the medium itself, as the means to generate profound, often challenging sensory experiences'.[2] Accordingly, Palmer calls for an approach that takes the *cinéma du corps* on its own terms and analyses its formal devices and (often highly ambitious) aesthetic strategies that create such a haptic and overwhelming cinematic experience. One area that Palmer does not however then comment upon is the way in which this cinema uses location, and how this may provoke and enhance the sensations this cinema produces.

Expanding upon Palmer's observations, in this chapter I consider the way in which the two *cinéma du corps* filmmakers that he explicitly names —Catherine Breillat and François Ozon— exploit filmic location in their *cinéma du corps*.

---

[1] Tim Palmer, *Brutal Intimacy: Analyzing Contemporary French Cinema*, Middletown, CT: Wesleyan University Press, 2011, 61-62.

[2] Ibid., 58.

Both Breillat and Ozon repeatedly make use of the beachscape in their films, and here I shall be examining what it is about the beach as location that makes it so suited to a cinema of the body. I have previously discussed Ozon's interest in the beachscape as a place that enables the reconfiguring of the body's relationship to time, mainly via the figure of the spectral Child, and Breillat's use of the beach as a space to question heteronormative positioning of the female adolescent.[3] Here I bring the two filmmakers together to demonstrate the common thread that links the recurrent use of beach settings in their films, that is to say the association of the beachscape with sexual violence against women. This chapter will analyse the construction of the beach as a site that anticipates (and possibly provokes?) rape in both *A Ma Soeur* (Breillat, 2001) and *5x2* (Ozon, 2004), as well as considering the way these films reflect upon their own investment in these forms of representation. The beach emerges in this account as a particularly rich site for the critique of cinematic representations of bodies and sex. This is especially the case in a cinematic movement that aims to undo sentimental accounts of sexuality in favour of sensory, confrontational engagements with bodies. It holds as one of its aims a desire to undo sentimental accounts of sexuality in favour of something wilder, less sanitised, and altogether more confrontational, and that aims to produce sensory experiences.

The beachscape has a uniquely privileged existence within culture as neither wholly natural nor totally cultural. It is neither an unspoiled desert; nor the blend of nature and culture synthesised by the countryside; nor the culturalized city, but 'in the margins of all that.'[4] It is a site in which there is great emphasis on the body and the flesh. Beaches enact a different kind of relationship to the body, providing a socially sanctioned space where nearly naked bodies can indulge in new types of sensory experience enabled by burning sand, freezing seawater, brackish smells and distant horizons. As Jennifer Webb argues, it is at the beach that we become most acutely aware of our body:

> as incorporated beings, it is at places like the beach, where we are so obviously embodied, that we can experience the relation of presence in the world, of belonging to and being possessed by the world, and of being attenuated as a consequence of this [...] even the weakest swimmer, when in the sea, experiences the sensation of being simultaneously dunked and supported [...] (delight and danger) [...] the inevitable engagement with the elements forces us to concentrate on the body as lived rather than observed, because all the while the burning of sun and water and wind textures the skin itself, the ingestion of salt water affects the interior, and in every way the self turns out to become and to be experienced more as body [...] less as machine.[5]

---

[3] See Fiona Handyside, 'The Feminist Beachscape: Catherine Breillat, Diane Kurys and Agnès Varda', *L'Esprit Créateur* 51:1, 2011, 83-96; 'The Possibilities of a Beach: Queerness and François Ozon's beaches', *Screen* 53:1, 2012, 54-71.

[4] Jean-Didier Urbain, *At the Beach*, trans. Catherine Porter, Minneapolis, MN: University of Minnesota Press, 2003, 154.

[5] Jennifer Webb, 'Beaches, Bodies, and Being in the World' in *Some Like it Hot: The*

As such it is perfectly suited to the needs of French extreme cinema, which combines an emphasis on the flesh with a desire for a brutal realism. Both Ozon and Breillat's films feature close-ups on body parts covered in (wet or dry) sand, medium shots of naked bodies on the beach, and long shots of beaches stretching to the horizon and marked by driftwood and small human figures, emphasising the imbrications of flesh, water and sand, the body and the beach, the human and the elemental. The close-up on Marie's hand pawing into the dry sand in *Under the Sand* (Ozon, 2001) or on Anaïs's hair and face covered in globules of wet sand in *A Ma Soeur* (Breillat, 2001), recalls for the viewer the physical sensations caused by the strange, alternating textures of dry or wet sand and its feel on our bodies, a haptic rendering of the beachscape. Indeed, Laura Marks comments that 'the term haptic emerges in Deleuze and Guattari's description of "smooth space", a space that must be moved through by constant reference to the immediate environment, as when navigating an expanse of snow or sand. Close-range spaces are navigated not through reference to the abstractions of maps or compasses, but by haptic perception that attends to their particularity'.[6] The beachscape emerges in this description as an inherently haptic site that resists the camera's tendency to map and control space through techniques that mimic (or, in a broader context, permit) surveillance. Rather than panoramic or aerial view shots, we are offered close–ups of body parts on the beach, or sequence shots which stress in contrast the sheer expanse of the beachscape and its escape from borders and boundaries as it extends way beyond the frame.

Directly linking beaches and their haptic cinematic existence, the way these act as alibis for female nudity and sexuality on film, and cinematic rape narratives, Breillat and Ozon highlight the way European art-cinema and its modernist 'ambiguity' depend on a deliberate disembodiment and disavowal of the commercial and artistic (ab)use of the female. We can trace a complex resonance between European art-house representations of the (always potentially) violated female body and the use of the beachscape. In this way, the beachscape is not just an element of the *mise-en-scène*, but a codified spatial framework that evokes the ambiguity of rape in a patriarchal culture that mistrusts female sexuality. This largely hidden motif of the art-house is rendered strikingly, indeed horrifyingly, visible in Breillat and Ozon's body-conscious cinema.

An Art-House Tradition? Women and Beaches

In turning to the beach, and drawing our attention to the vulnerability of the female body here, both Ozon and Breillat are commenting on the gendered par-

---

Beach as a Cultural Dimension, eds. Allan Edwards, Keith Gilbert and James Skinner, Oxford: Meyer and Meyer Sport (UK), 2003, 83-85.

[6] Laura Marks, *Touch: Sensuous Theory and Multisensory Media*, Minneapolis, MN: University of Minnesota Press, 2002, xii.

adigm of European art-house cinema and the usual lack of attention paid to its exploitation/abuse of the female body. The interconnections between the beach and the (raped) female body are found in the striking alignment of women as 'ambiguous', 'enigmatic' and/or 'neurotic' with the beach. Examples include *Red Desert's* (Antonioni, 1964) Guiliana (Monica Vitti), whose fantasy space for leaving polluted Ravenna is a beach where a young girl plays among flesh-coloured rocks; *Persona's* (Bergman, 1966) seaside cottage where Alma (Bibi Andersson) recounts to Elisabeth (Liv Ullmann) her orgy on the beach with some teenage boys, an encounter that ended in pregnancy and abortion; and *Belle de jour's* (Buñuel, 1966) Séverine (Catherine Deneuve) who flees from the extreme sexual pleasure she feels at the brothel to a beach holiday with her husband. She wears a dark brown fur coat and a fur-trimmed leather cap with chinstraps tied as a bow, and the straps and crown have brass studs. The confining appeal of studs and leather shows Séverine's (unconscious?) desire to be at the brothel, even as she walks along the windswept deserted beach with Pierre. Beaches in all three examples come to stand as ideal locations for (male authored visions of) female sexual transgressions and fantasies.

Rape often occurs in the 'hallowed' European art films beloved of critics, from classics such as *Wild Strawberries* (Bergman, 1957), *L'Année dernière à Marienbad* (Resnais, 1959), *Rocco and his brothers* (Visconti, 1960), *Belle de jour* (Buñuel, 1967), *A Clockwork Orange* (Kubrick, 1971) and *Die Marquise von O* (Rohmer, 1972) to the more contemporary such as *Talk to Her* (Almodovar, 2000), *Irréversible* (Noé, 2002), *Dogville* (Von Trier, 2003) and *Don't Move* (Castillitto, 2004). The ubiquity of the trope of rape in this cinema should be evident from this list, yet as Dominique Russell contends, rape remains largely neglected in discussions of this cinema, with most discussions of sexual violence in film concentrating on issues of justice and/or rape revenge in films such as *The Accused* (Kaplan, 1988) or *Thelma and Louise* (Scott, 1991). Similarly, one can trace the importance and influence of the beachscape for such key directors of European art-house fare as Michaelangelo Antonioni (*L'Avventurra*, 1960 and *Red Desert*, 1964); Federico Fellini (*The White Sheik*, 1952, *I Vitelloni*, 1953, *La Dolce Vita*, 1960 and *8 and a Half*, 1962); François Truffaut (*The 400 Blows*, 1959); Jean-Luc Godard (*Pierrot le fou*, 1965), Ingmar Bergman (*Persona*, 1966) and Eric Rohmer (*La Collectionneuse*, 1967, *Ma nuit chez Maud*, 1969). Despite the recurring use of the beach by these directors as variously a place of death, drowning and disappearance; a location for the dispossessed and the marginal; and a Utopian space of yearning and nostalgia, the majority of studies of cinematic spatiality ignore the beach, arguing for the cinema as a site of *flânerie* and therefore identifying the city as its key mode of expression.[7]

---

[7] See as an example among many Mark Shiel and Tony Fitzmaurice, *Cinema and the City: Urban Societies in a Global Context*, Oxford: Blackwell, 2001.

This critical neglect of rape and beaches in European art-house cinema could of course be mere coincidence and it may seem somewhat far-fetched to argue for a deep and abiding connection between European art-house cinema's repeated deployment of the trope of rape and its frequent use of beachscapes. My argument rests on the fact that beaches and art-house cinema occupy a strikingly similar cultural role. They are both marginalised within mainstream urban-oriented cultures of modernity, which prioritise the entertainment cinema and the city which seems so intrinsic to its functioning (in terms of subject matter and distribution). Yet, beaches and art-house films are as relevant to modern life as urban environments and mainstream commercial films – indeed, one could see them as an essential by-product of them: the former as a place of relaxation and escape, the latter as enabling market differentiation. Beaches are an invention of modernity, only visited en masse following the invention of the railway and recorded as daringly modern environments for spectacle, display and *flânerie* by Impressionists.[8] Art-house films articulate 'modernist' concerns of alienation and dislocation. Indeed, the beach as the edge of the nation; the site of liminality, transgression and marginality; finds its full expression in art-house film. Their desire to avoid definitive closure finds spatial expression in the sea's contradictory role of barrier and threshold, paradigmatically made use of by Truffaut in his famous freeze-frame at the end of *The 400 Blows* (1959). The beach is an utterly contradictory and ambiguous site within cultural mythology:

> perceived within the ancient tradition of the abyss, a place filled with violence, with its horrors reflected in either an outside force (the monster) or an interior one (human violence). It's also, in a seemingly completely contradictory manner, seen as a place of natural harmony, where vigour and family bonds are rediscovered.
>
> [perçu dans la tradition de l'abyssos des Anciens comme un lieu investi de violence où se reflète l'horreur, extériorisée (le monstre) ou intériorisée (la violence humaine), mais aussi, de façon apparamment contradictoire, comme un lieu de harmonie naturelle, de rédecouverte de l'énergie ou de la tribu.][9]

Rape also affords a representational ambiguity and polyvalence, in that it depends on competing stories. Depending on who wins out, the rape itself can disappear, leaving behind only seduction and feminine misunderstanding. The beach and femininity are both sites marked by ambiguity. The beach thus offers

---

[8] The relative modernity of the beach as a place of enjoyment and pleasure is hard to realise, so normalised is its place within current leisure norms: Corbin refers to the gradual move from horror of the abyss to pleasure on the beach (which he links to the Enlightenment) as its 'invention'. Alain Corbin, *The Lure of the Sea: The Discovery of the Beach in the Western World 1750-1840*, trans. Jocelyn Phelps, Los Angeles, CA: University of California Press, 1994.

[9] Luc Rasson and Bruno Tritsmans, 'Écritures du rivage : mythes, idéologies, jeux', *L'Esprit Créateur* 51:2, 2011, 1.

a location that lays bare both literally and metaphorically the disavowed importance of the female body as the supreme site for the expression of modernist European cinematic values and practices.

We can find further evidence of this complex meeting of beaches and vulnerable/appealing female flesh in the art-house. 'From the beginning, art cinema appealed as much to the libido of its spectators as it did to their intelligence. Indeed, the breakthrough figure for foreign art films was Brigitte Bardot'.[10] Furthermore, Bardot's star image was established on the beach at the Cannes film festival, where she promoted films in which she had cameo roles from the early 1950s onwards, becoming famous even before she starred in *And God Created Woman* (Vadim, 1956). Bardot frequently featured in magazines such as *Cinémonde* frolicking on the beach with co-stars such as Kirk Douglas, so that her free and easy attitude to her sexuality, her 'naturalness' (unkempt hair, lack of jewellery and make-up, cheap clothing, bare feet) and her beauty became linked to a nascent international beach culture. Central to French/European cinema's promotion of itself to American and international markets as cosmopolitan, modern and sexy, the Cannes film festival shrewdly made use of the beach as locale where stars could be caught 'off-duty', often wearing bikinis (invented in the resort in 1946), and Bardot's habit of sunbathing, frequently photographed by the paparazzi, became a mass cultural idea of pleasure around the world.[11]

For the critics of the *Cahiers du cinéma*, Bardot's fresh, youthful body, presented by Vadim in *And God Created Woman* through the new technologies of widescope and Eastman color spoke to a 'new realism' in the cinema against the staid and conservative *cinéma du qualité* (predating the crest of the New Wave by some five years). Consider for example François Truffaut's panegyric:

> I can no longer stand those soppy, bland, false love scenes from Hollywood cinema, or the filthy, salacious and equally fake ones from French films. That's why I'm so grateful to Roger Vadim, who directed his young wife by asking her to perform everyday gestures in front of the camera. These could be as banal as playing with her sandal, or less banal like making love in full daylight, but they are both real. Instead of copying other films, Vadim wanted to forget cinema and copy life, real intimacy. Apart from two or three rather lax scene endings, he has perfectly achieved his goal.
>
> [[J]e ne puis plus supporter les scènes d'amour mièvres et mensongères du cinéma hollywoodien, crasseurs, grivoises et non moins truquées des films français. C'est pourquoi je remercie Vadim d'avoir dirigé sa jeune femme en lui faisant refaire devant l'objectif les gestes de tous les jours, gestes anodins comme jouer avec sa sandale ou moins anodins comme faire l'amour en plein jour, eh oui!, mais tout aussi réels. Au lieu d'imiter les autres films, Vadim a voulu oublier le

---

[10] Dominique Russell, ed. *Rape in Art Cinema*, New York, NY: Continuum, 2010, 5.

[11] Vanessa Schwartz, *It's so French! Hollywood, Paris, and the Making of Cosmopolitan Film Culture*, Chicago, IL: University of Chicago Press, 2007, 67-79.

cinéma pour 'copier la vie', l'intimité vraie, et à l'exception de deux ou trois fins de scénes un peu complaisantes, il a parfaitement atteint son but.]¹²

Truffaut explicitly contrasts mainstream, popular Hollywood and French cinema sex scenes with those performed by Bardot, where often the alibi for what Truffaut labels her 'authentic' and 'everyday' near-nudity and making love outdoors is her presence on a beach. In other words, European art-house cinema's specificity as a more 'realistic' cinema than that of Hollywood depends here on female flesh, its nudity naturalised via the beachscape. Because it makes female nudity 'natural', the beach blocks any questions we might want to ask about why the woman is naked, and any suggestions of abuse or exploitation are avoided.

Bardot and *Contempt*

Godard's *Contempt* (1963) acutely critiques the way in which Bardot's body is used as a creative and commercial launching pad for male success. Camille, (Bardot), Paul's (Michel Piccoli) wife, comes to despise him when he pawns her body for his career advancement. She reads Paul's behaviour as encouraging her to sleep with the producer Jeremiah 'Jerry' Prokosch (Jack Parlance) so that Paul will be employed to write the new screenplay. This is a producer who insists on as much naked female flesh in his films as possible, to enhance their commercial appeal (allegedly a spoof of Godard's own producer, Joseph Levine, who insisted that he put more 'sexy' shots of Bardot into the film).¹³ With its use of Greek myths, the reading of a book about erotic Greek art by Paul, and the presence of ancient statues of women, alongside more contemporary cinematic references, Godard's film suggests that this (ab)use of the offered naked female body for male commercial and creative success is historically determined. Bardot's 'modern' nude image cannot so easily discount or erase the ways in which the female body is generally used in western cultural production. In the light of my discussion, we can also read into its narrative a deft interweaving of questions of rape, representation, and beaches. The nude girls swimming in the sea that Jerry watches during the rushes, his face contorting in a lecherous close-up, have their presence explained to him by the director Fritz Lang as being that of mermaids, women whose nudity is explained by the cultural mythology of the shore. 'Fritz, that's wonderful for you and me, but do you think the public is gonna understand that?' asks Jerry, in a sentence that is then reinterpreted (rather than translated) by Francesca (Giorgia Moll) as 'c'est de l'art, mais est-ce

---

¹² François Truffaut, 'Les critiques du cinéma sont misogynes. BB est victime d'une cabale.' *Arts*, 12 décembre 1956, np.

¹³ Jacques Aumont, 'The Fall of the Gods: Jean-Luc Godard's *Le Mépris* (1963)' in *French Film: Texts and Contexts*, eds. Susan Hayward and Ginette Vincendeau, London: Routledge, 2000, 2nd edition, 176.

que le public comprendra?' [literally: it's art, but will the public understand?]. Francesca thus ironizes Jerry's use of the term 'that's great', choosing to translate it as 'art' when it is anything but (what's great for Jerry is commercial success). Lang's interpretation of nude women as mermaids is perhaps art, but it is also commercial expedience justifying itself via appeals to the natural and the coast.

Paul encourages Camille to take a car journey alone with Jerry, when he invites the two of them for lunch at his villa. The film insists on the importance of Camille's resistance to this suggestion, as we see her circling the red Alfa-Romeo (the car that will finally be the cause of her death), and it is after this event that Camille's attitude to Paul changes. Perhaps the reason for Camille's utter contempt for the way Paul encourages her to take a car journey with Jerry by herself while her husband travels by foot alone to the villa is because of the vulnerability to Jerry's predatory nature this engineered situation leaves her in. Furthermore, the film elides what happens on the journey, following Paul rather than Camille's perspective, masking what exactly may have happened on the journey and why Camille may be so reluctant to travel to Capri with the film company (a reluctance which leads to the film's famous lengthy sequence in Camille and Paul's flat). In their discussion of the film, Leo Bersani and Ulysse Dutoit warn against a psychologising reading, in which we try to find an explanation for Camille's contempt. 'The close-ups of Paul and Camille are either psychologically inexpressive or psychologically impenetrable. If we read 'contempt' into the close-ups of Camille's face, it is because the film's title and Camille herself [...] have identified the film's apparent subject for us [...] to say these looks express contempt is to speculate [...] on what the enigmatic signifier is concealing.' Yet, just a page later, Bersani and Dutoit themselves speculate that a close-up on Paul smoking a cigarette 'seems to tell a pathetic story not exactly of his pushing his wife into Jerry's arms, but simply of a certain relief of being free of her for the moment so that he can enjoy watching the naked actresses diving into the water.'[14] If the modernist ambiguity and deliberate flatness of the film, what Bersani and Dutoit label its 'enigmatic signifier[s]', does block off an interpretation that Camille could have been raped by Jerry, it nevertheless still provides plenty of opportunities for men to ogle female flesh. Under the guise of art-house cinema, set within the mythological universe of the sea voyage, sexual abuse of the female is invisible and uncommented upon (indeed, its being remarked upon is discouraged), even by those who in other ways may be the most ambitious and acute of critics. Bersani and Dutoit's deliberate silence on what Camille's contempt indicates (her possible rape by Jerry, or, at the very least, Paul's utter indifference to the fact this may have happened) replicates a more general wilful dismissal of rape culture's foundational role in western culture and the art it produces.

---

[14] Leo Bersani and Ulysse Dutoit, *Forms of Being: Cinema, Aesthetics, Subjectivity*, London: BFI, 2004, 49-51.

From Art-House to the New Extreme Cinema

Catherine Breillat's *A Ma Soeur* offers a series of intriguing allusions to *Contempt* which allows us to further tease out the complex meeting of art cinema, rape, and the beachscape setting in this film. Through a striking colour palette, a complex reference to Bardot, and a gently retro styling, Breillat reminds us of the links between the new French extremism and European art-house cinema. However, if the question of Camille's seduction/violation by Prokosch is blocked within the critical parameters set up by *Contempt* and what Bersani and Dutoit label its modernist enigmatic signifiers, i.e. its deliberate flatness and ambiguity, Breillat's cinema repurposes ambiguity in line with her feminist visual politics. Here, ambiguity works to capture 'the sexual moment as a scene of extreme ambivalence.'[15] While Godard/Lang/Prokosch/Levine's beach in *Contempt* functions as 'art' that ignores the female beyond her purpose as alluring/commercial flesh (even as it critiques this stance), Breillat's beachscape functions precisely as a site for Anaïs (Anaïs Reboux) to explore her own subjectivity and female sexuality as structured through fantasy and shame.

The *mise-en-scène* echoes that of *Contempt*: Frédéric Bonnaud comments on the overall stylisation of the film, arguing that Breillat 'envelopes her story with a '60s look, with snatches of old-fashioned Italian songs and slightly retro clothes' [nimbe son histoire d'un look culturel sixties, avec des bouffées de variété italienne désuète et des costumes délicatement rétros].[16] They share narrative similarities, both concentrating on the minutiae of events during a coastal holiday, and then dramatically terminating with a somewhat unmotivated car crash which kills one of the main female protagonists. Furthermore, *A Ma Soeur* copies *Contempt's* dominant colour palette of red, yellow and aquamarine, notably when Anaïs and Elena (Roxane Mesquida) wear yellow dressing gowns, a clear reference to the yellow gowns worn by Francesca and Camille. Breillat originally intended for the film to be set on the Italian Mediterranean coast, only switching to the French Atlantic coast for budgetary reasons, although in the end she welcomed the 'plus mystérieux, plus nostalgique, plus hostile' atmosphere of the Atlantic.[17] Italian influences remain in the film via the nationality of Elena's lover, Fernando (Libero de Rienzo). While the intended reference to *Contempt's* Italian setting has almost been lost in the final edit, it speaks both to the complex references *A Ma Soeur* makes to *Contempt* and the desire of both

---

[15] Tanya Horeck, 'Shame and the Sisters: Catherine Breillat's *A Ma Soeur* (*Fat Girl*)' in *Rape in Art Cinema*, ed. Dominique Russell, New York, NY: Continuum, 196.

[16] Frédéric Bonnaud, 'A l'ombre des jeunes filles en fleurs,' *Les Inrockuptibles* 280, 2001, 44.

[17] Stéphane Goudet and Claire Vasse, 'Une âme aux deux corps, entretien avec Catherine Breillat,' *Positif* 481, 2001, 27.

to critique the transnational European conception of the beachscape as alibi for the display of female flesh.[18]

Such echoes from the earlier film are confirmed in a sequence where the girls watch television together (the only programme we see them watch). We cut from a brief sequence where we have seen them lying on a beach together, the only noise on the soundtrack crashing waves and the calls of gulls, to the two girls sat on a red sofa, filmed from behind at a low angle, so that only the backs of their heads and their shoulders are visible, showing them again both clothed in yellow, and we watch the black-and-white television programme with them. The programme, that Bonnaud speculates is mid-late 1960s women's magazine programme *Dim Dam Dom*, features the actress Laura Betti discussing her 'scandalous' reputation. 'In my programme, there are sexual issues, there's no sex.' [Dans mon spectacle, il n'y que les problèmes sexuels, il n y'a pas de sexe] she asserts. Applying her train of thought to the French situation, Betti continues, 'You've got Bardot, haven't you? She's a sexual issue – you should read what Simone de Beauvoir has said about her' [Vous avez Bardot, non? C'est un problème sexuel, ça [...] Il faut lire ce que Simone de Beauvoir a écrit là-dessus.]

If we take this rather strange interlude in the film at face value, we should follow Betti/Breillat's advice, and turn to de Beauvoir's article, in an attempt to help us make sense more generally of the way Breillat's film uses this oblique reference to Bardot. Reading de Beauvoir, we can see an insistence on the presence of Bardot's body that echoes Truffaut's comments I cited above. 'Garbo was called "The Divine"; Bardot on the other hand, is of the earth earthy. Garbo's

---

[18] Work has been carried out on the significance of the beach in Italian cinema, both in art-house and popular contexts. France and Italy both enjoy long coastlines and a warm summer climate, so it is perhaps unsurprising that both countries have mass indigenous tourism and that their national cinemas have produced both art-house and popular films dedicated to the beach. Natalie Fullwood comments that the late 1950s-early 1960s Italy saw an explosion of popular comedies set on the beach, citing such titles as *Racconte d'estate* (1958), *Costa azzura* (1959), *Tipi de spiaggi* (1959), *Diciottenni al sole* (1962), *La voglia matta*, *Frenesia dell'estate* and *L'ombrellone* (1965). This beach is very much the site of mass tourist activity, aided and abetted by increased car ownership in the Post-War modernising country, and 'state organisation of leisure was increasingly replaced by private, motorised transport, as independent family holidays, rather than community outings, became more and more possible for ever greater numbers of Italians. The mobility of mass motorisation enabled the explosion in the use of beaches as leisure spaces.' Furthermore, Fullwood explains, the beach as alibi for the display of the body is as prevalent in this popular Italian setting as in the art-house location of Capri. 'In a genre dominated by male characters, leisure spaces represent a rare example of a sphere where female bodies dominate. But most often these are female bodies displayed for and enjoyed by onlooking men. In both beaches and nightclubs, the display and erotic enjoyment of female bodies become one of the central structuring elements of the leisure and pleasure offered by these spaces. Beach scenes construct a *commedia di costume* in the more literal sense of the term, where revealing swimming costumes and lingering camerawork construct the female body as the primary attraction of the leisure space.' Natalie Fullwood, *Cinema, Space, Gender, Commedia all'Italiana 1958-1970*, University of Cambridge PhD thesis, 2012, 3; 7.

visage had a kind of emptiness into which anything could be projected; nothing can be read into Bardot's face. It is what it is. It has the forthright presence of reality [...] With B.B. men get nowhere. She corners them and forces them to be honest with themselves. They are obliged to recognise the crudity of their desire, the object of which is very precise – that body, those thighs, that bottom, those breasts.'[19]

This collapsing of Bardot onto the 'forthright presence' of her body is reiterated by Godard in *Contempt's* famous opening sequence. Camille lies in bed with Paul, asking him if he loves various named parts of her body – her ankles, her feet, her legs, her thighs and her breasts. Echoing Truffaut's praise of her 'realism', Bardot's authenticity is mapped onto her body and absolutely linked to the natural world, here summarised by de Beauvoir as the earth. As she sunbathes, caught either on film or by paparazzi cameras, as the character of Juliette in *And God Created Woman*, Camille in *Contempt*, or as 'herself' at the film festival in Cannes or in her private beachside residence La Madrague, the 'earth' that supports and frames Bardot's body is that of sand. The beach is the support for her body's particular expression of cinematic realism, female nudity, and the aesthetic and commercial impact of that on French cinema, a realisation that is rendered explicit for us in this unlikely intervention by Laura Betti in the weave of Breillat's film.

In an extended beach sequence, while her sister Elena lies near the dunes kissing her boyfriend Fernando, Anaïs sits by the shore. First we see her, filmed from behind, sitting fully clothed and allowing the sea to lap over her legs as she sings her morbid songs of death and boredom. Breillat cuts to a long-duration close-up on Anaïs' face and shoulders, her hair wet, her hair, face and clothes covered in blobs of wet sand. As Anaïs' song speaks of a desire for annihilation, we cut to a silent image of her lying flat in the surf, her green dress rucked up around her stomach and her yellow pants clearly visible. Her body becomes corpse-like, washed over by the ocean, dissolving into sand and water, both separate from and part of the elements. We then cut to another image of her sister and Fernando on the beach, their heavy petting but a pale imitation of the extreme bodily experience Anaïs undergoes at the beach and that anticipates the *mise-en-scène* of her violation at the end of the film, when her black dress will be forcibly pulled up toward her shoulders and her mouth stuffed with her yellow pants. If the latter image is one of horrific violence, the former suggests elements of pleasure and desire in Anaïs's annihilation. This ambivalence maps onto Breillat's representation of rape, permitting her film to complicate the affective and emotional responses this act provokes. As Tanya Horeck explains, the film's final rape scene only makes sense in the context of the defloration

---

[19] Simone de Beauvoir, *Brigitte Bardot and the Lolita Syndrome*, London: André Deutsch/ Weidenfeld and Nicholson, 1960, 23-24.

scene which precedes it.[20] Elena's need to believe in Fernando's romantic discourse, revealed by Laura Betti, who plays his mother, to have been a tissue of lies, is a form of violence.[21] Elena's consent was not given in full knowledge of the truth: Breillat terms it a mental rape. In contrast, Anaïs' refusal to call herself a victim of rape despite the fact we have just witnessed her sexual attack demonstrates her refusal to be read as a fragile girl, indelibly damaged and broken. The ambiguity that Breillat captures here is not then that of *Contempt*, (where the question might be what happened to Camille?) but a specifically feminist visual politics. She refuses to settle the boundaries between rape and heterosexual intercourse, violence and love in the crucible of fantasy, desire and shame her film outlines. Here, the question becomes one of how can male sexual violence be understood and countered in the context of a patriarchy in which women are educated to be ashamed of their own desire? Far from being merely an element of *mise-en-scène*, the beachscape functions as fundamental to the way in which Breillat tackles these themes, enabling her to carve out a space in which bodies become fantastical and ambiguous as sea, surf, sand and flesh mingle together in the very grain of the image.

The Beach as Meta-Cinematic Space

A similar series of motifs mark the use of the beach in Ozon's *Under the Sand* (2001), where Marie's (Charlotte Rampling) husband Jean (Bruno Crémer) disappears while swimming. Although the film explains his disappearance as a probable drowning (a body, genetically identified as that of Jean, is recovered from the ocean late in the film), the title of the film also evokes the possibility that he has been swallowed up by the sands. At the end of the film, Marie returns to the beach that was the site of her husband's disappearance. Sobbing, she plunges her hand into the sand, as if she hopes to somehow recover him. Ozon's camera catches in close-up an image of her hand covered in grains of sand, a intermingling of flesh with the stuff of the beach. Jean-Didier Urbain explains that in the nineteenth and early twentieth century, the sand itself was a source of fantasy and anxiety as a place where one could be swallowed up whole, a power that

---

[20] Horeck, 'Shame and the Sisters', 207.

[21] The decision to cast Laura Betti as Fernando's mother is important. She rings the doorbell only moments after we have seen archive footage of her discussing Bardot on television, as I discuss above. As well as reinforcing the idea that Betti is the voice of feminist critique in this film, it also facilitates a rather perverse and cruel wish fulfilment by Breillat. Anaïs has just said of the televisual Betti that she wishes she could meet her, only for her to turn up on her door-step (!), but as Fernando's mother, not stepping outside of the diegesis. Furthermore, her role here is to precipitate the film's final disaster, as she reveals the engagement ring Elena thought was a lover's gift was in fact stolen, and that Elena's consent is thus compromised.

has now shifted to the ocean, although sand still has important symbolic and emotional potential. He goes on to comment that, 'sand is a strange substance [...] liquid when dry, solid when wet, quasi-volatile under water, it is soft on the beach and hard as cement under surf. It is an undecideable form of matter, at once fluid and solid, in which the ephemeral and eternal, traces and their absence, form and formlessness blend – for in it everything is erased.'[22] Ozon's film plays with these resonances as the beach becomes the site of Jean's total erasure but also possibly, the film's final image suggests to us, his resurrection, as Marie runs towards a distant male figure standing by the surf, too distant in the image for us to understand his significance. We can only speculate as to whether this male figure represents the continuation of Marie's fantasy that Jean is still alive, whether it could in fact be Jean himself (an unlikely but not impossible reading), or a potential new partner. Bodies themselves are undecideable matter at the beach, caught in complex webs of fantasy and ambivalence, shifting between form and formlessness.

Ozon's *5x2* and Breillat's *Sex is Comedy* both provide ample material to further these reflections on the beach as a space that calls for a particular fragmented, partial, haptic relation to the image and thus resists mapping and control. In the case of *Sex is Comedy* (which has of course also another reference to *Contempt* via the trope of a film-within-a-film, as discussed by Keesey),[23] this is through the opening sequence of the film which features the director Jeanne (Anne Parillaud) attempting to direct an amorous encounter on the beach between Fernando (Grégoire Colin) and Elena (Roxane Mesquida). The film starts with a dark screen and the sound of lapping waves, alerting us from the start to the importance of the beach. We then see its opening image of a beach at dawn. Jeanne and her assistant Léo (Ashley Wanninger) stand on the edge of a wide expanse of sand undulating to a distant sea discussing the problems the location presents – they hadn't realised that the low tide would mean much more sand was visible than when the location was scouted, and that therefore the beach would have changed in character. 'Merde' exclaims Léo twice within a few seconds, while Jeanne decides she will lose her extras, make the scene more deserted, and reassures him that 'la mer, c'est toujours beau'. During the credit sequence, as the sun rises, we see the crew, wearing bulky coats, scarves and hats, struggling over the sands, carrying heavy equipment – cameras, tracking rails, reflectors, booms, tripods and so on, making us aware that the beach is an exacting location for a filmmaker in practical terms alone. The difficulty of their progress is accompanied by the plaintive, beautiful music playing on the soundtrack. A traditional Portuguese folk song (*A Sombra*) in which a woman sings of being saved from the depths of the sea fades up from the sound of waves

---

[22] Urbain, *At the Beach*, 266.

[23] Douglas Keesey, *Catherine Breillat,* Manchester: Manchester University Press, 2009, 67.

crashing, a romantic evocation of the beach that contrasts to the pragmatic lugging of equipment that we can see.

As the scene progresses, despite the undeniable beauty of the location, emphasised by sweeping camera shots over the sand dunes reflecting back the pinkish glow of the sunrise, Jeanne's problems multiply, until filming is finally terminated by a downpour. Although the 'comedy' to which Breillat refers in her title refers more generally to its sense as masquerade or performance, as Breillat explains *Sex is Comedy* 'is also just a comedy' [est aussi une comédie, au sens comique du terme'].[24] This comedy finds particular expression through the director's tribulations at the beach. As Kate Ince summarises, 'laughter [...] arises spontaneously in the opening "beach" sequence from the misery of two scantily clad actors trying to create an atmosphere of oblivious sexual passion in a freezing Atlantic wind.'[25] In a film that generally stresses the agency and control of the film director, the opening sequence on the beach places this into a context in which actors' bodies are vulnerable to the elements, and in which the struggle between the female director and the male actor for power is undercut through a setting which defeats both of them.

Ozon's *5x2* shares some of *Sex is Comedy's* meta-cinematic reflections upon the possibilities and problems the landscape of the beach offers the filmmaker. Although Ozon does not self-reflexively refer to a film-within-a-film or show us crew and equipment, he deliberately uses highly varied cinematic techniques for each of his film's five sections, varying tone, lighting and pace. He explains on his website that:

> I also wanted each episode to reflect a different style of cinema. We start with an intense psychological drama, then move into the second part, which is more socially anchored, in the tradition of French cinema. For the wedding, American films were my reference, and for the couple's initial encounter I aimed for something along the lines of Rohmer's summer films. I wanted the film to evolve in such a way that the tone and issues would change from chapter to chapter.[26]

Such shifts distance the audience from the film, drawing our attention to its status as representation rather than having us lose ourselves in its story. Furthermore, these shifts in the formal cinematographic structures echo the changing

---

[24] Quoted in Kate Ince, 'Is Sex Comedy or Tragedy? Directing Desire and Female Authorship in the Cinema of Catherine Breillat,' *Journal of Aesthetics and Art Criticism* 64:1, 2006, 162.

[25] Ibid.

[26] François Ozon, 'Interviews about *5x2*', *François Ozon: Le Site Officiel*. Available: http://www.francois-ozon.com/en/interviews-5x2-five-times-two. Accessed 23/05/2015. Rohmer's summer film *Pauline à la plage* (1983) is also an important reference for Breillat, who used some of its dialogue in her screen tests for *A Ma Soeur*. Although *Pauline à la plage* is as one would expect a more restrained film than either Breillat's or Ozon's, it nevertheless provides an important intertext, dealing as it does with sexual infidelity and betrayal during a seaside vacation.

appearance over time of Marion (Valeria Bruni-Tedeschi) and Gilles (Stéphane Freiss), suggesting the instability and friability of the body itself.

The film fragments the bodies of its actors through its narrative structure, which concentrates on five individual episodes in the lives of a married couple, Marion and Gilles, over a period of around five years. As its mathematical, formulaic title suggests, this is a film which seeks to analyse not only an individual couple, but also to consider the very nature of (heterosexual) coupledom itself, and the repetitious nature of its reproduction. If we multiply 5 by 2, we will always have the same result. Similarly, whatever the individual contingencies of the couple, normative heterosexual culture tends to operate via a universal narrative of meeting, marriage and reproduction. *5x2* tells the story of the demise of its relationship, thus of course recalling through this theme *Contempt*, a resonance that Andrew Asibong also finds in Marion's 'essential blankness and unreadability' so that she starts to 'emerge as a character we must be content merely to observe, never to comprehend' and as Asibong further suggests, its numerical title alludes to other films by Godard that examine male-female relations such as *Numéro deux* (1975).[27] The film is told in reverse, so that we begin with their divorce and final painful love-making in a hotel room in Paris, where Gilles anally rapes Marion, and we finish with their first meeting at a Sardinian beach resort, and the very final image of the film is a gorgeously photographed, long-lasting shot of the two walking into the sea as the sun sets. Although Ozon claims that the beach sunset scene wasn't ironic for him, it seems hard to miss the biting contrast between the idyllic beach, the pink/orange glow of the sky, and the happy, flirtatious complicity that is being set up between Marion and Gilles, and the functional hotel room, its dark, sombre colours, and the pain and misery of Marion and Gilles' final meeting. As Asibong comments:

> [I]t seems difficult to get rid of the sense that what the film really does is draw the viewer's attention, in a starkly distancing manner, to the fundamental mendacity of idealised images [...] the entire film is [...] haunted by the early sequence of Marion's post-divorce rape by Gilles, a sequence that has occurred just ninety minutes before the blissful Italian sunset. What viewer is likely to have simply forgotten those images of humiliation and horror just because his or her attention is now being directed to the same couple's first stirrings of romance?[28]

Indeed, within the sequence itself, Marion has drawn our attention to the dangers as well as the pleasures of the beach, as she comments that 'on this beach, the sea can be dangerous, there are strong currents' [sur cette plage, la mer peut être dangereuse. Il y a pas mal de courants.] The seemingly calm waters contain

---

[27] Andrew Asibong, *François Ozon*, Manchester: University of Manchester Press, 2007, 101. The connection between these two films is further enhanced on the French DVD menu sequence, which features images from each sequence of the film coloured by strident filters.

[28] Ibid., 99.

their own threat to the future of the couple, as we will of course remember from Ozon's earlier film *Under the Sand*. Threats to the couple are not only from the physical dangers presented by the beach. Nor do we need to think back to the opening sequence to comprehend possible dissolution of couples in situations of pain and violence. As Thibaut Schilt comments, 'what could be a nascent story of love is tarnished by the fact that Gilles is on vacation with his girlfriend of four years, Valérie (Géraldine Pailhas).'[29] Several times she comments on the sadness and loneliness of the single women at the holiday resort, but she seems dissatisfied and lonely herself, and our final image of Valérie is a close-up of her face staring out to sea while she is alone on a hike. Furthermore, the scene where Gilles and Valérie have sex starts in their hotel room, in a harsh white light, with her wearing a white dress, and the camera pans over Gilles' back to a close up on Valérie's face and darting eyes.[30] This is an ambivalent image that recalls Marion's facial expressions at the start of the rape sequence, filmed from an identical angle. Both the scenes with Marion and Valérie begin with this image of Gilles on top, and at this moment, neither woman is protesting nor expressing enthusiasm, a blurring of the line between consensual and coercive sex that echoes the ambivalence of Breillat's film. Marion will then struggle away from Gilles before he violently flips her over and enters her anally, causing her to shriek in pain. In contrast, here the image of Valerie's face ends the shot and on the cut the lighting changes entirely, so that Gilles and Valérie are surrounded by dark shadow, their now naked bodies a highly contrasting white emerging from the gloom, and non-diegetic piano music plays, suggesting that in fact we have shifted ontological register and are here in a fantasy of fulfilling sexual union, although it is uncertain whether this fantasy belongs to Gilles or Valérie.[31] In what then seems to be a less radical or challenging film than *A Ma Soeur*, a deliberately 'banal' concentration on the universal norms of heterosexuality, finishes then on an extremely disturbing note in which Gilles' violent rape of his ex-wife comes to seem a repetition of his past behaviour in sexual relations. The way that Gilles repeatedly coerces his lovers into sexual relations is both statistically more likely and emotionally more disturbing than the fantastical figure of the bogeyman in the woods conjured up in Breillat's film.[32]

---

[29] Thibaut Schilt, *François Ozon*, Urbana, IL: University of Illinois Press, 2011, 133.

[30] The ambivalence of Valérie's response is indicated in the published screen play: 'Ils font l'amour. Valérie semble ailleurs. Gilles est agressif et directe'. François Ozon, *5x2*, Paris: L'Arche, 2004.

[31] As Alice Stanley points out, there are several moments in the film that defy narrative plausibility and could be read as fantastical: the decision to have farewell sex in the hotel; the orgy that Gilles recounts; Gilles' failure to attend the birth of his son; Marion's one night stand with a stranger on her wedding night. Alice Stanley, *Representations of Sexuality in the Films of François Ozon*, unpublished PhD thesis, University of Warwick, 2009.

[32] Rape Crisis reports that 'many people believe that adult sexual violence and child

The complex chronology of Ozon's film, where the image of Marion and Gilles swimming in the sea functions as both the beginning of their story, but also the end of the film, links the beach directly to the act of rape, which functions as the beginning of the film, but the end of the story. The French DVD of *5x2* includes a bonus feature, *2x5*, which tells the story of Marion and Gilles in the correct chronological order. Although this may seem a pointless technical exercise, it demonstrates nevertheless the circularity of the story and in the end its utter interchangeability: whether we multiply 2 by 5, or 5 by 2, we get the same result. The idyllic beach provides Ozon with a location in which he idealises the meeting of a man and a woman and the 'happy beginning' of a heterosexual relation, but it also merges into a hotel room and a violent rape. This demonstrates the way that seduction and violation blur within a patriarchal society in which women's bodies are objects and in which female sexuality is a source of shame.

This persistent ambiguity between feminine 'seduction' and violation and its tenacious expression in film was articulated as recently as May 2013 at the Cannes film festival, where François Ozon presented *Jeune et jolie* (2013). He created a media scandal as he declared in an interview with the *Hollywood Reporter* that: 'I think women can really be connected with this girl because it's a fantasy of many women to do prostitution. That doesn't mean they do it, but the fact to be paid to have sex is something which is very obvious in feminine sexuality.'[33] Although he then took to Twitter to refute the allegation of misogyny, claiming 'inept and misunderstood remarks. Obviously I wasn't talking about women in general, just the characters in my film'['Propos maladroits et mal compris. Evidemment je ne voulais pas parler des femmes en général, juste des personnages de mon film'], Ozon's remarks reveal the tenacity of the 'happy hooker' myth in film if not in society at large. The *Le Monde* blog that reported the spat finished its discussion by providing a link to a youtube clip of *Belle de jour*, making explicit the continuity between Ozon's commentary and the European art-house tradition (Ozon's film begins its story of a 17 year old call-girl with a family beach holiday, the beach remaining propitious to female sexual transgressions).[34]

Such trite and universalising misogyny in an interview from a director whose films work to showcase queer desires is troubling but perhaps rather pre-

---

sexual abuse is normally committed by a stranger. In fact, perpetrators are normally known to the victim and many are partners or family members' (http://www.rapecrisis.org.uk/mythsampfacts2.php).

[33] Rhonda Richford, 'Cannes: Francois Ozon Says "It's a Fantasy of Many Women to Do Prostitution" (Q&A)', *Hollywood Reporter*, 20 May 2013. Available: http://www.hollywoodreporter.com/news/cannes-francois-ozon-says-a-525566. Accessed 21/05/2015.

[34] *Le Monde*, 'TERRAIN GLISSANT - François Ozon s'excuse pour ses propos sur la prostitution,' 21 May 2013. Available: http://bigbrowser.blog.lemonde.fr/2013/05/21/terrain-glissant-pour-francois-ozon-la-prostitution-est-le-fantasme-de-beaucoup-de-femmes/. Accessed 21/05/2015.

dictable, although clearly Ozon felt himself to have been misrepresented. What is more interesting here is not the accuracy of the interview, but rather its perfect illustration of how film still operates within a male-dominated imaginary where female sexuality remains bound up in ideas of passivity, masochism and seduction. Beaches on film enable directors to justify the *mise-en-scène* of a sexualised female body, while operating as a mythical space of (gender neutral) bodily violation and vulnerability. Attending to the dangers and pleasures that beaches pose for the bodies that lay upon them, both Ozon's and Breillat's films render visible the way in which European art cinema, and its critical tradition, laud a narrative ambiguity which still depends on a sexual double standard.

References

Asibong, Andrew, *François Ozon*, Manchester: University of Manchester Press, 2007.

Aumont, Jacques, 'The Fall of the Gods: Jean-Luc Godard's Le Mépris (1963)' in *French Film: Texts and Contexts*, eds. Susan Hayward and Ginette Vincendeau, London: Routledge, 2000, 2nd edition, 174-187.

de Beauvoir, Simone, *Brigitte Bardot and the Lolita Syndrome*, London: André Deutsch/ Weidenfield and Nicholson, 1960.

Bersani, Leo and Dutoit, Ulysse, *Forms of Being: Cinema, Aesthetics, Subjectivity*, London: BFI, 2004.

Bonnaud, Frédéric, 'A l'ombre des jeunes filles en fleurs,' *Les Inrockuptibles* 280, 2001, 44-45.

Fullwood, Natalie, *Cinema, Space, Gender, Commedia all'Italiana 1958-1970*, University of Cambridge PhD thesis, 2012.

Goudet, Stéphane and Vasse, Claire, 'Une âme aux deux corps, entretien avec Catherine Breillat,' *Positif* 481, 2001, 26-30.

Handyside, Fiona, 'The Feminist Beachscape: Catherine Breillat, Diane Kurys and Agnès Varda', *L'Esprit Créateur* 51:1, 2011, 83-96.

_____ , 'The Possibilities of a Beach: Queerness and François Ozon's beaches', *Screen* 53:1, 2012, 54-71.

Horeck, Tanya, 'Shame and the Sisters: Catherine Breillat's *A Ma Soeur* (*Fat Girl*)' in *Rape in Art Cinema*, ed. Dominique Russell, New York, NY: Continuum, 195-210.

Ince, Kate, 'Is Sex Comedy or Tragedy? Directing Desire and Female Authorship in the Cinema of Catherine Breillat,' *Journal of Aesthetics and Art Criticism* 64:1, 2006, 157-164.

Keesey, Douglas, *Catherine Breillat*, Manchester: Manchester University Press, 2009.

Le Monde, 'TERRAIN GLISSANT - François Ozon s'excuse pour ses propos sur la prostitution', 21 May 2013. Available: http://bigbrowser.blog.lemonde.fr/2013/05/21/terrain-glissant-pour-francois-ozon-la-prostitution-est-le-fantasme-de-beaucoup-de-femmes/. Accessed 21/05/2015.

Marks, Laura, *Touch: Sensuous Theory and Multisensory Media*, Minneapolis, MN: University of Minnesota Press, 2002.

Ozon, François, 'Interviews about *5x2*', *François Ozon: Le Site Officiel*. Available: http://www.francois-ozon.com/en/interviews-5x2-five-times-two. Accessed 23/05/2015.

Palmer, Tim, *Brutal Intimacy: Analyzing Contemporary French Cinema*, Middletown, CT: Wesleyan University Press, 2011.

Rasson, Luc and Tritsmans, Bruno, 'Écritures du rivage: mythes, idéologies, jeux', *L'Esprit Créateur* 51:2, 2011, 1-3.

Richford, Rhonda, 'Cannes: Francois Ozon Says "It's a Fantasy of Many Women to Do Prostitution" (Q&A)', *Hollywood Reporter*, 20 May 2013. Available: http://www.hollywoodreporter.com/news/cannes-francois-ozon-says-a-525566. Accessed 21/05/2015.

Russell, Dominique, ed., *Rape in Art Cinema*, New York, NY: Continuum, 2010.

Schilt, Thibaut, *François Ozon*, Urbana, IL: University of Illinois Press, 2011.

Schwartz, Vanessa, *It's so French! Hollywood, Paris, and the Making of Cosmopolitan Film Culture*, Chicago, IL: University of Chicago Press, 2007.

Shiel, Mark, and Fitzmaurice, Tony, *Cinema and the City: Urban Societies in a Global Context*, Oxford: Blackwell, 2001.

Stanley, Alice, *Representations of Sexuality in the Films of François Ozon*, unpublished PhD thesis, University of Warwick, 2009.

Truffaut, François, 'Les critiques du cinéma sont misogynes. BB est victime d'une cabale,' *Arts*, 12 décembre 1956, np.

Urbain, Jean-Didier, *At the Beach*, trans. Catherine Porter, Minneapolis, MN: University of Minnesota Press, 2003.

Jennifer Webb, 'Beaches, Bodies, and Being in the World' in *Some Like it Hot: The Beach as a Cultural Dimension*, eds. Allan Edwards, Keith Gilbert and James Skinner, Oxford: Meyer and Meyer Sport (UK), 2003, 75-89.

7.

COLONIES DE VACANCES

Sophie Fuggle

A battered bus arrives in the middle of the night during a storm. Palm trees sway precariously and disheveled passengers disembark, stretching, bitching and moaning and gather their luggage together before being allocated their beach huts. Luggage is missing and huts are lacking. The viewer feels the same lack of sympathy towards the desperate, whining holidaymakers as these holidaymakers do towards each other. This is *Les Bronzés*, Patrice Leconte's 1978 parody of Club Med and the aspirational upper-lower middle classes opting to spend their vacations in its dilapidated resorts in search of perfect tans and casual sex.

Providing clarification to the remark that all 'great world-historic facts and personages appear, so to speak, twice', Marx informs us that what Hegel omitted to tell us here is that this occurs 'first as tragedy, the second time as farce.'[1] If *Les Bronzés* is farce then what of the tragedy? Where the doubling of farce and tragedy might be aptly identified with the dark tourism of the early twenty-first century in the form of prison and slavery museums, war memorials and tours of disaster zones, in the latter half of the twentieth century, a different yet equally notable version of this doubling occurs in the form of the camp. From refugee camp, labour camp and death camp we pass to the all-inclusive holiday resort with its regimented activities timetable, buffet queues and alcohol rations. More recently, the 'boot' camp has come to represent the apotheosis of the leisure industry. One no longer goes on holiday with the objective of escaping the constraints of work and its disciplinary regime but, rather, precisely to reaffirm and reinforce these constraints free from the very messy, unpredictable 'productivity' of work as it perpetually exceeds and contradicts its own limits.

The 'simulation' of military training in the form of physical exercise and dietary regime also marks an open acknowledgment of the link between war and tourism beyond simply visiting sites of historical conflict and violence. Both forms of leisure embody an endemic anxiety about modernity which has come

---

[1] Karl Marx, *The Eighteenth Brumaire of Louis Bonaparte* (1852). Available: http://www.marxists.org.

to define late capitalism.² Moreover, if war was once considered to suspend tourism as it did industry, its exceptionalism is now recognized as the *status quo*. Dark tourism, ecotourism, NGO charity work and international activism are all emerging 'leisure' economies predicated upon ongoing war, political unrest and natural disaster. At the same time, the habitual flows of voluntary migration are efficiently redirected, rechanneled according to a deterritorialised, global economic market. Holiday hotspot becomes political hotspot. Voluntary migration is offset against forced migration. First, business and economy class travel are now supplemented by what William Walters and others have termed a 'deportation class'.³

To proceed so swiftly from the concentration camp to the all-inclusive resort might appear as at once brutal and flippant. Yet, the short trajectory from one to the other is, in fact, underpinned by a certain utopian logic which binds post-war economic and emotional recovery together. This is the story of Club Méditerranée.

Whether described as 'camp', 'colonies de vacances' or, in the case of Club Med, 'village', the enclosed holiday resort might be defined as a space of exception. This is a space which Diken and Laustsen, following Giorgio Agamben's 1998 account of *Homo Sacer*, claim attests to the 'convergence between the biopolitics of totalitarianism (abandonment to violence and death) and mass hedonism (abandonment to sun, sea, sex and drugs).'⁴ In its celebration of the sovereign core of Western biopolitics, the camp proliferates within modernity, as a site which, in offering itself up to the suspension and transgression of established cultural values and social norms, exists precisely to affirm such norms and values. Thus, while the holiday camp is promoted in terms of the 'liberation' of the natural, animalistic body (*zoē*) from its political rendering as *bios* within the space of the *polis*, the possibilities for such 'liberation' are increasingly limited. The exceptional space of the resort is at once inside and outside the *polis*, itself recreating at a micro-level the inclusions/exclusions of everyday socio-political existence. As such it is a space where *zoē* is 'captured' by the *polis* as it strives to extend the 'range of the biopolitical paradigm.'⁵

Yet, in tracing the trajectory between war and tourism via the space of the 'camp', we run the danger of producing a 'theory of the camp' which identifies

---

² Lennon and Foley define 'dark tourism' in terms of this 'anxiety' which, they claim, has also rendered news of death and disaster as 'commodity'. John Lennon and Malcolm Foley, *Dark Tourism: The Attraction of Death and Disaster*, London: Continuum, 2000.

³ For a critical discussion of 'deportation class' see William Walters' chapter 'On the Road with Michel Foucault: Migration, Deportation and Viapolitics' in *Foucault and the History of Our Present*, edited by Sophie Fuggle, Yari Lanci and Martina Tazzioli, London and New York, NY: Palgrave, 2015, 94-110.

⁴ Bülent Diken and Carsten Bagge Laustsen, *The Culture of Exception: Sociology Facing the Camp*, London: Routledge, 2005, 113.

⁵ Ibid., 113; 119.

everything in terms of this marginal, liminal site of exception. In doing so we risk reducing all experience to the suspended logic of existence within the camp, failing to take account of the hugely divergent sets of relationships and acts occurring within different spaces termed 'camp'. In the face of such a reduction, it becomes difficult to locate any possibility for sustained critical and political engagement. This is clear from Diken and Lauststen's conclusion to their penultimate chapter on 'sociology after the camp' where their recourse to Gilles Deleuze's 'difference machines' as conceptual tool fails to offer more than further abstraction to the genuine problematic of the camp in late capitalist society as does their call for a 'politics of pity'.[6] To predicate one's politics on 'pity' seems to assume a Western model of imperialist guilt rather than demand a reconfiguration of existing political and economic paradigms. Consequently, the ethics of risk-taking they go on to propose in their final chapter constitutes a reactionary position which seeks to limit the damage of the camp, any camp, rather than actively contest the construction and operation of camp as simultaneously specific, exceptional and paradigmatic space. The camp is not the *non-place* [non-lieu] defined by anthropologist Marc Augé.[7]

At stake in this chapter, therefore, is an examination of how nationalism and its discontents continue to map themselves onto the beach. Here, my focus is on a 'beach' which exceeds hexagonal framing yet, at the same time, is predicated upon an understanding of the French beach which is as mythical as it is socio-historical. In considering the complex relationship between war and tourism inscribed onto the surface of the beach, destined to be washed away and redrawn *ad infinitum*, particular attention is given to the French holiday resort chain Club Med with reference to the specific myths it has engendered and parodies it has spawned. Here, the beach becomes the space where tragedy repeats itself as postmodern cynicism.

Beach as Battlefield

The beach, as attested elsewhere in this volume, functions both metaphorically and metonymically as site of violent encounter between different sets of forces, identities and ideologies. Emerging from such encounters are various forms of colonization: appropriation, erasure, reclamation. In seeking to explore the links between war and tourism and the specific forms of neocolonization operating within the space of the Club Med village, a note of caution is required. It is all too easy to replicate the scathing mockery of Leconte's *Les Bronzés* in our critique of beach vacations along with the more recent indictments of tourism *qua*

---

[6] Ibid., 170.

[7] Marc Augé, *Non-Lieux: Introduction à une anthropologie de la surmodernité*, Paris: Seuil, 1992.

human traffic in the novels of Michel Houellebecq. As satire pure and simple, Leconte's film replicates the elitist snobbery of his French middle class audiences whom no doubt would have failed to see themselves in his caricatures. Leconte himself is not unaware of this potential response and writes this into the narrative itself most notably in the relationship set up between two single females, Christiane and Gigi.

Christiane embodies the wealthy bohemian who, in seeking out an 'authentic' encounter with other cultures finds herself on a package holiday with the socially inferior Gigi whom, as Christiane puts it, 'will do anything to make herself seem interesting.' There is a double irony here due to the comic timing of the statement which follows Gigi's reaction to the news that Bourseault, the *animateur* she was sleeping with, has died in a freak accident. Here, there is no time allowed to move from tragedy to farce. There is no authenticity under the superficiality. Only farce, only surface.

A similar self-reflexivity can be found in Marc Augé's *L'Impossible Voyage*, in which the anthropologist turns his gaze upon the French tourist. Adopting a personal tone, Augé's affectionate criticism of French holiday practices which include Disneyland Paris and Center Parcs along with La Baule, is situated between a nostalgia for childhood vacations spent in the French countryside and an 'urgent' call to a more enlightened form of travel which resists the tag of 'tourism.'[8]

Where both Augé and Leconte position themselves at a critical distance from those they are representing, Leconte's attack is based on the law of small differences maintaining social hierarchies; differences which are intellectual as much as economic. The overriding message of the film, embodied by the decision of the GOs, Popeye and Bobo, to stay for another season despite their ennui and disillusionment, is that rather than strive for a more fulfilling vacation experience whether this is predicated on the sexual, social or cultural, French society needs to stop taking itself and its tourism so seriously. Such a position no doubt endorses low-budget hedonism and the reckless consumerism of global tourism as a way of shedding French cultural stereotypes of colonial shame along with its intellectual and artistic elitism. In this respect, Leconte offers a playful riposte to the apocalyptic tone of Jean-Luc Godard's *Weekend* (1967).

Augé's position, on the other hand, is more sinister in its critique of mass tourism through the awkward and reductive distinction he makes between 'tourist' and 'traveller'. Frequently, he makes his photographer companion, Catherine, scapegoat here thus setting up an additional gaze in between his own and that of the 'ordinary' tourists. This occurs most notably when he recounts Catherine's attempt to distance herself from the other camera-wielding tourists in Disneyland Paris, anxious not to be mistaken for yet another trigger-happy

---

[8] Marc Augé, *L'Impossible Voyage: Le tourisme et ses images*, Paris: Éditions Payot et Rivages, 2013, 15.

parent. Ironically, it is thanks to the ubiquity of cameras within the theme park that she can photograph Disneyland unimpeded.[9]

Whether the distance one attempts to place between oneself and other 'tourists' or travellers is critical, reflective or knowingly ironic, the risk is a reproduction of the same inertia, a confrontation taking place within the space of a mirror. Fear of one's own superficiality is mitigated by reducing the experience and engagement of others with a space or practice to the vacuous and superficial.[10] As such the anthropologist is limited by his or her own gaze, caught up in defining the authenticity or validity of their own set of experiences as much as in capturing, classifying and denigrating the experiences of others. One goes to the beach with the precise aim of rendering oneself object. The refracted gaze of Augé constitutes less a meta-critique than a *mise-en-abîme* in which the possibility of 'authenticity' and self-legitimisation is endlessly deferred.

The suggestion proposed by Augé that it is possible to engage in a form of voluntary, temporary migration without being a 'tourist' has, in recent years, become increasingly problematized. Nevertheless, charity work, ecotourism and the spread of NGOs with their endless supply of gap year students continue to be affirmed by public discourse and academic scholarship alike as responsible forms of tourism which counteract the damage done to planet and populations alike in the construction and frequentation of holiday resorts and hotel complexes. Yet, where the work of NGOs and humanitarian charities pursue the 'mission civilisatrice' of colonialism under the auspices of Western guilt *qua* responsibility, the beach resort continues to operate as site and process of unabashed neo-colonization. Moreover, to revisit the beach resort in the wake of more diverse studies and accounts of tourism is to insist upon its ongoing ideological function in conjunction rather than opposition to emerging and alternative forms of tourism.

What is required is a more engaged analysis of mass tourism which unpacks rather than reiterates the notion of tourists as a homogeneous, global mass. As Ellen Furlough makes clear in her article 'Making Mass Vacations', the emergence and development of specific tourist practices is bound very closely to the economic, political and social structures and ideologies of individual nations and states. Thus, where mass tourism in the U.S. can be linked to the notion of 'employee benefits' which developed under Fordism, in France and other European countries, annual vacation entitlement was defined in more overtly political terms.[11] *Congés payés* were first introduced in France by the Popular Front Government in 1936, the original 15 days (12 working days) paid vacation were

---

[9] Ibid., 24; 26.

[10] See, for example, Dean MacCannell, *The Tourist: A New Theory of the Leisure Class*, New York, NY: Schocken Books: 1989 [1976], 10.

[11] Ellen Furlough, 'Making Mass Vacations: Tourism and Consumer Culture in France, 1930s to 1970s', *Comparative Studies in Society and History* 40:2, April 1998, 249.

extended by the government to four weeks in 1969 and then to five weeks in 1981.[12] The relationship between paid vacation as assuring the double role of worker as producer-consumer thus needs to be thought alongside and in distinction to the function of the *grandes vacances* in affirming a notion of citizenship that embodied a sense of belonging at the same time as enabling freedom of movement. Such freedoms must be thought of in terms of a neocolonial project which seeks to capture leisure alongside industry in its retention, acquisition and control of overseas territories and their natural and human resources.

Mission Civilisatrice

> The discovery of the sea is a precious experience that bears thought. Seeing the oceanic horizon is indeed anything but a secondary experience; it is in fact an event in consciousness of underestimated consequences.
>
> I have forgotten none of the sequences of this finding in the course of a summer when recovering peace and access to the beach were one and the same event.[13]

As the powerful opening to Virilio's *Bunker Archeology* makes apparent, the beach as site of suspended logic, as state of exception is inherently linked to its spectral double, war. If access to the beach is predicated on the arrival of peace, the rest of *Bunker Archaeology* bears witness to the scars left by war upon the French coastline, transformed under Nazi occupation into an Atlantic Wall composed of around 1500 bunkers. For Virilio, therefore, understanding what he refers to as the 'liquid continent' is predicated on the recently departed army who had used it as a frontier. '[T]he meaning of this oceanic immensity' he tells us 'was intertwined with this aspect of the deserted battlefield.'[14]

In a similar vein and with implicit reference to the same strip of coastline, La Baule, Augé has suggested 'Le tourisme, c'est la forme achevée de la guerre' [Tourism is the finished form of war]. Moreover, like Virilio, he is attentive to the acceleration of this process: 'De ce point de vue, les choses s'accélèrent' [From this point of view, things are speeding up].[15] Augé is, of course, referring specifically to the dark tourism of recent decades and the increasing speed with which sites of disaster are transformed into tours and monuments.[16] Yet we might begin to chart this from further back. Where the development of the beach resort

---

[12] Ibid., 261.

[13] Paul Virilio, *Bunker Archaeology*, trans. George Collins, New York, NY: Princeton Architectural Press, 2012 [1994], 9.

[14] Ibid.

[15] Augé, *L'Impossible Voyage*, 10. My translation.

[16] For specific discussion of war memorial tourism in France, see, for example, Jennifer Iles, 'Recalling Ghosts of War: Performing Tourism on the Battlefields of the Western Front,' *Text and Performance Quarterly* 26:2, April 2006, 162-80.

is linked to the industrial revolution and urbanism, the first and second world wars intensified the role of the beach as both witness and counterpoint to the anxieties and atrocities of modernity.[17] Lenček and Bosker make reference to the fantasies of tropical beaches held onto by those fighting inland in the cold and muddy trenches during the First World War. Likewise, following WWII, the beach turned battlefield is reimagined as a site of healing and rejuvenation. This is not simply as a result of the restorative qualities of the sea and the air which constituted the focus of eighteenth and nineteenth century trips to the coast.[18] Where the complex social hierarchies and strict lines between public and private were both reaffirmed and contested on the nineteenth century beach, the beach is reconceived in post-war France as a space in which such hierarchies can be erased in favour of collective freedom.

This was Gerard Blitz's vision which led to the founding of Club Med in 1950. In the aftermath of the Second World War, Blitz worked in a rehabilitation centre for survivors of the concentration camps. His work there led him to reflect on the collective trauma of war and recognize the therapeutic role vacations could play in alleviating such trauma. Moreover, to be truly effective, such vacations needed to be made available to all members of society and erase rather than reinforce social hierarchies and conventions. As Victor Franco writes of Blitz's vision in his biography of Club Med:

> His idea was not merely to transport, house, feed and amuse holidaymakers. In his view anybody could do that job. What he wanted to do was create a new kind of holiday, to make a stand in the name of fresh air, sport, the principles of the amateur Club, wind, sand and a warm translucent sea. He hoped at the same time to express his opposition to pre-war society, the society which had emerged from the holocaust having learned nothing and understood nothing. He rejected the rules of conduct laid down by this society. The pattern on which he would build his club was an expression of this anti-bourgeois reaction.[19]

This 'anti-bourgeois' reaction was echoed by Gilbert Trigano, a former communist who, having supplied camping equipment to Blitz, subsequently became a partner in the organization, becoming President in 1963 and running Club Med for several decades afterwards before his son, Serge took over in 1993.

Drawing on one of the best-known claims made by Club Med marketing that its villages provided an 'antidote to civilisation', Furlough has argued that the organisation embodied the mass tourism and consumer culture of post-war Europe rather than provided a space in which to resist this.[20] At the same time,

---

[17] Lena Lenček and Gideon Bosker, *The Beach: The History of Paradise on Earth*, London: Pimlico, 1999.

[18] Ibid., Ch. 3 and 4.

[19] Victor Franco, *The Club Méditerranée*, trans. by Michael Perl, Guilford: Shepheard-Walwyn, 1972, 12.

[20] Ellen Furlough, 'Packaging Pleasures: Club Méditerranée and French Consumer

we might read this idea of 'antidote' posited as cure for the traumas of the various wars waged by the so-called civilized world against the notion of a 'mission civilisatrice' inherent in Club Med's establishment and development beyond the borders of France itself. As Franco points out, there were important reasons why Blitz opened his first resort in Alcudia in Majorca rather than on the French coast:

> Now traditionally, so far as holidays were concerned, their horizons were limited to the blue line of the Vosges, and that of the Pyrenees…the Atlantic stopped at Hendaye, the Mediterranean at Menton, while from Cape Gris-Nez to the Gulf of Gascony the bunkers of the Atlantic defence system loomed sinister on the beaches.[21]

The bunkers which were so fascinating to the young Virilio, functioned as a permanent reminder of the pathologies of war to the French population. To move beyond such pathologies required the temporary displacement of the French population outside of the traditional limits of their world. 'The World as it is does not suit us', Blitz claimed. 'So we must build a new one.'[22] This construction of a new world was simultaneously an attempt to efface an old one.

The history of Club Med tends to be recited within wider accounts of *Les Trente Glorieuses* and the absorption of American notions of consumerism into French cultural practice. However, attention should also be paid to the fact that Club Med grew at a time when France, along with the rest of Western Europe, was undergoing an intense period of decolonization. Club Med opened its resort in Tunisia in 1954, two years before the country's independence from French rule. The Club's first permanent resort was opened in Agadir, Morocco in 1965. As Furlough suggests, 'Club Med was a reconfigured colonialist adventure…vacationers could continue to partake of colonialist "exoticism" even if their country no longer controlled the region politically.'[23]

Similarly, the resorts in France's overseas departments, such as Les Boucaniers which opened in Martinique in 1969, were part of the development of tourism which frequently, as Pascal Perri has argued, reaffirmed the enslavement of North African and DOM-TOM inhabitants to their former slave masters and colonisers. The rapid transition from slave colony to assimilation into the Republic ensured and demanded the maintenance of certain colonial hierarchies and forms of oppression.[24] Subsequently, the shift from a plantation-based economy to one focused on tourism reinforced these old hierarchies which required

---

Culture, 1950-1968', *French Historical Studies* 18:1, Spring 1993, 65-81.

[21] Franco, Op.cit., 12.

[22] Quoted in ibid., 13.

[23] Furlough, 'Packaging Pleasures', 77.

[24] Pascal Perri, *Le tourisme à la Martinique: Sous la plage…les conflits*, Paris: Éditions Karthala, 2004, 143.

black slaves to labour for their white masters. According to Perri, two in three visitors to Martinique are from mainland France.[25] Thus, for those working in the tourist and service industries, working for white French tourists is a reality as much as an impression. As Perri puts it: 'Les métiers du tourisme, eux, sont avilissants car on produit pour un autre, souvent un Blanc, un service sans grand valeur ajoutée.' [Tourist jobs are degrading in that one carries out a service for another, often a White, with little value attached to it.][26]

For Perri, tourism continues to function as a 'catalyst' for conflict and tension in Martinique. Here he cites as a notable example the problematic dialectic established between the 'neo-colonial' attitude of the French tourists vacationing in the Antilles and the local population often described as *'enfants gatés'* [spoilt children] for their refusal to embrace tourism as a viable economy or reconcile themselves to the low level of pay accepted by workers in other Caribbean countries. In 2002, the French hotel chain Accor withdrew its presence from Martinique as a result of problems with local labour. Strikes at Les Boucaniers in early 2007 lasted 3 weeks and led to 300 French guests being sent home early. The common response from tour operators and French media embodies a colonial discourse which condemns those making up the labour force for their failure to appreciate a form of work and industry which has been imposed upon them and which fails to serve their own communities who benefit little from the concrete jungles and infrastructure set up to facilitate the arrival and departure of overseas visitors. On their withdrawal from Martinique, then Accor boss, Gérard Pélisson, described the Antilles as *'un climat social détestable.'*[27]

In defining such animosity towards tourism as a form of 'ingratitude', such discourses continue to affirm the 'mission civilisatrice' of mainland France towards its outlying territories. And when such a mission fails, it is those who have refused or contested its oppressive demands and called out its colonial project that are punished most heavily. Investment in France's DOM-TOM encouraged by substantial tax breaks[28] has focused on tourism, the construction of hotel complexes and resorts. To alienate tourists is to alienate the financial support of mainland France rather than propose alternative economies and industries. Rather than withdrawing from Martinique along with Accor and others in 2002, Club Med decided to operate a sale and lease back system. In the transferal of the operation of the Club to local business, the state contributed 35 million Euros towards the '*défiscalisation*' process with local organisations paying 16 million Euros. Club Med limited their contribution to 3 million Euros. While

---

[25] Ibid., 17.

[26] Ibid., 27.

[27] Quoted in ibid., 9.

[28] For example, the '*Loi Pons*' was introduced in 1986 in order to encourage investment in DOM-TOM property development. Investors were given tax reductions of around 45% on properties in the region.

this move may be seen as alleviating tensions by giving local populations greater agency in the running of their service industries, what this actually points to is a huge reduction in the Club's responsibility for the finance and management of Les Boucaniers whilst ensuring it continues to obtain maximum profits. There is no real redistribution of wealth here since it is only rich Martinican business owners such as Yan Monplaisir benefitting in the process.[29]

Furthermore, at the same time as assuring the continuation of France's own colonial legacy, Club Med's decision to open a resort in the Arziv region of Israel's north Mediterranean coast in 1961 at the invitation of Ben Gurion attests to its complicity with the Israeli occupation and the Western powers which continue to endorse this. As Peter Lagerquist has suggested, the empty coastline which was partly given over to the club by the Israeli government is both a physical and symbolic embodiment of a revisionist history aimed at forgetting.[30] The dominant narrative of Arab migration to Lebanon following the arrival of Israeli forces in 1948 glosses over the ethnic cleansing and genocide which resulted in the idyllic, unpopulated beaches. The coastal village of al-Zib was deserted and its thousand year Arab history bracketed out.[31] Club Med became Israel's only private beach via special legislation. Thus, where Blitz and Trigano perceived the role of the club in Israel as in keeping with its therapeutic ideology following the specific atrocities of the Holocaust, the exceptionalism granted to the Club in Israel might, in fact, be considered as an obscene joke. The exceptional space of the camp reconfigured to exclude rather than include *homo sacer*.

*

In the opening decade of its operation, Club Med's occupation of overseas territories moved from that of encampment to colony. Despite Blitz's concept of creating a vacation space which removed French society entirely from the spectres of war, his first resorts relied on army surplus supplies, tents and campbeds, provided by the Trigano family. Later the army tents were replaced with Polynesian huts enacting the shift from territorial occupation to cultural appropriation as sarongs and other Polynesian inspired motifs were assimilated into the 'mode de vie' at Club Med villages around the world. Describing his own experience of a Club Med resort, sociologist Henri Raymond comments on the use of the appellation 'village' suggesting it evokes a sense of permanence or longevity in relation to the vacation,[32] something which might also be compared to the lon-

---

[29] Jean-Jacques Manceau, *Le Club Med: Réinventer la machine à rêves*, Paris: Editions Perrin, 2010, 108-9.

[30] Peter Lagerquist, 'Vacation from History: Ethnic Cleansing as the Club Med Experience,' *Journal of Palestinian Studies* 36:1, Autumn 2006, 43-53.

[31] Ibid., 49.

[32] Henri Raymond, 'Recherches sur un village de vacances', *Revue Française de Sociolo-*

gevity of a colonial occupation. At the same time, such 'villages' are situated apart from actual villages which assume the form of ghettos or excursion sites.

The introduction of Polynesian style huts was intended to inspire a primordial simplicity, aimed at reinforcing the idea of abandoning the constraints and conventions of Western civilization. Jean-Didier Urbain describes this in terms of a passage from simulacra to simulation. Where the hotels and guesthouses of the nineteenth century were taken up with reproducing the social hierarchies of city life, at stake here is the simulation of a different world. Sleeping on the beach, shedding the trappings of civilization, one 'plays' at being the other, the down-and-out, the negro.[33] Yet, Urbain's observation of the decontextualisation does not go far enough. This 'playing' the other is neither innocent nor unmotivated.[34] Moreover, we should be wary in defining it simply in terms of the apathy of late capitalism in which all experience is reduced to simulacra and, as Augé and Virilio suggest, all tourism is constitutive of a form of inertia. Something more complex is at work in this reenactment of Tahitian village life, in this 'playing' the homeless or the negro. It is not simply the acquisition of real estate that defines Club Med's 'mission civilisatrice'. This also occurs in the emptying out of meaning of cultural signifiers, the celebration of Polynesian cultural representations, architecture, clothing and so on, as empty signifiers, waiting to be appropriated according to individual fantasies of relaxation, hedonism, exoticism.

Club Med's 'mission civilisatrice' might thus be considered as a reenactment of Bougainville in Tahiti. Describing Bougainville's travel journal published in 1771 as 'one of the most influential publications shaping attitudes toward the beach', Lenček and Bosker suggest how his narratives of Tahiti project Western ideals and fantasies onto the islanders and their way of life rather than provide accurate accounts:

> [Bougainville's] glowing descriptions of native islanders were instantly seized upon by intellectuals seeking support for the myth of the 'noble savage' – the idea so popular in the eighteenth century that man in his natural state is both good and happy, and that all his vices and miseries stem from the greed and sophistry of civilization. Both Bougainville and his readers were all too glad to think of the Polynesians as incarnations of an ideal. On the beaches of Tahiti, they imagined idyllic islanders whom they endowed not with actual virtues, but with virtues they thought, as noble savages, they ought to have.[35]

---

gie 1:3, July-Sept 1960, 323.

[33] Jean-Didier Urbain, S*ur la plage: Mœurs et coutumes balnéaires XIXe-XXe siècles*, Paris: Payot, 2002, 197ff.

[34] A further irony is at work here in the repetition of nineteenth century French artist, Paul Gauguin's original quest for the purity and innocence of an island lifestyle as source of aesthetic inspiration. Tahiti was thus already marked on French cultural consciousness less as an escape from corrupt civilization than as a space in which the exoticised, untouched other (in the form of Gauguin's child wives) is forced to yield to the violent, transgressive desires of the European colonizer.

[35] Lenček and Bosker, Op. Cit., 49.

Lenček and Bosker make the connection between the promiscuity promised by Club Med's advertising and encouraged within its villages and the sexual favours supposedly offered as a welcome to French sailors arriving in Tahiti (rather than assumed and demanded from them). However, the link here is more complex and more important than a basic association of sex and beach. Imbuing local traditions with its own values and ideology, reshaping the landscape and imposing social and racial hierarchies akin to a colonial project, Club Med involves a similar act of projection to the one found in Bougainville's encounter with the Tahitian population and his subsequent representation of this encounter to those back in France.

One of the major paradoxes here is the affirmation of the body within the Club's discourse. For Blitz, sport and other forms of exercise were an inherent part of mental and physical recuperation following the war. However, scholarly reflection on the privileging of the body is often taken up with the scantily clad body of the bronzed sunbather and his or her sexual exploits. Urbain, Furlough, Littlewood and others have all commented on the implicit and explicit promiscuity of encounters within the Club facilitated by the purported erasure of social hierarchies and the reduction of dress codes to swimming trunks or sarongs.[36] Yet, Club Med affirms the space of the beach not simply as site to be colonized by towels and sun loungers. From the outset the Club embodied a specific reification of the body which finds its origins in military training and performance documented in 19th and early 20th century manuals such as Georges Hébert's *Méthode Naturelle* (1912) along with texts such as Victorin Raymond's *Manuel des Baigneurs* (1840). As Urbain points out, Dr Raymond is quick to distinguish swimming as a technical exercise from that of the 'singe, nègre ou quadrupède' [monkey, negro or four-legged animal].[37] An acquired technical superiority is emphasized in certain races in contradistinction to the 'animal-like' naturalness of movement attributed to others.

Herein lies the inherent contradiction of Club Med's claim to reject civilization and its discontents whilst not only reaffirming existing socio-economic distinctions but also the very discourses underpinning Western Imperialism and, more specifically, National Socialism. The 'technicity' required by many of the activities on offer in the Club Med villages re-establishes social hierarchies at the same time as reenacting a fascistic reification of the young, male athletic body not simply in itself but via the mastery and performance of a series of technical pursuits such as scuba diving, sailing, windsurfing together with the competitions that were regularly organized.[38] Where international competitions and tournaments such as the Olympics offer a receptacle for displays of

---

[36] Furlough, Op. cit.; Urbain, Op. cit.; Ian Littlewood, *Sultry Climates: Travel and Sex since the Grand Tour*, John Murray: London, 2001, 208ff.

[37] Quoted in Urbain, Op. cit., 172.

[38] See Raymond, Op. cit., 328-9.

national prowess and a way of channeling xenophobic sentiments into 'healthy' patriotism, the recruitment of former Olympic and professional sportsmen and women as GOs extended such patriotism beyond the televised spectacle to the space of the vacation.

Finally, if anything affirms the colonization project of the club against its slogans then this must surely be its logo. In contrast to the therapeutic, egalitarian claims of its advertising copy, the logo chosen for Club Med, Neptune's trident, is immediately associated with the conquest of the Mediterranean. Such symbolism does not simply reimagine the myths of the sea but, instead, represents first a desire to conquer and rule the Mediterranean coastline and, second, to transpose the (phallocentric) power of this rule onto the beaches of the entire world. It has been claimed that the French comedian, Guy Bedos, used to make the joke that:

> On nous dit qu'on ira bientôt dans la lune ? La lune, ce sera comme l'Espagne… Quand on pourra y aller, on tombera sur le Club Méditerranée !
>
> [They're telling us we'll soon be able to go to the moon? The moon will be like Spain…The moment we're able to go, we'll find Club Med already there!][39]

A trident is a three-pronged fishing spear and despite reworkings of the logo in 1980 and 1995 to make it appear first softer and more casual and then, in 2010, cleaner and neater in keeping with brands such as Apple,[40] it nevertheless continues to provide an inadvertent reminder of the plundering of natural and human resources involved in the constructing and operating of holiday resorts throughout the developing world. In this respect, the prongs might be further reimagined as arrows, evoking those appearing on imperial maps and strategic military plans. It is also important to note the deliberate resemblance of the prongs to the roofs of the Polynesian-style huts. The reduction of representation to a set of simple lines parallels the emptying-out of meaning that is essential to the 'mission civilisatrice' transposed to mass tourism.

Factory of Desire

If Club Med provides one of the most salient examples of the neo-colonization project of French tourism during a period of major decolonization in the decades following WWII, such a project is, as Furlough and others have argued, closely intertwined with the unprecedented economic growth and rise of

---

[39] Quoted in Christiane Peyre and Yves Raynouard, *Histoire et légendes du club méditerranée*, Paris : Seuil, 1971, 8. My translation.

[40] Here, see Manceau, Op. cit. [middle plates].

consumer culture associated with *Les Trente Glorieuses*. Moreover, the shifting ideology underpinning Club Med as it evolved from non-profit organization to a company of shareholders in the mid-1960s when the Baron de Rothschild came to its financial rescue, can be neatly mapped onto the marked change in the general notion of 'vacances' as a right for all, to a product to be desired and consumed by those who have 'earned' it. This is something Raymond already observes in his early ethnographic study of the 'village de vacances' in 1960.[41] Moreover, the saturation of images of the beach in mainstream media and advertising consolidate the idea of the vacation as a product which extended beyond the temporal and spatial limits of its consumption. Indeed, in this respect Club Med seems to prefigure as much as to emulate brands such as Apple which have come to predicate themselves on lifestyle aspirations which do not simply exceed specific products being sold but, also, offer up possibilities of exceeding the very notion of a 'lifestyle' itself.

It is fairly obvious perhaps that a company offering beach vacations would be able to extend customer experience and consciousness of the brand beyond the product itself in ways not immediately available or intuitive for other products. On the one hand, the 'empty' beach featured in Club Med's magazine, *Le Trident*, and other advertising, provides a *tabula rasa*, open to individual interpretation and desire rather than evoking a clearly defined set of behaviours and achievements to aspire to. It matters little whether the 'actual' experience of a specific resort lives up to the marketed images since such images dominate public consciousness for the greater part of the year and thus do much to blur and erase specific memories of sunburn and overcrowded beaches. On the other hand, Club Med offers its GMs the opportunity to 'consume' their vacation via its clothing ranges and other merchandise both before and after the vacation.[42] Thus, where a washing powder advertisement might offer up the myth of bourgeois domesticity,[43] a Club Med holiday can be marketed as providing an escape from such domesticity while its merchandise and magazines ensure this escape remains a perpetual possibility even when one returns to everyday life in the city or suburbs. The quotidian becomes the time and place where one remembers, dreams, plans and prepares for one's vacation. Again, like war, the vacation has ceased to constitute a hiatus in usual economic production and consumption and has now become its defining, structuring objective.

Of equal importance here is the role of a brand like Club Med in the construction not only of consumer myths but, at the same time, its creation and perpetuation of nationalist myths of vacation and, furthermore, the culturally

---

[41] Raymond, Op. cit., 326.

[42] In addition to its on-site gift shops, Club Med launched a mail order catalogue in 1959 exclusively for GMs. See Furlough, 'Packaging Pleasures', 78.

[43] See Roland Barthes, 'Saponides et détergents' in *Mythologies*, Paris: Seuil, 1957, 36-38.

and socially-inflected figure of the French tourist. This does not simply involve an erosion of politically-charged notions of vacations for all workers and their families. And, this affirmation of national identity occurs precisely as a result of Club Med's success as an international corporation rather than in spite of this.

A recent biography of Club Med describes the organization as a 'monument nationale', comparing it to the French football team.[44] Writing about *the* 'monument nationale', the Eiffel Tower, in 1964, Roland Barthes unpacks the construction of myth via mythical construction. According to Barthes, for Guy de Maupassant, like many of his fellow Parisians now and then, the only way to escape the visual profanation to his beloved Paris was to climb the Tower and dine in its passable restaurant. Yet, as Barthes points out, the Eiffel Tower has come to constitute the ultimate symbol of Paris and, moreover, France to the rest of the world. The cosmopolitan glamour the Tower has come to embody cannot be attributed to its construction, its function as a radio mast or even the irresistible pleasure inspired by its hourly light show.[45] There are other TV masts elsewhere, Berlin, Seattle, Tokyo with comparable aesthetics, other towers, the Empire State Building, the Petronas Towers, with similar stories of architectural genius and engineering prowess but none of which replicate to anything near the same degree the very specific myths produced by the Eiffel Tower. Implicit in Barthes' text is not simply the variety of myths belonging to the Tower but also the way in which the Tower lends itself to all of these. The same applies to Club Med. Its mythical status is also predicated upon multiple perspectives which operate from within and without in seeming opposition. On the one hand, it operates, like the Eiffel Tower, as a symbol of French national identity. To vacation in a Club Med village is frequently perceived by non-French guests as vacationing as the French do. On the other hand, the Club is mocked and derided from within as vulgar manifestation of modernity and Republicanism.

However, rather than simply echoing claims made by biographers and scholars alike concerning the 'mythical' status of Club Med, it is more interesting to consider the way in which this mythical status continues to be affirmed by such accounts. One of the most notable ways in which this occurs, is via the notion of collective storytelling. As Manceau suggests in his biography: 'L'esprit est entretenu par oral' [The spirit is maintained by word of mouth].[46] The decision to define customers as *gentils membres* (GMs), thus including them in the narrative of the organization, has become a staple – used both to champion the socialist origins of the Club within a history of French tourism as well as by those more critical of the role the club played in developing mass consumerism via brand loyalty. Furlough, for example, documents the ubiquitous presence of the Club

---

[44] Manceau, Op. Cit., 17.

[45] Roland Barthes, *The Eiffel Tower and Other Mythologies*, trans. Richard Howard, New York, NY: Hill and Wang, 1979.

[46] Manceau, Op. Cit., 8.

via its publications, marketing campaigns and social networks. In their 1971 biography of the Club, Peyre and Raynouard suggest this ubiquity extends beyond those patronising the Club and is a matter of national concern :

> Le Club Méditerranée est la seule organisation en France qui partage avec le Parti communiste l'étrange privilège de ne laisser personne indifférent. On est pour ou on est contre, sans trop savoir pourquoi.
>
> [Club Med is the only organisation to share with the Communist Party the strange privilege of leaving no one indifferent. You are either for or against without really knowing why.][47]

The comparison with the PCF is important. Not only does it maintain Club Med's association with a socialist, egalitarian agenda but, at the same time, it defines the Club as a matter of nationalist, political interest. This is less a case of actually demonstrating that Club Med *was* a matter of interest for the entire French population and more of arguing that Club Med *should be* a matter of interest as a national brand and global symbol of a particular aspect of French identity as produced by leisure and consumption.

This notion of public responsibility and implication in a national brand is echoed in Manceau's more recent book focused on Henri Giscard d'Estaing's management of the club since 2002. For Manceau, Club Med is a fundamental part of the French psyche to the point that he suggests that : 'Depuis sa création le Club Med est au cœur de toutes les grandes questions philosophiques qui ont animé la société française.' [Since its creation, Club Med has been at the heart of every philosophical question inspiring French society.][48] Yet, here public complicity and responsibility for the club's future takes on a slightly different inflection. For Manceau the public's sense of ownership of the Club instilled in them by Blitz and Trigano, is something to be treated with suspicion. In this respect, his account includes reference to the damaging role of parodies like *Les Bronzés* as well as social media sites like Trip Advisor. At stake here is a different interpellation of the French public, one that limits this public to a certain financial elite, affirming French exceptionalism above inclusivity. Thus, despite Giscard d'Estaing's failure to make the club profitable by 2010, Manceau's objective is to demonstrate how his management strategies have put the Club 'sur la bonne voie'.[49] Such strategies are presented by Manceau in terms of an ethico-moral responsibility which, it becomes apparent, have the objective of affirming the club's 'mission civilisatrice' both above its economic success and as fundamental to this.

---

[47] Peyre and Raynouard, Op. cit., 7.

[48] Manceau, Op, cit., 13.

[49] Ibid., 217.

Manceau's narrative involves a revisionist history of Club Med, a rewriting which enables him to position Giscard d'Estaing's 'vision' as a continuation rather than radical departure from the one conceived by Blitz and Trigano. The book's subtitle 'reinventer la machine à rêves' might be translated as 'reinventing the dream machine' focusing on the possibility of having a 'vision', risk taking, and the image of an innovative yet well-oiled machine required to set such a 'vision' in motion. Here, a double-doubling occurs in which the fantasy of Giscard d'Estaing like that of Blitz is defined as the realization of the fantasies of the Club's patrons. Yet, we might also read this reference to a 'machine à rêves' via a different translation, the notion of a 'factory of desire' in which Fordism gives way to a post-Fordist configuration of desire based on the very same narcissism of small differences underpinning Leconte's parody of the Club. And, for Manceau it is precisely the small differences that enable Giscard d'Estaing to redefine Club Med as a 'marque de luxe' where previous radical changes to the Club's business model and product by his predecessors simply impoverished the brand.

One of the main ways this revisionist history is constructed is by assuming the tradition established in earlier biographies of setting up an opposition between the Club's heroes and its villains. If Blitz and Trigano were the original heroes, the Baron de Rothschild was the first villain. If Rothschild assured the Club's growth and success by bankrolling the operation during the 1960s, he is also credited with turning the resorts into 'factories', losing sight of the club's original values and *raison d'être*.[50] In Manceau's book, Philippe Bourguignon plays a similar role. Having become President of Club Med in 1997 after running Disneyland Paris, Bourguignon is associated with a cheap americanisation of the Club via an endless recounting of his unsuccessful projects and campaigns. As 'antidote' to this *disneyfication*, Giscard d'Estaing is cast as perfect embodiment of French sophistication.[51]

In setting up these oppositions, Manceau is able to situate Giscard d'Estaing within the Club Med myth. His revisioning of the Club as a luxury brand aimed at the top 4% of the French population[52] is credited by Manceau as somehow in keeping with the all-inclusive ideology of Blitz and Trigano. Manceau achieves this by focusing on what I have already termed the 'mission civilisatrice' of Blitz and Trigano. Where for Club Med's founders, this 'mission' enabled the French population to collectively exceed the horizons of the 'hexagone' along with the

---

[50] See Peyre and Raynouard, Op. cit., 257.

[51] At the same time as being reified as the Club's founding fathers, Blitz and Trigano are conjured up but not dwelt upon by Manceau. Where various global events of the opening decade of the 21st century, 911, SARS, the 2004 Tsunami, play a major role for Manceau in the Club's recent narrative of survival and reinvention, almost no mention is made of the manslaughter sentences served by the Triganos in 2000 following an aircraft accident off the coast of Senegal.

[52] Manceau, Op. cit., 53-4.

limits of everyday life such a mission takes on a different form with Giscard d'Estaing. The French tourist is no longer the primary focus but is instead displaced by a global elite. The 'all-inclusive' discourse of the early Club Med gives way to a 'multi-culturalisme' composed of the new moneyed middle classes of emerging super-powers China, Russia and Brazil.[53]

Moreover, this claim of continuity coupled with innovation is affirmed via an incessant rhetoric of colonization. On the one hand, this rhetoric is described as fundamental to Giscard d'Estaing's plan for the club. His two major strategies as recounted by Manceau, 'Cap sur l'incomparable' and 'Magellan', employ an overtly colonist vernacular as does his 'carte de transformation.'[54] At the same time, such language is echoed by Manceau's own narrative as he refers Giscard d'Estaing as 'capitaine'[55] and to the Club's success as predicated upon 'un monde à construire' [a world to be built][56] and, in particular, 'la future conquête sur la Chine' [the future conquest of China].[57] Thus it becomes apparent that, at least for Manceau, Giscard d'Estaing's salvation of Club Med lies precisely in a reinstatement of the 'mission civilisatrice' of the French tourist industry. Such a reinstatement, in turn, redefines France in terms of an old world, aristocratic sense of privilege and taste. His love of hunting in rural France is evoked in contrast to the Club's raucous 'Crazy Signs' dance routines.[58] At numerous points in his book, Manceau plays on the deliberate ambiguity of the appellation of 'president' to link Giscard d'Estaing to his father's political legacy creating a direct link between the management of the Club and the government of the Republic. 'Les pâtes et les foies gras poêlés sont désormais au goût du président.' [Pasta and foie gras are henceforth cooked according to the tastes of a president.][59]

Thus, as France continues to subsidise its flag carrier, Air France, while other European airlines have long been privatized or, in the case of Sabena and others, abandoned by government and tax payers, it is possible to see a very specific French colonial desire at work in Giscard d'Estaing's 'projet Magellan'. Leisure continues to function as a symbol of French national identity. Yet, inclusion within this identity becomes carefully refined, aligned with luxury brands such as Dior and Hermes that are increasingly marketed to the new wealth of Asia and South America. Consequently, the 'multiculturalism' of Giscard d'Estaing's

---

[53] According to Manceau five 'essential' values were agreed upon as part of Giscard d'Estaing's new vision: 'multiculturalité, esprit pionnier, gentillesse, liberté, responsabilité.' [multiculturalism, a pioneering spirit, kindness, freedom and responsibility], Op. cit., 84. My translation.

[54] Ibid., 55-6.

[55] Ibid., 55.

[56] Ibid., 103.

[57] Ibid., 208.

[58] Ibid., 32.

[59] Ibid., 68. My translation.

marketing discourse assures the global myth of the French-citizen-tourist as monocultural, solely predicated upon economic wealth and a homogenized image of global consumerism.

Reclaimed Land

Since the late 1980s, the need to critique the neocolonial desires enacted through global tourism has taken on a double imperative. Western operated resorts and tour companies have often justified their plundering of resources and occupation of prime coastal real estate in terms of the (questionable) economic benefits and employment opportunities afforded to local populations. However, such justification becomes harder to maintain in the face of today's discourses on global warming and the already widely evident threats to coastal areas around the planet. Short-term financial gains no longer serve as legitimation for the strain placed on water supplies and other resources along with the irreversible damage caused to coastlines by concrete developments and infrastructures set up to benefit a visiting rather than local population.

As indicated above, Manceau's desire to align Club Med's history and identity with that of France manifests itself most excruciatingly in his references, both implicit and explicit, to Giscard d'Estaing's father, Valéry. There is a certain irony in this forced linking not least in its open celebration of old money as appropriate embodiment of French civilization versus the vulgarity of mass tourism as symbol of impoverished Republican ideals. A different link might be set up here via father and son. As Maurice Burac has argued, the aggressive tourism development program announced by Giscard d'Estaing at the start of his presidency failed to translate to the needs and circumstances of France's Outre-Mer where over-population was already a major issue.[60] In addition to the misplaced incentives of the *Loi Pons* mentioned above, urban planning policies defined in mainland France failed to be applied with the same level of consistency in the overseas territories leading to what Perri has termed a 'tourisme anarchique'[61] and what Aimé Césaire and others have criticized as the 'bétonnisation' [concretization] of the Antilles by European and North American developers. According to Burac, tourism in Martinique during the 1970s and 1980s 'seemed like a new form of human pollution within a structure of neglect.'[62]

A similar attitude might be identified in Henri Giscard d'Estaing's 'tokenism' concerning the Club's perceived championing of sustainable development

---

[60] Maurice Burac, 'The Struggle for Sustainable Tourism in Martinique' in Sherrie L. Baver and Barbara Deutsch Lynch (eds), *Beyond Sun and Sand: Caribbean Environmentalists*, New Brunswick, NJ and London: Rutgers University Press, 2006, 67.

[61] Perri, Op. cit., 24.

[62] Burac, Op. cit., 68.

juxtaposed with his own aggressive development programme. Manceau makes it clear in his biography of the Club that questions of environment, local labour and sustainable development are little more than marketing tools at best, impediments to economic growth at worst. He cites the multiple environmental awards the Club has won as an exercise in branding rather than an ethical obligation. The cynicism at work here is palpable and epitomized by a statement from the Club's director of sustainable development, Agnès Weil:

> Sans savoir encore si nous souhaitons aller jusqu'a l'obtention d'un écolabel pour chacun de nos villages, nous voulons être exemplaires en accélérant les démarches de management environnemental et en donnant des *guide lines* de construction pour nos villages futurs.
>
> [Without knowing yet if we want to go down the path of obtaining an eco-badge for all our villages, we want to be exemplary in speeding up the process of environmental management and providing guidelines for the construction of our future villages.][63]

It is clear from this statement that the focus here is on speedy construction with sustainable development merely a means to achieving this. The environment like local labour is something to be managed not respected and protected in itself. Moreover, Club Med's specific conservation projects seem to embody one of the major paradoxes of a more broadly defined ecotourism as explained by Sherrie L. Baver and Barbara Deutsch Lynch:

> [E]cotourism projects may meet narrowly defined conservation objectives, but privatization of natural resources and enclosure in support of ecotourism exacerbates problems of inequality and access.[64]

Elsewhere, debates over land leased to the Club demonstrate the extent to which the 'mission civilisatrice' has been internalized by local communities. In the case of Phuket in Thailand, discussions in 2014 as to the future of the land leased to the club since 1985 highlighted divergent opinions as to the validity of Club Med's presence. Where certain groups spoke out in favour of making the land which is part of Kata beach available for the use of the local community, there were also those that welcomed the presence of a foreign investor whom they view as circumventing the possibilities for corruption amongst local officials and developers and the destruction of coastal parkland by the general public. As local news source, *Phuket Wan* stated:

> While Club Med is about as international in outlook as any resort gets, it is regrettable that little of that international approach has permeated the surrounding

---

[63] Quoted in Manceau, Op. cit., 183. My translation.

[64] Sherrie L. Baver and Barbara Deutsch Lynch, 'The Political Ecology of Paradise' in Baver and Lynch, Op. cit., 14.

village mentality, which is still locked into the same way of operating as in 1985.[65]

Similarly, readers' comments following the *Phuket Gazette*'s reporting on the negotiations included the following type of statements:

> Because of the Club Med, the Kata Beach Road is the cleanest, prettiest beach road on the entire island. Park? I guess the locals just want to ruin it as quickly as possible. They'll set up massage tents, street food vendors, tuk-tuk stations, etc, and generally make the place filthy. Has anyone noticed how run down the beach is in Kamala?[66]

The outspokenness of critics of Phuket's government along with an indictment of the local Thai population based on the crudest of stereotypes seems to reproduce a 'colonial' discourse in which indigenous communities cannot be trusted to look after their land and resources thus requiring intervention from the developed world.

In August 2014 it was agreed that Club Med would develop 5 rai (8000m2) of land into a public park in exchange for a renewal of their lease for just 3 years. The symbolism of this gesture should nevertheless be noted within the context of global operations, in particular, their stakes in the Chinese market but also, their lack of commitment to local communities elsewhere as demonstrated in their minimal investment in Les Boucaniers.

Conclusion: Les Vieux Crabes

For a number of years, singles tour operator, *Club 18-35 ans* has used the tagline 'interdit aux vieux crabes.' [old crabs prohibited] The pun referencing STIs as well as Club Med's ageing brand and customer base affirms the role and indeed the necessity of parody within today's increasingly stratified beach resort industry. Moreover, parody, it seems does not damage a brand but rather assures its status in public consciousness. A critique of tourism and more specifically, the tourist, is built into the tourism of late capitalism. It is this critique which enables organisations like Club Med to turn any attack on their operation onto their customers at the same time as demanding public responsibility for the interests of a brand as symbol of their own national and class identity. This circumven-

---

[65] Sert Tongdee and Alan Morison, 'Fairway to Heaven: Phuket Scores Park for the Club Med Course,' *Phuket Wan*, 14 August 2014. Available: http://phuketwan.com/property/fairway-heaven-phuket-scores-park-club-med-course-20824/. Accessed 16/09/2014.

[66] Comment made by 'artistman' in response to Saran Mitrarat, 'Phuket officials threaten protest over Club Med lease,' *Phuket Gazette*, 18 April 2014. Available: http://www.phuketgazette.net/phuket-news/Phuket-officials-threaten-protest-Club-Med-lease/29170. Accessed 16/09/2014.

tion of sustained critique not simply of tourism *per se* but the neocolonial ideologies which continue to underpin it, works in tandem with the inertia of global travel identified by Virilio and others.

However, if the respective takes on weekenders and tourists by Godard and Leconte represent the descent into ironic self-parody of Western consumerism in the post-war decades, Michel Houellebecq's reimagining of France's global tourist industry in *Plateforme* (2001) marks a limit in which farce flips over into tragedy once more. In the novel, the postmodern cynicism which enables the open promotion of sex tourism as respectable and mainstream meets the violent necropolitics of an Islamic fundamentalism responding to this reenacting of Western colonialism. Where Houellebecq's anti-Islam stance is deeply problematic, the novel nevertheless is worth noting here for taking irreconcilable global tensions to their logical conclusion in order to reaffirm the perpetual link between war and tourism.

In early autumn of 2014, the future ownership and management of Club Med was uncertain. A complex set of negotiations had taken place over the preceding months between two different potential investors, Chinese conglomerate Fosun and Italian tycoon Andrea Bonomi. Both investors were highly sensitized to the mythical status of Club Med within French national identity as perceived both inside and outside of France. Fosun had their bid supported by Ardian, a French private equity firm and proposed to keep Giscard d'Estaing as Director General. Bonomi was backed by Serge Trigano who would be reinstated as Club chairman if their bid had been successful. In the end, Bonomi withdrew after the bidding war saw him make a tidy profit from Club Med's elevated share price.

As part of its reporting on the 'saga' between the two sets of investors, *Le Nouvel Observateur* ran the headline 'Le Club Med devrait devenir le Club Chinois' [Club Med would have to become Club Chinese].[67] If anything this simply reiterates the Club's own stirring up of nationalist sentiment and the legitimization of its neocolonial projects in Asia now presented as counterpoint to the designs China has on the European tourist industry. Moreover, the 'revisioning' of history in order to write the new owner into the Club's narrative will not attest to a 'betrayal' or 'affirmation' of the Club's values and identity. What is at stake here is the acknowledgment not so much of the myths produced by Club Med but, rather, the ability of the beach, other beaches, and those appropriating these spaces, to *produce* a whole series of myths. In its 'colonisation' of beaches worldwide, Club Med not only ensures the longevity of France's 'mission civilisatrice' long after its loss of empire, but also enables this mission to redefine itself along with French identity according to the pathological anxieties of global consumerism.

---

[67] Claude Soula, 'Le Club Med devrait devenir le Club Chinois', *Le Nouvel Observateur*, 12 September 2014. Available: http://tempsreel.nouvelobs.com/societe/20140912.OBS9034/le-club-med-devrait-devenir-le-club-chinois.html. Accessed 16/09/2014.

Thus, if the beach represents the site of multiple encounters, actual and imaginary, encounters largely defined as violent and transgressive and as such, celebrated and mourned in equal measure, it is nevertheless the image of the empty beach, a beach free from the detritus of human existence that persists in Western consciousness. But never *only* an empty beach and a phone number. Gérard Blitz's first poster for Club Med has come to frame the beach dialectically since the post-war years. No matter the rising sea levels, hurricanes and tsunamis affecting coastal life around the world. No matter the pollution caused by hotel chains worldwide, the damaged coral reefs, the extinction of coastal wildlife. No matter the ghettoization of local populations and the persistence of slave economies produced by the tourist and service industries, the neo-colonisation and ethnic cleansing. As colonial guilt and post-war shame are washed away with the tides, military strategy is rewritten as risk assessment and brand management policy. Despite appearances, the beach continues to operate as battlefield, camp and colony.

References

Agamben, Giorgio, *Homo Sacer: Sovereign Power and Bare Life*, Stanford, CA: Stanford University Press, 1998.

'Artistman', Comment in response to Saran Mitrarat, 'Phuket officials threaten protest over Club Med lease,' *Phuket Gazette*, 18 April 2014. Available: http://www.phuketgazette.net/phuket-news/Phuket-officials-threaten-protest-Club-Med-lease/29170. Accessed 16/09/2014.

Augé, Marc, *Non-Lieux: Introduction à une anthropologie de la surmodernité*, Paris: Seuil, 1992.

_____, *L'Impossible Voyage: Le tourisme et ses images*, Paris: Éditions Payot et Rivages, 2013.

Barthes, Roland, 'Saponides et détergents' in *Mythologies*, Paris: Seuil, 1957.

_____, *The Eiffel Tower and Other Mythologies*, trans. Richard Howard, New York, NY: Hill and Wang, 1979.

Baver, Sherrie L. and Deutsch Lynch, Barbara, 'The Political Ecology of Paradise' in Sherrie L. Baver and Barbara Deutsch Lynch (eds), *Beyond Sun and Sand: Caribbean Environmentalisms*, New Brunswick, NJ and London: Rutgers University Press, 2006, 3-16.

Burac, Maurice, 'The Struggle for Sustainable Tourism in Martinique' in Sherrie L. Baver and Barbara Deutsch Lynch (eds), *Beyond Sun and Sand: Caribbean Environmentalisms*, New Brunswick, NJ and London: Rutgers University Press, 2006, 65-74.

Diken, Bülent and Laustsen, Carsten Bagge, *The Culture of Exception: Sociology Facing the Camp*, London: Routledge, 2005.

Franco, Victor, *The Club Méditerranée*, trans. Michael Perl, Guilford: Shepheard-Walwyn, 1972.

Furlough, Ellen, 'Packaging Pleasures: Club Méditerranée and French Consumer Culture, 1950-1968', *French Historical Studies* 18:1, Spring 1993, 65-81.

_____ , 'Making Mass Vacations: Tourism and Consumer Culture in France, 1930s to 1970s', *Comparative Studies in Society and History* 40:2, April 1998, 247-286.

Hébert, Georges, *L'éducation physique ou l'entrainement complet par la méthode naturelle*, Paris: Librairie Vuibert, 1912.

Iles, Jennifer, 'Recalling Ghosts of War: Performing Tourism on the Battlefields of the Western Front', *Text and Performance Quarterly* 26:2, April 2006, 162-80.

Lagerquist, Peter, 'Vacation from History: Ethnic Cleansing as the Club Med Experience', *Journal of Palestinian Studies* 36:1, Autumn 2006, 43-53.

Lenček, Lena and Bosker, Gideon, *The Beach: The History of Paradise on Earth*, London: Pimlico, 1999.

Lennon, John and Foley, Malcolm, *Dark Tourism: The Attraction of Death and Disaster*, London: Continuum, 2000.

MacCannell, Dean, *The Tourist: A New Theory of the Leisure Class*, New York, NY: Schocken Books: 1989 [1976].

Manceau, Jean-Jacques, *Le Club Med: Réinventer la machine à rêves*, Paris: Editions Perrin, 2010.

Marx, Karl, *The Eighteenth Brumaire of Louis Bonaparte (1852)*. Available: http://www.marxists.org.

Perri, Pascal, *Le tourisme à la Martinique: Sous la plage...les conflits*, Paris: Éditions Karthala, 2004.

Raymond, Henri, 'L'Utopie Concrète: Recherches sur un village de vacances', *Revue Française de Sociologie* 1:3, July-Sept 1960, 323-333.

Raymond, Victorin, *Manuel des Baigneurs*, Paris: Desloges, 1840.

Soula, Claude, 'Le Club Med devrait devenir le Club Chinois', *Le Nouvel Observateur*, 12 September 2014. Available: http://tempsreel.nouvelobs.com/societe/20140912.OBS9034/le-club-med-devrait-devenir-le-club-chinois.html. Accessed 16/09/2014.

Tongdee, Sert and Morison, Alan, 'Fairway to Heaven: Phuket Scores Park for the Club Med Course', *Phuket Wan*, 14 August 2014. Available: http://phuketwan.com/property/fairway-heaven-phuket-scores-park-club-med-course-20824/. Accessed 16/09/2014.

Urbain, Jean-Didier, *Sur la plage: Mœurs et coutumes balnéaires XIXe-XXe siècles*, Paris: Payot, 2002.

Virilio, Paul, *Bunker Archaeology*, trans. George Collins, New York, NY: Princeton Architectural Press, 2012 [1994].

Walters, William, 'On the Road with Michel Foucault: Migration, Deportation and Viapolitics' in *Foucault and the History of Our Present* edited by Sophie Fuggle, Yari Lanci and Martina Tazzioli, London and New York, NY: Palgrave, 2015, 94-110.

8.

'ELLE NE SERA BIENTÔT QU'UNE ÉPAVE SOUDÉE À SES ROCHERS': WOMEN WRITING THE WRECK OF BEIRUT

Claire Launchbury

> Et mes yeux sont un port
> d'où partent des navires
> dont on dit qu'ils sont beaux
> comme un enfant qui pleure
> dans la nuit des miroirs.
>
> Nadia Tuéni, 'Pour que la haine soit légitime'

Beirut occupies a rich yet relatively under-explored place in the francophone imagination. Under French mandate from 1922 to 1943, Lebanon, and its capital in particular, reveals postcolonial traces in both cultural and urban fabrics. Rivalling Haifa in British-mandated Palestine as the major port of the Eastern Mediterranean under Western control, the relationship between the city and the sea has worked to define elements of Beirut's identity for centuries — a trading port since Phoenician times, the destruction of Berytus by a tsunami in 551CE, and more recently as a luxury resort for the international jet-set, or a city under siege during Israeli sea blockades. The urban seafront is best known for the gilded palm-lined avenues which form the Corniche, a long curving promenade, the Avenue de Paris which runs from the central district along the coast from the Baie Saint-Georges up to the Raouché district and the symbolic Grotte aux pigeons where it becomes the Avenue Général de Gaulle. A democratic space in some ways, it is non-sectarian and classless, but also one whose expensive and exclusive private beaches are distinct from the appropriation of rocky outcrops almost exclusively by men; the fishermen who line the stretch and the kaak sellers on their bicycles. The Corniche can and has been interpreted in many different ways: as an outward looking departure point from Beirut towards the shared trading space of the Mediterranean, or as something to look inwards from during the various sieges or seaborne attacks of the civil war: the sea and its shore have variously been haven, threat, waste dump, escape and pleasure ground.

The Beirut shoreline is a location of multiple encounters: between the city and sea, leisure and work, between the West and the Arab world. This is not without parallels, as Ann Davis explores in her study of Spanish spaces, the site of the beach works as a double space of exoticism, and relevant here is the trope of available 'orientalised' sexuality for the visiting northern European tourist, as well as of work.[1] Within this space, she identifies an ambivalence of subjecthood, particularly female, which is articulated in a way that 'on the one hand, attempts to overturn the stereotype of the Spanish beach as the place of sun, sand and sex, and yet, on the other hand, sees the Spanish consenting to participate in their own othering, and at times finding both sexual and other satisfactions in so doing.'[2] Such contrasts are also explored by Fiona Handyside in relation to Eric Rohmer's cinema where the beach represents a site of mass cultural leisure and pleasure yet also forms the site of narrative ambivalence, isolation and loneliness.[3] Conceived as a place of escape from the city, relationships are unplanned and temporary, provisional and mobile. While Rohmer maintains a focus on the beach's reality as a site produced by labour, he is all the while, as Handyside points out, alert to these contingencies.[4] While both Davis and Handyside discuss the beach as a zone which is different or separated from the city, Beirut, of course, is the location of an important encounter between the urban and the beach: the proximity of sandy shores at the city limits or the pools and beaches constructed on the western edge along the Corniche means city-based office workers are no more than ten minutes from desk to deckchair.[5] The encounter between the West and the Arab world was increased by the development of large luxury hotels and nightclubs. Their proximity to the beaches provided visiting tourists with a Western form of leisure, reaching its apogee in the 1960s when economic growth combined with Beirut becoming the fashionable destination for the jet-set of the Occident and the wealthy of the Gulf States.[6] Indeed, this development, along with changes in women's fashion – the bikini, the mini skirt – led to what Samir Kassir observed as the summertime unveiling of the female body by the sea. This, he argued was emblematic of the progressive modernism

---

[1] Ann Davis, *Spanish Places: Landscape, Space and Place in Contemporary Spanish Culture*, Liverpool: Liverpool University Press, 2012.

[2] Ibid., 128.

[3] Fiona Handyside, 'Rohmer à la plage: The role of the beach in three films by Eric Rohmer', *Studies in French Cinema* 9:2, 2009, 148.

[4] Ibid., 155.

[5] Samir Kassir, *Beirut*, trans. M. DeBevoise, Berkeley, CA: University of California Press, 2010 [2003], 396.

[6] See Bruno Dewailly and Jean-Marc Ovazza, 'Le tourisme au Liban: quand l'action ne fait plus système' in *Tourisme des nationaux, tourisme des étrangers: quelles articulations en Méditerranée?* edited by M. Berriane, Florence: Institut européen de Florence, 2004, 1-37.

in which the collective identity of the city at this time was rooted.⁷ The transition from urban work clothes to beachwear over such tiny distances played into the cosmopolitan, liberal notions of the Lebanese capital as playground.

Developing beach resorts in Beirut was strongly encouraged by the French mandatory authorities in the context of promoting tourism to the region from the end of the First World War. As an indication of the sometimes strange linguistic topography of Beirut, Edward Said observed how the naming of a new beach, Saint-Picot, occurred through misunderstanding 'Saint' as the French word for beach —older established beaches known as Saint-Michel and Saint-Simon were something entirely different in Arabic. Georges Picot along with Sir Mark Sykes signed off the divisions of the region between French and British mandatory authorities at the fall of the Ottoman Empire and his mistaken beatification here was politically loaded in post-independent Lebanon. Said continues: 'in a small way the endowment of Picot's name (to which the Arabs have no reason to be grateful) with sainthood, and the entitlement of a Lebanese beach to so oddly decorated European name, was a reflection [...] of Beirut's unique status as a place of natural entry from the West onto the confusing modern topography of the Arab world.'⁸

The outbreak of the civil war in 1975 killed off the international tourist industry and the beach resorts in south Beirut closed. Yet, this did not stop local populations from visiting the sea: Christian populations took refuge in Jounieh Bay, and according to Dewailly and Ovazza, apart from periods of especially violent fighting, the region just north of Beirut, Keserwan, was secure enough for residents of the mountain region of Metn to holiday on the coast.⁹ Within the city itself, one of the major effects was to limit the potential for urban excursion. The civil war introduced a new and violent dividing border to the urban landscape: the demarcation line which divided Beirut between east and west with only perilous crossing points open at limited times during the day. Schools and workplaces on the other side were impossible to access and daily life became circumscribed by the sectarian borders of the immediate district. Children were unable to go to school; people were unable to go to work. Families and friendships were split, life or execution at a checkpoint was dependent upon ID checks: whether the religion on your national identity card was acceptable or not to whichever faction was in charge. The everyday became subject to the arbitrary decisions of self-appointed militia leaders, or to the actions of international intervention, the Israeli invasion. The central area of the city became inaccessible because of fighting militia, snipers and mines.

---

⁷ Kassir, Op. cit., 398.

⁸ Edward Said, 'The Palestinian Experience (1968-69)' in *The Edward Said Reader*, edited by Moustafa Dayoumi and Andrew Rubin, New York, NY: Vintage, 2000, 17.

⁹ Dewailly and Ovazza, Op. cit., 5.

So in this chapter, the contrasting, paradoxical sites represented by the urban beaches of Beirut are explored, in particular how sea and shore are configured in wartime francophone narratives by two Lebanese writers: Evelyne Accad, *L'Excisée* (1982), *Coquelicot du massacre* (1988) and Etel Adnan, *Sitt Marie-Rose* (1977). Miriam Cooke has documented how through the act of writing the war, women forged new senses of identity and, moreover, of responsibility in their negotiations of a radically disturbed everyday. She identifies this self-assertion of female identity as coinciding with the disintegration of Lebanon's identity as an independent patriarchal polity.[10] An emancipatory vortex created an opportunity for women to undertake transformative processes of self-realisation in the act of writing and of writing of and about themselves. The Beirut decentrists, the group of women writers defined by Miriam Cooke, existed on the margins of a divided city, on the edges of sectarian conflict, and they chose narrative —which is far from anodyne in a non-European context — in order to write against and thus contest historical and personal trauma.[11] In a corollary to the later work of Marguerite Duras, their work forms an interrogation into the status of writing in the face of catastrophe.[12] Women writing narrative in French, but even more so in Arabic, marks, for Accad, the re-appropriation of a Eurocentric genre but one in which the novelists necessarily work in a contradictory mode, a form of schizophrenia expressed with originality, and a process through which women discover a unique voice that constructs their own identity (EA, 6). A postcolonial condition, then, in which the influence of surrealism, along with its often violent rhetoric, operates as means of encoding, expressing the absurd and taking irony to its extreme as 'a refuge from the war's cruelty and inhumanity' (EA, 6).

Each of these case studies presents women characters in their struggle to negotiate a cityscape that has been reformulated, divided and destroyed. The wreck of Beirut becomes a significant, often gendered figure, both Accad and Adnan depict the wounds of patriarchal violence — including the primal crimes of rape, female circumcision and honour killing — as inflicted upon the characters themselves but also metaphorically upon the cityscape too. Contrastingly, there is a sense in which the fluidity of the sea plays into tropes of feminine sexuality, the homophonic concordance of *mer* and *mère* in French is telling here and, as such, represents a place of resistance to violence when it is a space appropriated by women. Etel Adnan writes of the sea in her contemplation of women and cities: 'J'attends beaucoup d'elle, comme je faisais à Beyrouth quand j'étais enfant, mais l'innocence est partie. Nous avons enterré tant de morts, et

---

[10] Miriam Cooke, *War's Other Voices: Women Writers on the Lebanese Civil War*, Syracuse, NY: Syracuse University Press, 1996 [1987], 12.

[11] Ibid.

[12] Martin Crowley, *Duras, Writing and the Ethical: Making the Broken Whole*, Oxford: Oxford University Press, 2000, 148.

lui demandons toujours du secours.' [I expect a lot from her [the sea], as I used to in Beyrouth when I was a child, but the innocence has gone. We buried so many dead and always asked her for help.]¹³ Adnan has written widely in Arabic, English and French and is an established visual artist. Her work represents displacement and alienation and the struggles of articulating identity, particularly in languages which, although permitting a sense of writing back, suggest some level of complicity with a colonial or patriarchal authority against which she is seeking to protest.

In Evelyne Accad's writing on sexuality and war, she is seeking to assess the 'necessary changes Lebanon must undergo to solve its tragedy and to become, once again, the area for democratic tolerance and freedom.'¹⁴ For her, it is through the transposition of personal into political relationships that ultimately such a solution becomes possible; in short, through a new understanding of love. Defining the issue at a regional level, Accad suggests that sexual relations which can be read as the sexual politics of the Mediterranean and Middle East always operate in dysfunction because the phallus and gun are collapsed into the same violent configuration. A need to replace this by a new understanding of a feminine consciousness would lead, she contests, to the opportunity to (re)establish peaceful coexistence. In her novels, sexual violence — castration, circumcision and the repressive preservation of virginity for honour purposes — are demonstrative of when the penis is used to 'conquer, control, possess'.¹⁵ From this she then draws a stratified analogy between the violence of warfare in its destruction of life and the pain of childbirth in producing it. Such stark oppositions arise through the polarising effects of internecine conflict and the fractures and fault lines of its many atrocities.

Furthering the contrast between fractured urban space and the liminal shore, the appropriation of the sea as feminine space in Accad's narrative *L'Excisée* (1982) sets up the contrast in wartime Beirut between the area of the city immediately around the demarcation line known as 'la ligne verte' which divided the city into Muslim West and Christian East. This deadly partition ran a vertical axis from the coast along the Rue de Damas from north to south of the city. It forms the centre point of Accad's novel, *Cocquelicot du massacre* (1988) in which a mother and her child endeavour to cross to the other side of the line and whose success is dependent upon a soldier sacrificing his own life, symbolically being killed rather than killing. Borders such as these denote transgression in their crossing and the symbolic act of getting to the other side of the city is, once more for Accad, an expression of sexuality, symbolising 'the bridge

---

¹³ Etel Adnan, *Des Villes et des femmes, lettres à Fawwaz*, Beirut: Tamyras, 2014, 39. Unless otherwise indicated all translations are my own.

¹⁴ Evelyne Accad, *War and Sexuality: Literary Masks of the Middle East*, New York, NY: New York University Press, 1990, 4.

¹⁵ Ibid., 32.

between opposing forces'.[16] In Etel Adnan's *Sitt Marie-Rose*, the female protagonist's bold transgression into the masculine imagination is described as being like 'un océan déchaîné'.[17] Where Beirut met the sea, during the war, a liminal site was formed from where the city could look inland toward its own partition, but the resistance presented by these narratives, I argue, is to invert this gaze: the wreck of Beirut is grounded upon the rocks and the city vomits its atavistic violence out into the sea.

Evelyne Accad, *L'Excisée* (1982) [*The Excised*]

Accad's writing both attests to the necessity of remembrance and the challenges of survival in societies where the internecine war becomes the crucible for human relationships. Her often semi-autobiographical writing (locations and careers, for example, corroborate with situations in her own life) plays with polyphonic subjecthood. Aspects of E, Nour and the mysterious 'Egyptienne' can all to some extent be mapped onto the same character. The multiple selfhoods correspond to Accad's own identification as *métisse* after Françoise Lionnet who describes *métissage* as a dialogical hybrid that fuses together heterogeneous elements.[18] There is a sense in Accad's writing that her relationship with both city and coast lends itself to this hybrid form of lifewriting. The beach functions as useful space for evoking shared experiences between author and reader at the same time as its topography allows for metaphorical and literal freedoms, the opportunity to invent new narratives, to clear away and begin again.

In *L'Excisée*, Accad presents a cautionary tale in which the hopes and ideals of a young woman, known only as 'E', are destroyed by the patriarchal dictates first of her father, a Christian preacher, and then by her Palestinian lover and later subsequent husband, whose apparently shared ideals of liberal equality disappear upon their marriage: she is physically sequestered by both. Such a paradoxical repression alongside the initiation of an anonymised figure, consensually subject to sexual violence resonates with earlier literary figurations such as the 'O' of Pauline Réage's *Histoire*. The figure of circumcision and women's complicity and agency in its perpetuation is used to illustrate violence and repression while the sectarian hostilities of 1958 form the symptomatic backdrop. In choosing to write of the 1958 crisis, Accad here throws 1975 civil war into relief as she is writing at the height of the conflict in 1982 during the Israeli invasion and siege. While the American warships bombed the city from the sea in 1958, it is the cityscape that retains the palimpsestic memorial structure in

---

[16] Ibid., 2.

[17] Etel Adnan, *Sitt Marie-Rose*, Beirut: Tamyras, [1977] 2010, 76.

[18] See Françoise Lionnet 'The Politics and Aesthetics of Métissage' in *Autobiographical Voices: Race, Gender, Self-Portraiture*, Ithaca, NY: Cornell University Press, 1989, 1–29.

contrast to the coastline, where traces are inevitably eventually washed away. Beirut, through the representations here, highlights the tensions between these two spaces where memory, trace and effacement are in perpetual negotiation. Indeed, the 'liberation' symbolised in characters such as Rima, the friend who introduces 'E' to her Palestinian lover, is shown only the fallacy of being caught up in an Americanised false consciousness of freedom as represented by Coca Cola, rock 'n' roll, Elvis Presley and blue jeans.

Accad's semi-autobiographical narrative emerges through poetic digressions reflecting upon the rituals and teachings of Christianity and Islam. Neither is privileged and both are represented as repressive structures in society at large and for women, in particular. Opening with a foundation myth, the novel begins with a short tableau depicting a furious dragon seeking vengeance upon a woman who is saved in an elemental battle between river and earth. The dragon, infuriated, sinks to rest on the seabed. Setting the scene then for passages which resound with biblical and qu'aranic references, the figure of the sea becomes a representation of safety and peace and a place towards which a way must always be found. Again the contrast between the border of the coast and the violent fault line of demarcation are highlighted as the initial tableau breaks into lyric poetry. The text 'Et la femme prend l'enfant et court, Elle court, elle court vers la mer' (*L'éxcisée*, 7) [And the woman takes the child, she runs, she runs towards the sea] is used again in Accad's *Coquelicot du massacre* by Nour (a reappearance) 'J'ai pris l'enfant loin de la ville, Et j'ai couru vers la mer' [I took the child far from the city, and I ran towards the sea](CM, 119) sung by Nour with her child, Raja as they approach the demarcation line through the ruins of the city.

'E' (referring to Elle or Eve, even Evelyne) refers to her parents as simply Mère and Père avoiding any form of possessive article as she enters seemingly against her will into a series of lies about her relationship with the 'musulman blond aux yeux bleus' [the Muslim with blue eyes] (28) whose tender look is the 'bleu de la mer retrouvée' [the blue of the regained sea] (29).[19] Her frustrating impasse is transmuted to symbolise women's oppression more broadly as patriarchal imprisonment obfuscates female desire represented here in a universalising metaphor of searching for the sea:

> Femme devant un mur, Femme qui triche pour vivre. Femme qui s'arrange pour vivre. Femme qui troue le mur avec une épingle pour pouvoir apercevoir l'autre côté de sa prison, le côté liberté, le côté espace. Femme qui travaille avec lenteur et patience pour respirer, pour ne pas suffoquer, pour retrouver l'espace qui conduit à la mer et aux vagues infinies (31).

> [Woman in front of a wall, Woman who cheats to live. Woman who adapts to live. Woman who pierces the wall with a needle to see the other side of her prison, the side of freedom, of space. Woman who works slowly and with patience

---

[19] See Evelyne Accad, 'Excision: Practices, Discourses and Feminist Commitment', *Feminist Issues*, Fall 1993, 47-68.

in order to breath, to not suffocate, to find the space which leads to the sea and its infinite waves.]

This didactic passage is contrasted with a description of her love object, known only as 'P', prefiguring the inevitable deception as their relationship falters. Mastery through penetration leads to both pregnancy, alluding to the fecund imagery here, yet ultimately, violence and then abandonment:

> Homme sûr de lui, de son pouvoir, de sa force. Homme pénétrant la femme pour s'assurer qu'il est le Maître, qu'il est le créateur des jardins, des plaines et des moissons (35).
>
> [Man, sure of himself, of his power, of his strength. Man penetrating woman to reassure himself that he is the Master, the creator of gardens, plains and harvests.]

The backdrop of war, 'a woman excised symbolically by fanatic religion in war-torn Lebanon' provides the inauspicious indication of personal and political catastrophe again represented by a reference to the sea: 'La mer a rougi, puis elle est devenue d'encre, ravalant au loin sa honte' (9). [the sea has blushed, then she became ink, swallowing her shame in the distance], as the women, seemingly helpless in the face of masculine violence raise their arms to 'Dieu miséricorde' their tears 'coulent jusqu'à la mer qui semble attendre' (12). [Running to the sea which seems to wait for them]. Yet, the sea provides some sense of hope and reconciliation providing an alternative outward-facing backdrop, where the prospect of new relationships between men and women, Christians and Muslims, might be possible. In this respect the coast attached to the city becomes a 'contre-espace' in Foucauldian terms one of the 'lieux qui sont hors de tous les lieux' [real places outside of all places] (25), a heterotopia which is absolutely other from the rest of the city.[20]

When sitting on a rock next to the cliffs with 'P' the sound of the sea becomes 'le bruit de la guérison' (39). The sea is further personified as something which is free to roam: 'libre de gronder, libre d'écumer, libre d'être calme' (40) [Free to rumble, to foam, to be calm] to which is added a rejection of Christian imagery, such as the 'système d'anges, de rues d'or, d'habits blancs, de cantiques' (40) [system of angels, of golden streets, of white habits and canticles]. The contrast between sea and city is constantly put into focus as the shore becomes the liminal zone where love across two religions can be expressed without restriction unlike in the sectarian divided city:

> Ils sont de nouveau au bord de la mer, couchés dans le sable, enlacés dans leur vision. Ils ont laissé derrière eux le camp et ses problèmes, ses enfants aux regards chargés de questions. Ils ont aussi laissé la ville et la chaleur, ses poussières et ses cadavres, ses rues gorgées de sang et de haine (62).

---

[20] Michel Foucault, *Les Hétérotopies*, Paris: Lignes, 2009, 25.

[They were again at the sea front, lying in the sand, embraced in their sight. They left behind the camp and its problems, its children with questioning faces. They also left behind the city and the heat, its dust and its corpses, its streets full of blood and hate.]

It is by the sea that 'E' has the hope that 'peut-être que l'amour triomphera après tout' (63) [perhaps love will triumph after all]. The poetic hope expressed by the sea fails to survive however, in escaping the rule of her father she exchanges one masculine tyranny for another. It is however the sea, once more, that offers a means of transition and a dual encounter with an older, wiser woman that ultimately seals the narrative of *L'excisée*. The woman is an Egyptian whom 'E' meets on the boat on her way to Switzerland where she has been sent by her father. When E tells of her plans to elope with her Palestinian lover, the woman – who is fleeing an oppressive domestic scene herself – tries to warn her against her plans. She shows E her circumcised wound of a sex, and in some form of metaphoric exchange, E tells of the horrors of the fanaticism that are behind the war in the city she has left. But, the woman insists:

> Pourquoi ne te révoltes-tu pas avant qu'il ne soit trop tard, avant que toi aussi tu ne deviennes une excisée? Tu as vécu la guerre. Tu as vu l'horreur du sang versé dans les rues, sur la terre, à l'extérieur de toi, mais si tu devais vivre ce sang et cette honte et ces horreurs que tu m'as décrites, ces corps mutilés, ces sexes arrachés, ces cadavres violés, si tu devais vivre tout cela à l'intérieur de toi, dans ta chair même, alors que ferais-tu? (85-6).

> [Why don't you rebel before it's too late, before you also become excised? You've lived through the war. You've seen the horror of blood running down the streets, on the ground, outside of you, but if you must live of this blood and this shame and these horrors that you've told to me, these mutilated bodies, the castrated sexes, the raped bodies, if you have to live all of that within yourself, in your own flesh even, what will you do then?]

This mysterious prolepsis who doubles 'E' is found at the end of the novel once more. Enclosed within a secured compound, E spends her time in the company of the other wives and their children. A culminating point arrives at the ritual of circumcision. She is physically revolted by both the blood and horror but also by the collective female complicity in perpetuating the torturous procedure:

> Elle vomit le sang et elle vomit la peur. Elle vomit les chairs sacrifiées et elle vomit le dégoût de devoir être ce qu'elle est, cette femme pliée en deux et qui ne peut que s'agenouiller devant son Maître et Seigneur, devant le Père tout-puissant, devant tout les P. du monde. (124)

> [She vomits blood and she vomits fear. She vomits the sacrificed flesh and she vomits the disgust at what she has become, this woman folded in two and who can only kneel before her Lord and Master, before the all powerful Father, before all the 'Ps' of the world.]

Her liberating hopes of new ways of communication between men and women across traditions and religions are here at their most abject. As one of the women approaches her and attempts to lift her robes and see whether she too had undergone the excision, 'E' makes her decision to escape following a violent encounter with her drunken husband. At this point, Accad introduces the character of Nour, who reappears in *Cocquelicot du massacre*, as a young child who has not yet been subjected to circumcision and with precocious wisdom seeks to help 'E' in her flight from the compound. It is in the final stages of the narrative that the various doublings coalesce; the 'Egyptienne' is re-encountered and mutual understanding of trauma now acknowledged without enunciation. Nour is delivered to this double and taken to board a boat and travel to Switzerland. 'E' meanwhile commits effectively her double suicide as pregnant with her unborn child she drowns herself in the sea.

The site here of the sea as transition point between oppression and freedom of voyage and liberation for Nour and of life and death for 'E' becomes the location of an inversion of the intergenerational perpetuation of female circumcision. At this point, the opportunity for limited salvation in the next generation is suggested even as her suicide seems to preclude the possibility of a 'next' generation and liberation occurs by travelling to a 'neutral' and Western territory, something that might also be read as a form of complicit exclusion and erasure enabled via the sea rather than acts of autonomous emancipation. This is reinforced when Nour reappears in Accad's later novel, *Coquelicot du massacre*, as a woman trying to take her baby, Raja, across the divided city. Further supported by textual overlaps means that the two novels form a diptych precisely at moments which evoke the sea. As the ship leaves the harbour, Nour overhears the bargeman singing a song and sings along:

> Elle était née pour les étoiles
> Pour le souffle qui coule en elle
> Elle était née pour le voyage
> De la terre et du ciel et des mers
> Elle est restée, seule et brisée
> Elle n'a pas su où s'en aller
> Elle est allée jusqu'à la mer
> Et la mer l'a acceptée (*L'Excisée*, 163)
>
> [She was born for the stars
> For the whisper which runs in her.
> She was born to travel
> The earth, the sky and the seas
> She remained, alone and broken,
> She didn't know how to go away
> She went up to the sea
> And the sea accepted her in.]

This same poem is repeated by the later incarnation of Nour in *Coquelicot* (128) on the occasion of the arranged marriage of one of her students, Najmé, a recovering drug addict, for whom the oppressive marriage is effectively envisaged as a form of suicide. These doublings, the fate of the women who find in the sea a desperate form of rebirth and emancipation represented by the act of drowning, codify the repressive patriarchal structures of the urban war-torn cityscape - overrun with blood, bodies, mutilation - and the necessity to escape from it. The sea then on the fringes of the urban here, the shipwreck of a city, undermines feminine tropes of motherhood and fertility as it swallows up a pregnant woman. Etel Adnan, as demonstrated below, also meditates on representations of the coalescence of sea and city in Beirut. Again, the horror of the wars and of unrestrained atavistic primal drives leads to the destruction of both the female avatar of Beirut and the eponymous character, Marie-Rose.

Etel Adnan, *Sitt Marie Rose*

With its roots in the true story of a Syrian woman murdered for her support of the Palestinian cause, Adnan's polyphonic text is organised in two separate temporal phases. The first contextualises an ultimately rejected proposition of making a film about Syrian migrant workers involved in unregulated building projects which takes us around the city to the outbreak of war in April 1975, closing with a digest of the newspaper's 'colonne quotidienne des derniers "incidents"' from 3 July, read 'en guise d'oraison funèbre' (31). The second is divided into three acts that account for the events that take place over the course of two days documenting the kidnap and execution of Marie-Rose in front of her deaf-mute pupils in the classroom where she teaches. Individual chapters portray the scene from the point of view of the pupils, Marie-Rose, Mounir and the other figures in a form of quasi-theatrical presentation where each character offers an individual monologue in relation to the narrative events.

Adnan configures the city as a gendered site of decadence, '…dans ce centre de toutes les prostitutions qu'est la Ville…' (17) [in the centre of all prostitution which is the City], or as 'une épave soudée à ses rochers' (23) [a shipwreck soldered to its rocks], which works both to transmit the symbolic transgression of Marie-Rose as she transgresses the green line: 'on m'avait bien dit de ne pas traverser la ligne qui divise la ville en deux camps ennemis' (41) [they were right to tell me not to cross the line that divides the city into two enemy camps] from Christian to Palestinian resistance and to embody the cityscape as an organism in utter, uncontrolled, runaway distress: 'La ville est un champ électromagnétique auquel chacun veut s'embrancher. Ce n'est plus un lieu d'habitation, c'est un être qui ressemble à un train lancé' (21). [The city is an electromagnetic field to which everyone was to connect. It is no longer a place to live, it's a being resembling a runaway train]. Such destruction of the city, termed 'urbicide', in which the city is both subject to forces from outside as well as turning in on itself is witnessed by Adnan as narrator:

> Rue après rue, je traverse la ville. Beyrouth est une ville humiliée. Elle a essuyé une défaite. C'est elle qui a perdu. Elle ressemble à un chien qui a la queue entre les pattes. Elle a été insouciante jusqu'à la folie. Elle a ramassé les us et coutumes, les tares et les vengeances, la cupidité, la débauche du monde entier, dans son propre ventre. Et maintenant elle a vomi et ses vomissures remplissent chacun de ses espaces (28).
>
> [Street after street I cross the city. Beirut is humiliated. She has suffered a defeat. It is she who has lost. She resembles a dog with its tail between its legs. She had been carefree to the point of madness. She had swallowed habits and customs, crimes and vengeances, cupidity, the debauchery of the whole world, into her own belly. And now she has vomited and her vomit fills all of her spaces.]

Adnan acutely describes the physicality of the destruction as though the city is a living creature that vomits and incarnates; as a body which is violated and subjected to the primal crime of rape.

> C'est la ville en tant que grand être qui souffre, trop folle et trop survoltée, et qui maintenant matée, éventrée, violée, comme ces filles que les diverses milices ont violées, à trente et à quarante, qui sont folles dans les asiles, que les familles, méditerranéennes jusqu'au bout, cachent au lieu de soigner....mais comment soigner la mémoire? Cette ville, comme ces filles, a été violée (30).
>
> [It is the city as a great being who suffers, too mad, overexcited, and now, disciplined, dissected, raped, as those young women that the different milita raped, at thirty, at forty, who are insane in the asylums, whose families, Mediterranean to the last, hide away rather than care for.... But how do you administer care to memory? This city, like these women, has been raped.]

The blockaded city leaves hundreds of illuminated ships waiting to enter the port and deliver their goods creating an impression during the night that the city has slipped into the sea (23) and this reflection is reinforced by the observation of a young couple who make love in the afternoon on the veranda: 'Les événements ont dû les étourdir. Jamais ils n'avaient eu cette désinvolture en temps normal. Ils essayent peut-être de surmonter leur angoisse, à leur façon' (26). [The events must have dazed them. They would never have had such unselfconsciousness in normal times. Perhaps they are trying to get over their anxiety, in their own way].

In the 'second time' of the novel, the polyphony and theatricality of different participants in the narrative is articulated. Marie-Rose's deaf-mute pupils describe their love for her and its reciprocation as 'comme l'horizon sur la mer' (55), [like the horizon of the sea]. Though their loss of innocence as they witness her execution lead to the disturbing description of a *danse macabre*: Les sourds-muets se lèvent et, soutenus par les rythmes transmis à leurs corps par la terre martelée à nouveau par les bombes, ils se mettent à danser (111). [The deaf-mute children get up and supported by the rhythms transmitted to their bodies by the hammering of the earth, again by the bombs, they begin to dance]. The figure of Marie-Rose is also put into a ritournelle with the character Mounir sent with the other men to murder her. Sexually obsessed with her from an encounter many years before he describes: 'Un désir plus chaud que la chaleur du mois d'août à Beyrouth avait alors exaspéré mon sang et dans les masturbations successives de cette nuit j'ai connu un degré de Bonheur que je n'ai jamais atteint depuis' (63). [A desire hotter than the month of August in Beirut had exhausted my blood and in the successsive masturbations of that night I knew a degree of happiness which I have never again encountered]; which lines up a trajectory towards the inevitably fatal violence: 'La morale est une violence. Une violence invisible au début. L'amour est la violence suprême caché dans la nuit de nos atomes' (65). [Morality is violent. An invisible violence at the beginning. Love is the supreme violence hiding in the night of our atoms].

The sea, as for 'E' in L'Excisée becomes the final destination for the victims of violence. The city is described in terms of light and sea during the long 'mise à mort' Marie-Rose endures:

> Je veux dire à jamais que la mer est belle, et bien plus, depuis que du sang lavé par la pluie avare s'ouvre dans cette mer des chemins rougeoyants et ce n'est qu'en elle, dans son bleu immémorial, que celui des uns et des autres arrive enfin à se mêler. (104)

> [I want to say as never before that the sea is beautiful, and moreover, since the blood cleaned by the greedy rain opens up into the sea reddened paths and it is only in her, in her unforgettable blue, that those of one side and the other are able to mix together.]

The sea has become all the more beautiful through the trails of blood where, in contrast to the sectarian violence in the city, people are mixed together again. The victory and violence of death, terror and injustice will make of Beirut 'qu'une épave soudée à ses rochers' (23). [A shipwreck soldered to its rocks] Both Accad and Adnan, I argue, through the dissident acts represented here in creative narrative work to achieve a raising of women's consciousness whereby, in Nawal Al Saadawi's terms, they work to 'lift the veils off their minds and enhance this resistance against patriarchal violence and inequalities in the family in particular and society at large.'[21] The city itself is represented as a wreck, a wounded creature or a violated woman that is tied to the sea in some form of re-generational hope. As Accad states in her article 'Beirut, the city that moves me' the urban centre is asphyxiated, crushed, put to death so many times, yet

---

[21] Nawal El Saadawi, 'Women, Creativity and Difference' in *The Essential Nawal El Saadawi: A Reader*, ed. by Adele Newson-Horst, London : Zed Books, 1988, 73.

always rising again from its ashes and from the sea.'²²

In these two narratives, the violence perpetrated against women is presented as both symbolic of patriarchal oppression and symptomatic of the failure of Beirut's communities to peacefully co-exist. Sectarian violence is reconfigured to represent struggles between gender and the hopes of peace, love and kinship across borders (religious and topographical) are given voice even as they are ultimately symbolically dashed upon the rocks of the wreck of the city. The sea as a location for escape from destruction, as a beautiful horizon, figures in these texts by women who through their writing seek to contest the bitter tribal hatred of the civil wars.

References

Accad, Evelyne, 'Beirut, the city that moves me', *World Literature Today* 76:1, Winter 2002, 85–89.

———, 'Excision: Practices, Discourses and Feminist Commitment', *Feminist Issues*, Fall 1993, 47-68.

———, *War and Sexuality: Literary Masks of the Middle East*, New York, NY: New York University Press, 1990.

———, *Coqulicot du massacre*, Paris: L'Harmattan, 1988.

———, *L'Excisée*, Paris: L'Harmattan, 1982.

Adnan, Etel, *Des Villes et des femmes, lettres à Fawwaz*, Beirut: Tamyras, 2014.

———, *Sitt Marie-Rose*, Beirut: Tamyras, [1977] 2010.

Cooke, Miriam, *War's Other Voices: Women Writers on the Lebanese Civil War*, Syracuse, NY: Syracuse University Press, 1996 [1987].

Davis, Ann, *Spanish Places: Landscape, Space and Place in Contemporary Spanish Culture*, Liverpool: Liverpool University Press, 2012.

Dewailly, Bruno and Ovazza, Jean-Marc, 'Le tourisme au Liban: quand l'action ne fait plus système' in *Tourisme des nationaux, tourisme des étrangers: quelles articulations en Méditerranée?* edited by M. Berriane, Florence: Institut européen de Florence, 2004, 1-37.

Foucault, Michel, *Les Hétérotopies*, Paris: Lignes, 2009.

Handyside, Fiona, 'Rohmer à la plage: The role of the beach in three films by Eric Rohmer', *Studies in French Cinema* 9:2, 2009, 147-160.

Kassir, Samir, *Beirut*, trans. M. DeBevoise, Berkeley, CA: University of California Press, [2003] 2010.

Lionnet, Françoise, *Autobiographical Voices: Race, Gender, Self-Portraiture*, Ithaca, NY: Cornell University Press, 1989.

---

[22] Evelyne Accad, 'Beirut, the city that moves me', *World Literature Today* 76.1, Winter 2002, 89.

El Saadawi, Nawal, 'Women, Creativity and Difference' in *The Essential Nawal El Saadawi: A Reader*, edited by Adele Newson-Horst, London: Zed Books, 1988.

Said, Edward, 'The Palestinian Experience (1968-69)' in *The Edward Said Reader*, edited by Moustafa Dayoumi and Andrew Rubin, New York, NY: Vintage, 2000, 14-37.

IV. Eroded Identities

9.

BETWEEN REAL AND IDEAL SPACE: WRITING, EMBODIMENT AND THE BEACH IN MICHEL HOUELLEBECQ

Zoë Roth

With nearly 5,000 kilometres of coastline bordering four different oceans and seas, a well-developed tourist infrastructure, generous holiday entitlement, and iconic *stations balnéaires*, the French beach inhabits a special place in the country's national imaginary. It is a realm of collective consciousness bound up with France's past and its possible futures. The sociologist Alain Corbin has charted the social and cultural forces - from the industrial revolution to transportation technology - that led to 'the invention of the beach' as a nineteenth-century leisure destination.[1] In the 1950s, Club Med tapped into this growing consumerism by styling itself as the 'antidote to civilization'.[2] Its ersatz Polynesian beach paradise naturalised the artificial, oiling the comfort of recognisable social relations with an exotic sheen.[3] Reflecting the beach's *mis-en-scène* as an erotic site of sexual encounters, Brigitte Bardot made love on the sands of St. Tropez in Roger Vadim's *Et Dieu créa la femme* [*And God Created Woman*] (1955).[4] Played out against the backdrop of post-war reconstruction, this sexual confidence guaranteed the beach's ascendancy to France's primary leisure destination. The French beach became a 'democratic' space promising affluence and 'a return to order'.[5]

---

[1] Alain Corbin, *The Lure of the Sea: The Discovery of the Seaside in the Western World*, 1750-1840, Berkeley and Los Angeles, CA: University of California Press, 1994, 250. See in particular Chapter 5.

[2] Ellen Furlough, 'Packaging Pleasures: Club Méditerranée and French Consumer Culture, 1950-1968', *French Historical Studies* 18, 1993, 65. See also Chapter 7 of this volume for an extended discussion of Club Med.

[3] Ibid., 68.

[4] For an extended discussion see, Fiona Handyside, 'The Feminist Beachscape: Catherine Breillat, Diane Kurys and Agnès Varda', *L'Esprit Créateur* 5, 2011, 83–96 (88). Also Chapter 6 of this volume.

[5] Jean-Didier Urbain, *At the Beach*, Minneapolis, MN: University of Minnesota Press, 2003, 125.

But darker undertows pull at its shores. Man-made disasters - the 1978 Amoco Cadiz oil spill or the toxic *algues vertes* on the Brittany coast - disrupt man's fantasy of a bucolic synthesis with the coast, reminding us, however briefly, of the permanent imprints our steps leave in the sand. Our dismay at the long-term effects of such accidents belies our historical myopia of the beach. John Gillis has underlined how contemporary littoral leisure habits conceal the beach's previous existence as a site of labour, a source of danger, and a symbol of the unknown; not until the eighteenth century was the discrete line separating land and sea baptized a coastline.[6] Similarly, the modern beach is often artificially formed, replenished with foreign sand to cover up its diminishing width and cigarette butts. Despite this, we endow the beach with an ahistorical quality, desperate it will remain the same, while each year we return more weathered and aged. This freeze-frame image of the beach contradicts the movement - from erosion to the ebb and flow of tides and the migration of shore species - that defines it as a liminal, mobile space. As Gillis notes, 'the shore used to be the most fluctuant of all boundaries, terra incognita on most maps, a place of constant comings and goings, not just of waves and tides, but of an infinite variety of edge species, including our own. [...] Today, the tide line is where human movement stops.'[7] What he terms our 'anthropogenic shores' prohibit the movement, and thus interaction, inherent to natural beaches 'where sand stops for a moment to rest before moving on'.[8] Immobilizing the beach not only destroys wildlife and aquatic life, but also precludes the emergence of new experiences arising from threshold spaces.

The transnational landscape that now frames the French beach reflects this homogenization. As decolonization shrank the French Empire, globalization enabled another form of cultural imperialism, expanding the beach's imagined horizon to include both foreign and domestic coasts. From Tunisia and Senegal's once-French climes to Haiti's hinterlands and Thailand's soft-core exoticism, the incorporation of the periphery into the metropolitan centre has flattened the beach into a global sand pit that collapses political and social hierarchies. The waxing and waning shores of the French beach, then, encode anxieties about national exceptionalism and decline. And nostalgia for the beach emerges in the space between these real and ideal narratives of the past and the future.

In rhetoric, nostalgia is closely associated with anachronism. Derived from the Middle Greek term *anachronismos*, meaning 'late in time',[9] anachronism

---

[6] John R. Gillis, 'Life and Death of the Beach', *The New York Times*, 29 June 2012. Available: http://www.nytimes.com/2012/06/30/opinion/life-and-death-of-the-beach.html. Accessed 05/06/2015.

[7] Ibid.

[8] Ibid.

[9] Srinivas Aravamudan, 'The Return of Anachronism', *Modern Language Quarterly* 62, 2001, 331.

designates both an error in time and the condition of being out of date.[10] In his discussion of how the rhetorical figure represents historical obsolescence or reveals 'the otherness of the past',[11] Joseph Luzzi declares:

> [T]he rhetoric of anachronism provides a corrective against any attempt to reduce the formal matter of literary discourse to the status of mere reflector or mirror of its contextual referents; correspondingly, it resists the isolation or separation of this same formal component from the historical discourses in which it not only participates but also, in some cases, actively shapes.[12]

The anachronistic space of the beach - its ability to project both an ideal, unattainable past and ineluctable future decline - corresponds to the beach's historic location in French thought and territory as a constantly shifting and evolving topography of anxieties of decline and devolution. By revealing the otherness of the past, it reflects back to us our angst about the authenticity of an existence premised on the false continuity of time. Anachronism foregrounds the organic, technological, and historical processes that construct the beach, while tying it to the temporality of narrative.

If natural, historical, and narrative time is mapped onto the beach's physical geography, the human body incarnates anachronism through experiences of physical decline and nostalgia. It is unsurprising, then, that the beach constitutes an important topos in the œuvre of Michel Houellebecq, the foremost chronicler of modern French anxieties about obsolescence. For Houellebecq, social space is always an allegory for individual experience - an experience that is frequently embodied in the sovereign individual's regrets about the body's vulnerability. Sovereignty in Houellebecq refers to both the highly individualistic, 'atomised' nature of personal and social relations and the archetypal 'democratic' subject of late capitalism.

This dichotomy carries over into the way anachronism functions in his work. Just as it characterises the tension between French anxieties about decline and fantasies of exceptionalism, Houellebecq's representations of the beach - and the body - revolve around the disjunction between the real and the ideal. And though the beach's carefree climes may seem antithetical to Houellebecq's famous disenchantment, it encapsulates the tension between cynicism and sentimentality that defines his work: 'un peu sentimental, un peu cynique', is the aphorism the narrator of *La Possibilité d'une île* [*The Possibility of an Island*] (2005) uses to classify this mode.[13] The beach's disjunctive temporality frames

---

[10] 'anachronism, n.' *OED Online*, June 2012. Available: http://www.oed.com/view/Entry/6908?redirectedFrom=anachronism&. Accessed 01/07/2012.

[11] Joseph Luzzi, 'The Rhetoric of Anachronism', *Comparative Literature* 61, 2009, 72.

[12] Ibid., 70-1.

[13] Michel Houellebecq, *La Possibilité d'une île*, Paris: Livre de Poche, 2007, 391. Hereafter referred to parenthetically.

bodily sensations and emotions, particularly ageing and nostalgia. The anachronistic space of the beach is 'the representation of obsolescence' in Houellebecq's œuvre;[14] it inscribes the temporality and materiality of the body in a socially symbolic space of existence.

In this chapter, I will argue that the anachronistic space of the beach embodies the decline and decay of the ageing body, while also offering a tantalising glimpse at an ideal landscape of social and emotional regeneration. I will trace the evolution of the beach across Houellebecq's corpus beginning with its conception as an external space of social exclusion represented by the tacky trappings of the *stations balnéaires* frequented by ageing *retraités*, libertine couples, and unattainable teenage girls in *Poésies* and *Extension du domaine de la lutte* [*Whatever*] (1994). The foreign shores of *Lanzarote* (2000) and *Plateforme* [*Platform*] (2001) then hold out the promise of an erotic escape that ultimately infects the global beach with the banality of the *Hexagone*. Lastly, I will explore in detail the limitless, empty expanse of sand the immortal neo-human confronts in *La Possibilité d'une île*, which culminates in an acutely individualized space of both self-alienation and creative possibility. Just as the rhetorical figure of anachronism connects form and extradiegetic time, the act of writing in the novel provides an embodied thread connecting past and present, real and ideal bodies and shores.

*

Houellebecq's representations of the beach depict its multi-faceted realms and the subjective undercurrent of isolation that tugs at its shore. In *Poésies*, the marginal location of the observer vis-à-vis the social fellowship of the beach reinforces his isolation. In 'La lumière a lui sur les eaux...' the narrator observes from the margins of a beach scene, reminiscent of a viewer from one of Eugène Boudin's iconic beach tableaux[15]:

> Sur la plage il y avait une famille entière
> Autour d'un barbecue ils parlaient de leur viande,
> Riaient modérément et ouvraient quelques bières;
> Pour atteindre la plage, j'avais longé la lande. (131)

The narrator's tone - at once disdainful and plaintive - yearns for the group's comforting, banal conversation, even its laughter's strained sociability. The narrator's solitary arrival via *la lande* foregrounds the sense of his exclusion.[16] This image evokes the French poetic motif of a romantic *flâneur* strolling through a

---

[14] Joseph Luzzi, Op. cit., 70.

[15] For a further discussion of the relationship between Boudin's impressionist paintings and the construction of spaces of French modernity see Handyside, op. cit., 85.

[16] I would like to thank Léa Vuong for bringing this to my attention.

bucolic landscape, which sits in an uncomfortable poetic contrast to the raw, almost sexual nature of *la viande* through the alternating rhyming scheme. What emerges is a discordance constitutive of the subject himself. In characteristic Houellebecqian product placement, the *abab* rhyme of *entière* and *bières* encircles the stanza, suggesting that the family unit is as complete as the proverbial six-pack, leaving him superfluous to their self-contained unit:

> J'ai vraiment l'impression que ces gens se connaissent,
> Car des sons modulés s'échappent de leur groupe.
> J'aimerais me sentir membre de leur espèce;
> Brouillage accentué, puis le contact se coupe. (131)

The final stanza cements the narrator's awareness of his isolation. The alternating rhyme of staccato p-sounds signifies his detachment. These are in sharp contrast to the soft alliteration of s-sounds dispersed in the verse, which emphasise the biological nature of belonging to family, or *espèce*.

Houellebecq's descriptions of the beach frequently evoke bodily sensations and emotions. In the poem 'Moments de la fin de journée…', Houellebecq ironically employs a clichéd sunset image as a metaphor for the disappointing twilight of middle age, embodied as a sensation of ageing:

> Moments de la fin de journée
> Après le soleil et la plage.
> La déception s'est incarnée;
> Je ressens à nouveau mon âge. (132)

The beach brings into focus the realities of ageing, allegorizing the painful disparity between the fantasy and reality of the body. Such beach vignettes juxtapose the desire for community against a social exclusion as corrosive as salt. The scene at les Sables d'Olonne in *Extension du domaine de la lutte*, for instance, in which the unnamed narrator urges the dejected Tisserand to kill a girl who has rejected his amorous advances in a nightclub, retains the liminal connotations of the beach in *Poésies*, while reconfiguring them as a confrontation with the abject nature of the self.

In the novel, Tisserand's physical nature embodies his social exclusion: 'le problème de Raphaël Tisserand - le fondement de sa personnalité, en fait - c'est qu'il est très laid. Tellement laid que son aspect rebute les femmes' [The problem with Raphaël Tisserand - the foundation of his personality, indeed - is that he is extremely ugly. So ugly that his appearance repels women].[17] But Tisserand is also a cipher for the narrator's desires. The two characters follow the couple to the beach, which acts as a mirror, refracting the actions and desires of the

---

[17] Michel Houellebecq, *Éxtension du domaine de la lutte*, Paris: Maurice Nadeau, 1994, 54. Translated by Paul Hammond as *Whatever*, London: Serpent's Tail, 1998, 53. Henceforth page references will be given in parentheses.

characters off one another:

> La mer s'étendait à nos pieds, presque étale, formant une courbe immense; la lumière de la lune à son plein jouait doucement à sa surface. Le couple s'éloignait vers le sud, longeant la lisière des eaux. La température de l'air était de plus en plus douce, anormalement douce; on se serait cru au mois de juin. Dans ces conditions, bien sûr, je comprenais: faire l'amour au bord de l'océan, sous la splendeur des étoiles; je ne comprenais que trop bien; c'est exactement ce que j'aurais fait à leur place. Je tendis le couteau à Tisserand; il partit sans un mot. (120)
>
> [The sea extended to our feet; the light of the full moon was playing gently on its surface. The couple were making off towards the south, skirting the edge of the water. The air temperature was increasingly pleasant, abnormally pleasant; you'd have thought it was the month of June. In these conditions, well sure, I understood: to make love beside the ocean, under the splendour of the stars; I understood only too well; it's exactly what I'd have done in their place. I proffered the knife to Tisserand; he left without a word.] (119-120)

Yet the beach also transforms the poems' figurative violence of social exclusion into an exploration of the limits of experience. The beach stages a confrontation between sexual fantasy and possibility, bringing the subject to the point of no return, while simultaneously withholding final gratification. Jean-Louis Cornille has drawn attention to the numerous parallels between Albert Camus's *L'Étranger* and *Éxtension*,[18] casting Houellebecq's novel as an existentialist drama between the individual and society. When Tisserand is unable to carry out the crime, the ultimate act of nihilism is refigured as an onanistic gesture equally representative of his isolation. He masturbates in the dunes, returning with a knife covered in semen, rather than blood. The nihilistic void of the beach is abjected as a bodily trace of loss, prefiguring the violence of Tisserand's imminent suicide in a self-inflicted car accident on the way back to Paris.

In *Lanzarote* and *Plateforme*, Houellebecq moves away from representing the beach as an existentialist space. Both novels present the beach as sexualised domain governed by the laws of the market in which happiness results from a favourable cost-to-benefit ratio. In *Lanzarote*, the unnamed narrator's modest means circumscribe 'les conditions de possibilité de [...] bonheur [...] pendant ces quelques semaines' [your prospect of happiness [...] during those weeks].[19] The excellent deal that he receives on: '*le Bougainville Playa*. Trois mille deux cent quatre-vingt-dix francs la semaine tout compris [...] Hôtel quatre étoiles sup., normes du pays' (11) [Bougainville Playa. One week, all-inclusive, 3,290

---

[18] Jean-Louis Cornille, 'Extension du domaine de la littérature ou J'ai lu *L'Étranger*', in *Michel Houellebecq sous la loupe*, edited by Murielle Lucie Clément and Sabine van Wesemael, Amsterdam and New York, NY: Rodopi, 2007, 133-143. See also Nicholas Gledhill's discussion of Houellebecq's position within the literary canon of beach encounters in Chapter 3 of this volume.

[19] Michel Houellebecq, *Lanzarote: et autres textes*, Paris: Librio, 2008, 10. Translated by Frank Wynne as *Lanzarote*, New York, NY: Heinemann, 2003, 2. Henceforth page references will be given in parentheses.

francs [...] Superior four-star hotel] (3) anticipates his holiday's all-inclusive sexual triumph. The island's unearthly, lunar landscape, with its long deserted beaches encircling a volcanic interior, provides the ideal phantasmal landscape for the narrator's picaresque sexual encounters with a lesbian German couple on a deserted beach:

> Pam s'agenouilla au-dessus du visage de Barbara, lui offrant son sexe à lécher. Elle avait une jolie chatte épilée, avec une fente bien dessinée, pas très longue. J'effleurai les seins de Barbara. Leur rondeur était si agréable au contact que je fermai un long moment les yeux. Je rouvris, déplaçai ma main jusqu'à son ventre. Elle avait une chatte très différente, blonde et fournie, avec un clitoris épais. Le soleil était très haut. (41)

> [Pam crouched over Barbara's face, offering her pussy to be licked. She had a pretty little shaven pussy, with a well-shaped slit, not too long. I stroked Barbara's breasts lightly. Their roundness was so pleasant to the touch that I closed my eyes for a long moment. I opened them again, moved my hand to her stomach. Her pussy was very different, blonde and bushy with a fat clitoris. The sun was high.] (49)

Whereas the nocturnal beach setting in *Extension* mirrors the abject shame of Tisserand's body, the blinding sun of *Lanzarote* casts a pornographic visibility on the bodies on the beach,[20] exposing the most intimate details. Recalling Meursault's encounter in *L'Étranger*,[21] the effect of the sun and the beach on the narrator's vision serves as a metaphor for a subjective shift in consciousness. But in *Lanzarote* vision is tied to a bodily and sexual index. At the moment of the 'money-shot':[22]

> j'éjaculai violemment sur sa poitrine. J'étais dans une espèce de transe, je voyais trouble, c'est comme dans un brouillard que je vis Pam étaler le sperme sur les seins de sa compagne. Je me rallongeai sur la sable, épuisé; je voyais de plus en plus trouble. (43)

> [I ejaculated violently over her chest. I was in a sort of trance, my eyes blurred, I watched as through a mist as Pam spread my come over her partner's breasts. I lay back on the sand, exhausted; my vision seemed increasingly blurred.] (52)

Just as les Sables d'Olonne refracts the characters' desires and actions, the Lanzarote beach structures an economy of looks that place the body as the horizon of experience against the background of the beach.

If in *Lanzarote* the hyper-visibility of bodies results in an acute state of bodily

---

[20] Mads Anders Baggesgaard, 'Le corps en vue – trois images du corps chez Michel Houellebecq', in *Michel Houellebecq sous la loupe*, edited by Murielle Lucie Clément and Sabine van Wesemael, Amsterdam and New York, NY: Rodopi, 2007, 242.

[21] Cornille, op. cit., 137.

[22] Ibid.

awareness, the Thai beach in *Plateforme* to which the narrator, Michel, retreats after a terrorist attack kills his girlfriend, frames an embodied desensitization that exteriorizes Michel's inner state. Pattaya, where 'la nourriture et les caresses sont bon marché' [food and caresses are cheap],[23] crystallises the exclusion, abjection, and pornographic visuality of *Lanzarote*. Although he continues to visit massage parlours, 'ma vie était une forme vide, et il était préférable qu'elle le reste. Si je laissais la passion pénétrer dans mon corps, la douleur viendrait rapidement à sa suite' (349) [my life was an empty space, and it was better that it remain that way. If I allowed passion to penetrate my body, pain would quickly follow in its wake] (359). Pattaya embodies a global economic system, in which the buying and selling of bodies represents the apotheosis of consumer culture - and the death of desire.

Whereas the beach in these works acts as the microcosm of a contemporary society stratified by consumerism and sovereign individuality, in *La Possibilité d'une île* Houellebecq reflects on historical development as a specific temporality. He thus emphasizes, however obliquely, both the nostalgic and sentimental place of the beach in the French imagination, and its socially and historically constructed nature. The novel is narrated from the alternating points of view of Daniel, a contemporary French comedian, and his clones (or 'neo-humans') Daniel 24 and Daniel 25, who preside over a devastated landscape several thousand years in the future. Whereas Daniel experiences acutely the humiliation of ageing, the neo-humans' genetically modified and idealized bodies embody what Barbara Adams calls 'transcendent' time: the 'continuity of past, present, and future […] the permanent, the enduring and even the time-reversible'.[24]

Despite the novel's dystopian vision of the future, it illustrates the anachronistic space of the beach in cultural memory more than any of Houellebecq's other works. This 'outdated' topos - comprised of the beach's real and ideal shores - are presented as parallel spaces, 'before and after' versions of the same location, just as the parallel narratives of Daniel and his clones attest to two radically different, but contiguous, embodied experiences. For Daniel, his experience of the Andalusian beach closely resembles that of Houellebecq's other narrators: it is a recreational site where he walks his dog, a sexualised horizon he projects his fantasies on, a space of encounter, but also a reminder of his loneliness. Like the desultory onanistic practices of Houellebecq's other protagonists, Daniel goes to 'la plage, seul évidemment' where 'je me branlais un petit peu sur la terrasse en matant les adolescentes à poil' (95) [the beach, on my own, obviously [where] I wanked a little on the terrace whilst oggling naked teenage girls] (80). Akin to the narrator's threesome in Lanzarote, beaches are a place

---

[23] Michel Houellebecq, *Plateforme*, Paris: Flammarion, 2001, 349. Translated by Frank Wynne as *Platform*, London: Vintage: 2003, 360. Henceforth page references will be given in parentheses.

[24] Barbara Adam, *Time and Social Theory*, Cambridge: Polity, 1990, 127.

for bodies to be exhibited. Houellebecq underscores the visual dimension of this point of view as the narrator lingers over Esther's body on the beach:

> La mer était très calme. Une fois installée elle se déshabilla complètement, ouvrit largement ses cuisses, offrant son sexe au soleil. Je versai de l'huile sur son ventre et commençai à la caresser. […] je sais comment m'y prendre avec l'intérieur des cuisses, le périnée, c'est un de mes petits talents. (191)

> [The sea was very calm. Once she had sat down, she undressed completely, and opened her thighs wide, offering her sex to the sun. I poured some oil on her belly and began to caress her. [...] I know the best way to tackle the inside of the thighs, the perineum, it's one of my little talents.] (166)

But the visual scrutiny the beach symbolizes also induces feelings of physical inadequacy, which are profoundly unsettling. This is the case with Isabelle, Daniel's wife, for whom the act of putting on a bathing suit reflects her worst fears of ageing:

> lorsque nous nous préparions pour aller à la plage et qu'elle enfilait son maillot de bain […] je la sentais, au moment où mon regard se posait sur elle, s'affaisser légèrement, comme si elle avait reçu un coup de poing entre les omoplates. Une grimace de douleur vite réprimée déformait ses traits magnifiques. (52)

> [occasionally [...] when we were preparing to go to the beach, and she was putting on her swimsuit [...] I could feel her, at the moment I glanced at her, wincing slightly, as if she had felt a punch between the shoulder blades. A quickly stifled grimace of pain distorted her magnificent features.] (40)

The beach's social and sexual horizon calls attention to the imperfections of the body, foregrounding the inevitability of ageing.

Later in the narrative Daniel experiences a similar experience when walking along the beach with his new, much younger, girlfriend Esther:

> par moments […] j'étais envahi par une ivresse extraordinaire, j'avais l'impression d'être un garçon de son âge, et je marchais plus vite, je respirais profondément, je me tenais droit, je parlais fort. À d'autres moments par contre, en croissant nos reflets dans un miroir, j'étais envahi par la nausée et, le souffle coupé, je me recroquevillais entre les couvertures; d'un seul coup je me sentais si vieux, si flasque. (200)

> [sometimes [...] I was overwhelmed by an extraordinary drunkenness, I had the impression of being a boy of her age, and I walked more quickly, breathed deeply, walked upright and spoke loudly. At other times, however, on meeting our reflections in the mirror, I was filled with nausea, and, breathless, I shrivelled between the covers; in one fell swoop, I felt so old, so flaccid.] (174)

The beach acts like a mirror reflecting back two images of Daniel: one ideal, the other real. The division that tortures him resides in the difference between a body at once old before its time and 'out of place' (or time), and a throwback to a body that he never actually experienced in its ideal state. Daniel's awareness of the inequality of the system that vaunts the youthful body and disparages the old does not alleviate his pain. The contrast with Esther's youthful physicality only exacerbates the awareness of his ageing corporeality. The greatest crime of ageing is exclusion from desire and the consequent inescapable presence of the body to itself. Daniel's ageing body appears as an anachronism in the midst of the younger ones celebrating Esther's birthday:

> Ce que je ressentais, ces jeunes gens ne pouvaient ni le ressentir, ni même exactement le comprendre, et s'ils avaient pu ils en auraient éprouvé une espèce de gêne, comme devant quelque chose de ridicule et d'un peu honteux, comme devant un stigmate de temps plus anciens. Ils avaient réussi, après des décennies de conditionnement et d'efforts ils avaient finalement réussi à extirper de leur cœur un des plus vieux sentiments humains, et maintenant c'était fait, ce qui avait été détruit ne pourrait se reformer, pas davantage que les morceaux, ils avaient atteint leur objectif: à aucun moment de leur vie, ils ne connaîtraient l'amour. Ils étaient libres. (334)

> [What I was feeling, these young people could not feel, nor even exactly understand, and if they had been able to feel something like it, it would have made them uncomfortable, as if it were something ridiculous and a little shameful, like stigmata in ancient times. They had succeeded, after decades of conditioning and effort, they had finally succeeded in tearing from their hearts one of the oldest human feelings, and now it was done, what had been destroyed could no longer be put back together, no more than the pieces of a broken cup can be reassembled, they had reached their goal: at no moment in their lives would they ever know love. They were free.] (294-5)

Rather than emerging from the isolation of cloning, the disconnection of the neo-humans was already germinating in sovereign individuality; the only thing missing was the immutable body to accompany it. Equally, however, the yearning for an affective life remains as the anachronistic trace of the past.

Whereas Daniel is always situated *within* the landscape - a location that mirrors the inescapable immanence of his embodiment - his clone successors exist outside the coastal landscape they observe from a bird's eye view. The Almerian cliffs that jut over the beach where Daniel once walked his dog are an apt spatial metaphor for Daniel24/25's immortality:

> Les falaises, d'une noirceur intégrale, plongent aujourd'hui par paliers verticaux jusqu'à une profondeur de trois mille mètres. Cette vision, qui effraie les sauvages, ne m'inspire aucune terreur. Je sais qu'il n'y a pas de monstre dissimulé au fond de l'abîme. (112)

> [The rocks, completely black, today plunge through vertical stages to a depth of three thousand meters. This vision, which terrifies the savages, inspires no terror in me. I know that there is no monster hidden in the abyss.] (95)

The cliffs spatialize the clone's temporality through a vertical axis that represents his evolutionary superiority, his distance from both humans and other neo-humans, and his removal from the plane of bodily sensations and emotions. The bodies of the neo-human have attained a level of perfect equilibrium. Harnessing organic processes like photosynthesis and asexual reproduction, science has triumphed over the equally natural processes of erosion, decay, and decomposition. The neo-humans' immutable nature stands in stark contrast to the dramatic changes the landscape has undergone since their emergence. Watching from the evolutionary pedestal of his hermetically sealed existence, Daniel24 describes the Almerian landscape of his predecessor he sees on the screen:

> Les falaises dominent la mer, dans leur absurdité verticale, et il n'y aura pas de fin à la souffrance des hommes. Au premier plan je vois les roches, tranchantes et noires. Plus loin, pixellisant légèrement à la surface de l'écran, une surface boueuse, indistincte, que nous continuons à appeler la mer, et qui était autrefois la Méditerranée. (54)

> [The cliffs tower above the sea, in their vertical absurdity, and there will be no end to the suffering of man. In the foreground I see rocks, sharp and black. Further, pixelated slightly on the surface of the screen, is a muddy, indistinct area that we continue to call the sea, and which was once the Mediterranean.] (42)

In contrast to the distance - both actual and figurative - that separates Daniel24's embodied state and the natural world of the coast, the surviving humans are locked in a power struggle with the natural world, whose very composition gestures towards their insignificance. The temporal disjunction separating Daniel and his clones prevents a meaningful existential or embodied encounter; the beach separates, rather than joins them. As with the existential fissure in *Éxtension*, Isabelle's struggles with her body also play out against the backdrop of the coast, specifically 'des falaises de Carboneras, qui plongeaient, noires, dans des eaux d'un bleu éclatant' (56) [the cliffs of Carbonera, which plunged, pitch black, into sparkling blue water] (44), as if the cliff's dizzying heights anticipate her *chute*.

The day at the beach Daniel24 observes is an almost farcical caricature of antediluvian seaside activities such as strolling along the sand, tanning and swimming, or playing with groups of friends: 'des êtres avancent au premier plan, longeant la crête des falaises comme le faisaient leurs ancêtres plusieurs siècles auparavant' [Creatures advance in the foreground, along the crest of the cliffs, like their ancestors did, several centuries before] (42), only in this case the bikinis and packs of *Aoutiens* have been replaced by groups 'moins nombreux et plus sales' (54) [less numerous and more dirty](42). Instead of ball games and playful jostling, 'ils s'acharnent, tentent de se regrouper, forment des meutes ou des hordes' (54) [they fight, try to regroup, form packs or hordes] (42). Occasionally, the lassitude produced by their fighting causes them to 'tombent sur le dos [...] [é]lastique et blanc' (54) [they fall on their backs [...] elastic and white] (42), in a macabre parody of sunbathing. Their physical state reflects their brutal environment; exposed to the elements 'leur face antérieure est une surface de chair rouge, nue, à vif, attaquée par les vers' (54) [their faces are now just a surface of red flesh, bare and raw, attacked by worms] (42). The elemental association with flesh places them on the food chain below even insects and birds, which 'se posent sur la surface de chair nue, offerte au ciel, la picotent et la dévorent' (54) [land on bare flesh, peck at it and devour it] (42).

The digital transmission of these images, which Daniel24 subsequently narrates, simulates filmic representations of the beach. Cinema's framing of spatial relations converges with the temporality of narration, visualising the evolutionary leap from the human to the neo-human and the parallel transformation of the beach resort to a post-apocalyptic site of obsolescence. Rather than engendering sentimentality for a lost era, Daniel24's 'documentary' attests to the bodily alterations that have made nostalgia, and its source - compassion - redundant (62). Only at certain moments, when the (female) clone's body passes through 'intermediation' on the way to reincarnation, does this temporal blip provoke the shadow of a former embodied existence: 'certaines intermédiaires éprouvent sur la fin de leurs jours une nostalgie du membre viril, et aiment à le contempler durant leurs dernières minutes de vie effective' (140) [certain intermediary women feel a nostalgia at the end of their days for the virile member, and they like to contemplate it during the final minutes of actual life] (120). The neo-Daniel indulges in his interlocutor's desire by broadcasting images of himself masturbating. This sexually transmitted nostalgia, like the digital dissemination of images against the backdrop of what was once the Mediterranean, enables Daniel24 to visualise the evolutionary leap between human and neo-human bodies. But this insight does not seem to interest him anymore than his declared minor curiosity in the experience of sexual desire to which his forebear was so vulnerable. Indeed, one of Daniel24's poems, which he reads as he turns away from the scene, rejects the redemptive possibility of historical hindsight:

> Le bloc énuméré
> De l'œil qui se referme
> Dans l'espace écrasé
> Contient le dernier terme. (55)

Just as the beach's erosion parallels the decay of the human body, its eventual disappearance entrains a sensorial oblivion - 'le long fil d'oubli'[25] - that ultimately eliminates, like the disappearance of tears, laughter, or desire in the neo-human, even the primal 'extase mystique' of man's existential confrontation with the sea: 'la mer a disparu, et la mémoire des vagues. Nous disposons de documents sonores, et visuels; aucun ne nous permet de ressentir vraiment cette fascination têtue qui emplissaient l'homme, tant de poèmes en témoignent, devant

---

[25] Houellebecq, *Poésies*, 145.

le spectacle apparemment répétitif de l'océan s'écrasant sur le sable' (42) [The sea has disappeared, and with it the memory of waves. We possess audio and visual documents; none of them enable us to truly experience the tenacious fascination that gripped man, revealed in so many poems, in the face of the apparently repetitive spectacle of the ocean crashing upon the sand] (32). Whereas *Poesies*, *Éxtension*, *Lanzarote*, and Daniel's narrative strand in *La Possibilité* attest to the persistent - if unfulfilled - need for the touch of entangled bodies, the emergence of neo-human embodiment has effaced this desire, erasing the beach as a sentimental space of memory.

If existence has been entirely stripped of embodied experience, it is only writing that enables access to an anachronistic affective realm. As with the reconstruction of an imagined social space through a poetic horizon in *Poésies*, the intertextual references that create a shared existential literary space in *Éxtension*, and the filmic eye in *Lanzarote* that produces a common sexual space, writing in *La Possibilité* offers the possibility of rebuilding a physical terrain that mirrors the promise of the beach. Specifically, the novel's two parallel, first-person narratives delivered in the form of a confessional diary - or *récit de vie* - construct a dialectical form of communication between past and present selves. These embedded layers of narration begin with Daniel's account of his life until the point of his suicide; his clones then read his narrative and add their impressions, sometimes in the form of short vignettes they have composed themselves or which an interlocutor has transmitted. In this way a sense of continuity is retained in the absence of direct memorial transference - a metamorphosis of historical time into embodied memory. But in drawing attention to the yawning gulf between past and present selves, writing in *La Possibilité* also encodes a nostalgia that mirrors the evolution of the beach from an ideal space to an outdated (and eroded) space of memory. Like a line drawn in the sand, this writing trace corresponds to the anachronistic line of the beach which connects the 'before and after' narratives of Daniel and his clones, separated by over two thousand years.

Towards the end of the novel, Daniel's final clone sets out to discover the wasted landscape his predecessor once inhabited. Wandering in the expanse of what was once the Atlantic Ocean he comes across a note left by another neo-human in a futile search for the same sense of meaning. Included in the message is a torn, fragmented page from Plato's *Symposium* in which Aristophanes presents the complete nature of the self as the basis of love: 'la raison en est que notre ancienne nature était telle que nous formions un tout complet. C'est le désir et la poursuite de ce tout qui s'appelle amour' (468) [the reason for this is that our former nature was such that we formed a complete whole. It is the desire and pursuit of this whole that is called love] (417). Piecing together the fragments of a text in a world that can no longer read reflects the anachronistic nature of the desire to retrieve a mythical wholeness. The note and the decomposing page represent nothing less than the need 'présente chez les humains, est restée identique chez leur successeurs, de témoigner, de laisser une trace' (465) [present in humans and remaining identical in their successors, to bear witness, to leave a trace] (414). Leaving behind this unobtainable horizon of existence, Daniel's clone turns to the tangible realm of experience: the beach. After walking for several more days he encounters the ocean in the flesh:

> C'était donc cela que les hommes appelaient la mer, et qu'ils considéraient comme la grande consolatrice, comme la grande destructrice aussi, celle qui érode, qui met fin avec douceur. [...] Je comprenais mieux, à présent, comment l'idée de l'infini avait pu germer dans le cerveau de ces primates; l'idée d'un infini accessible, par transitions lentes ayant leur origine dans le fini. (473)

> [So this was what men had called the sea, what they had considered the great consoler, the great destroyer as well, the one that erodes, that gently puts an end to things. [...] I understood better, now, how the idea of the infinite had been able to germinate in the brain of these primates; the idea of an infinity that was accessible through slow transitions that had their origins in the finite.] (421)

This encounter with the shore brings together the different spaces of the French beach in Houellebecq's œuvre: it is a space of solace, ruination, and natural erosion - a space that opens up access to an anachronistic temporality that allows Daniel to represent his own obsolescence. In the final pages, he narrates the embodied experience of his approaching death as an extension of his *récit de vie*: 'Je me baignais longtemps, sous le soleil comme sous la lumière des étoiles, et je ne ressentais rien d'autre qu'une légère sensation obscure et nutritive. Le bonheur n'était pas un horizon possible. [...] Mon corps m'appartenait pour un bref laps de temps' (474) [I bathed for a long time under the sun and the starlight, and I felt nothing other than a slightly obscure and nutritive sensation. Happiness was not a possible horizon. [...] My body belonged to me for only a brief lapse of time] (423). Like the beach, 'la peau est un objet limite,'[26] constituting the limits of experience and the future horizon of possibilities. The beach thus represents not only a threshold in Houellebecq's work, but constitutes the shore on which the maturing writer meditates, promenades, and looks back.

References

Adam, Barbara, *Time and Social Theory*, Cambridge: Polity, 1990.
Aravamudan, Srinivas, 'The Return of Anachronism', *Modern Language Quarterly* 62:4, 2001, 331–53.

---

[26] Houellebecq, *Poésies*, 80.

Baggesgaard, Mads Anders, 'Le corps en vue – trois images du corps chez Michel Houellebecq' in *Michel Houellebecq sous la loupe*, edited by Murielle Lucie Clément and Sabine van Wesemael, Amsterdam and New York, NY: Rodopi, 2007, 241–52.

Corbin, Alain, *The Lure of the Sea: The Discovery of the Seaside in the Western World, 1750-1840*, Berkeley and Los Angeles, CA, University of California Press, 1994.

Cornille, Jean-Louis, '*Éxtension du domaine de la Littérature* ou J'ai Lu *L'Étranger*' in *Michel Houellebecq sous la loupe*, edited by Murielle Lucie Clément and Sabine van Wesemael, Amsterdam and New York, NY: Rodopi, 2007, 133–43.

Evans, David, '"On Transport Avec Soi Une Espèce de Gouffre": Textual Spaces and Literary Heritage in Michel Houellebecq's *Poésies*,' in *Narratives of French Modernity Themes, Forms and Metamorphosis*, edited by Lorna Milne and Mary Orr, Pieterlen: Peter Lang, 2011, 153–75.

Furlough, Ellen, 'Packaging Pleasures: Club Méditerranée and French Consumer Culture, 1950-1968', *French Historical Studies* 18:1, April 1993, 65–81.

Gantz, Katherine, 'Strolling with Houellebecq: The Textual Terrain of Postmodern Flânerie', *Journal of Modern Literature* 28:3, 2005, 149–161.

Gillis, John R, 'Life and Death of the Beach', *The New York Times*, 29 June 2012. Available: http://www.nytimes.com/2012/06/30/opinion/life-and-death-of-the-beach.html. Accessed 05/06/2015.

Grass, Delphine, 'Domesticating Hierarchies, Eugenic Hygiene and Exclusion Zones: The Dogs and Clones of Houellebecq's *La Possibilité D'une Île*', *L'Esprit Créateur* 52:2, 2012, 127–140.

Handyside, Fiona. 'The Feminist Beachscape: Catherine Breillat, Diane Kurys and Agnès Varda', *L'Esprit Créateur* 51:1, 2011, 83–96.

Houellebecq, Michel, *La Carte et le territoire*, Paris: Flammarion, 2010.

_____, *La Possibilité d'une île*, Paris: Livre de Poche, 2007.

_____, *Lanzarote: et autres textes*, Paris: Librio, 2008.

_____, *Plateforme*, Paris: Flammarion, 2001.

_____, *Poésies*, Paris: J'ai lu, 2000.

_____, *Éxtension du domaine de la lutte*, Paris: Maurice Nadeau, 1994.

Luzzi, Joseph, 'The Rhetoric of Anachronism', *Comparative Literature* 61:1, January 2009, 69–84.

Picard-Drillien, Anne-Marie, 'No Future ! Le Désistement mélancolique de Michel Houellebecq', in *Michel Houellebecq sous la loupe*, edited by Murielle Lucie Clément and Sabine van Wesemael, Amsterdam and New York, NY: Rodopi, 2007, 185–200.

Sweet, David Lehardy, 'Absentminded Prolepsis: Global Slackers before the Age of Terror in Alex Garland's *The Beach* and Michel Houellebecq's *Plateforme*', *Comparative Literature* 59:2, March 2007, 158–76.

Urbain, Jean-Didier, *At the Beach*. Minneapolis, MN: University of Minnesota Press, 2003.

10.

THE BEACH AS LIMINAL SITE IN ABDERRAHMANE SISSAKO'S *HEREMAKONO*

Thérèse De Raedt

Heremakono, which premiered in Cannes in 2002, is the third film by Mauritanian director Abderrahmane Sissako. It completes his autobiographical trilogy, which also comprises *Rostov-Luanda* (1997) and *La vie sur terre* (1998).[1] The film was shot on location in the desert city of Nouadhibou, Mauritania's second largest city, situated on the Northern peninsula at the border with the Western Sahara.[2] In 1980 Sissako, who grew up in Mali, spent some time in Nouadhibou with his mother, on his way to pursue his studies in cinematography at the Federal State Film Institute (VGIK) in Moscow.

Nouadhibou, called Port Etienne in the early twentieth century, was a stopover of the Latécoère Company, for whom Antoine de Saint-Exupéry, Jean Mer-

---

This essay is dedicated to my dear niece Clara, 2000-2012, who left this world because of an accident but whose light remains.
I would like to thank Sophie Fuggle for her insightful comments and Jerry Root for his careful reading of an earlier draft.

[1] Sissako has said that in his films he tried to find himself but that now (i.e. after having shot *Heremakono*) he feels that his life abroad has come to an end: 'ma vie à l'étranger prend fin. Je veux maintenant retourner à la maison. Je ne dis pas chez moi.' [my life abroad comes to an end. I now want to return to my house. I don't say to my home.] Interview with Sissako by Louis Danvers included in the DVD extras. Unless otherwise indicated, all translations from the French are my own.
Sissako was born in 1961 in Kiffa, Mauritania. When he was very young his family moved to Mali, where he grew up and learned Bambara. He stayed with his mother in Mauritania before going to Russia. He then lived in Paris and now resides in Mauritania. Fawzia, 'Nul n'est prophète dans son pays,' *Jeune Afrique*, 15 October 2006.

[2] For information about shooting the film in Nouadhibou, see Elisabeth Lequeret, 'Scènes de tournage à Nouadhibou', *Cahiers du cinéma* 560, September 2001, 42-43. The peninsula (called Ras Nouadhibou peninsula) on which Nouadhibou is located has been divided into two parts: the West (Western Sahara), the East (Mauritania). The divide is reminiscent of colonial powers (in this case Spain and France) scrambling for Africa and their creation of 'imagined communities' (to use Benedict Anderson's expression). La Güera in the Western part, located 15 km west of Nouadhibou, has become a ghost town since 2002 due to being partially overblown by sand. Nowadays the Western part is guarded by a Mauritanian military outpost despite not being Mauritanian territory.

moz, Henri Guillaumet, Emile Lécrivain, amongst others, are known to have worked as pilots. Throughout Sissako's film there are discrete allusions to planes (and airports), referring perhaps to the aircraft company.

Saint-Exupéry wrote *Terre des hommes* (published in 1939), in Port Etienne influenced by his experience with the Lateocère company.[3] For Saint-Exupéry the desert epitomized a place where people can discover who they are: 'Le désert pour nous? C'était ce qui naissait en nous. Ce que nous apprenions sur nous mêmes' [The desert for us? It was what was being born in us. What we learned about ourselves].[4] Sissako's film also transmits a reflection on life and, consequently, death. He inscribes his film in this broader literary tradition in which the desert functions as background for self-knowledge and philosophical enquiries. Saint-Exupéry's lyric realist style is found in the film *Heremakono*, which, surprisingly for a film where dialogues are rare, seems more closely related to literary works than cinema. Its aesthetic is marked by simplicity and ethereal beauty emphasized by its unpredictable and frequent sandstorms.[5]

In the peninsula, the sand of the beach seamlessly becomes the desert with its sand dunes. Since its creation and because of its porous borders, Nouadhibou, which is located very near the sea, has remained a city of transit where

---

[3] Lewis Galantière's English translation, published by Reynal and Hitchcock as *Wind, Sand and Stars*, also appeared in 1939. In this novel, Antoine de Saint-Exupéry described the city as: 'Situé à la lisière des territoires insoumis, Port-Etienne n'est pas une ville. On y trouve un fortin, un hangar et une baraque de bois pour les équipages de chez nous. Le désert, autour, est si absolu que, malgré ses faibles ressources militaries, Port-Etienne est presque invincible' [Port Etienne is situated on the edge of one of the unsubdued regions of the Sahara. It is not a town. There is a stockade, a hangar, and wooden quarters for the French crews. The desert all round is so absolute that despite its feeble military strength Port Etienne is practically invincible]. Antoine de Saint-Exupéry, *Terre des hommes*, Paris: Gallimard, 1939, 81.

[4] Ibid., 80. As is well known, Saint-Exupéry went on to use the magic of the Sahara as inspiration and background for his bestseller *Le Petit prince* [*The Little Prince*], published after the War in 1946. André Dubourdieu sees in the breakdown of Saint Exupéry's plane in the Sahara desert as narrated in *Terre des hommes*, the origin of *Le Petit Prince*. See Michel Autrand, 'Le Petit Prince. Notice', *Œuvres completes de Saint Exupéry*, t. 2, (Bibliothèque de la Pléiade) Paris: Gallimard, 1999, 1342.

[5] In Joseph Kessel's novel *Vent de sable* [*Sand Storms*], written in 1929, we find characteristics that are recognizable in Sissako's film: the emphasis on the beauty of the desert, the interstitial space between mobile and immobile elements, etc.: 'Sous un ciel implacable de pureté, d'un côté un ocean bleu, de l'autre un ocean fauve et notre avion glissant d'une marche insensible sur la ligne du rivage, mélange d'écume et d'or. Voilà ce que je retrouve dans mes souvenirs physiques. Mais dans les autres, les profonds, les véritables, quelle mobilité j'aperçois en face et à cause de l'immobile, avant que tout se soit joint et fondu!' [Under a sky of relentless purity, on one side a blue ocean, on the other a tawny ocean and our plane sliding insensibly on the shoreline, a mixture of foam and gold. That's what I find in my physical memories. But in the others, the deep and real ones, what a mobility I notice in front and because of the immobile, until everything has joined together and melted!] Joseph Kessel, *Vent de sable*, Paris: Gallimard, 1966 [1929], 100.

cultures mix.⁶ Sissako has described Nouadhibou as:

> une ville de transit où l'on trouve du travail. On y vient pour gagner un peu d'argent, avant de partir vers un ailleurs. […] Ces lieux sont comme des parenthèses, ce sont des lieux provisoires.
>
> [a transitory town where one finds a job. One goes there to earn some money before leaving for somewhere else. […] Those places are like parentheses, they are temporary places].⁷

Since the end of the twentieth century Nouadhibou has also been known as a point of departure for clandestine immigration to Europe.⁸

Like life in the peninsula, the rhythm of the film is slow.⁹ We follow several transnational people and watch their stories connect. Several scenes echo each other. All of these characters are living a transient situation partly triggered by the film's site in Nouadhibou. Their lives seem ordinary and narratively immobile but are rich with emotional and internal activity. There are the stories of Abdallah (Sissako's double) and his mother; of old Maata, an electrician and former fisherman and his apprentice Khatra; of the female griot and her little apprentice; of Nana, whom the Chinese Tchu pursues; of the Malian Makan, who lives at the seashore and his friends Omar and Mickaël. None of the actors who play these roles are professionals.¹⁰ Sissako encountered them accidentally, and worked with unscripted dialogues. He 'provoked situations in which he then allowed the actors to speak in their own words'.¹¹

Before discussing the film, I want to briefly focus on the prologue, which

---

⁶ In the film the protagonist Abdallah enters Mauritania via a level-crossing in the desert.

⁷ Jocelyne Streiff-Fénart and Philippe Poutignat 'De l'aventurier au commerçant transnational, trajectories croisées et lieux intermédiaires à Nouadhibou (Mauritanie)', *Cahiers de la Méditerranée* 73, December 2006, 130.

⁸ See Jocelyne Streiff-Fénart and Philippe Poutignat 'Nouadhibou "ville de transit"? Le rapport d'une ville à ses étrangers dans le contexte des politiques de contrôle des frontières de l'Europe', *Revue européenne des migrations nationales* 24:2, 2008, 193-217; esp. 200-3.

⁹ Sissako has said in an interview that he is aware that the film can put the spectator to sleep. (Interview with Sissako in the DVD bonus features).

¹⁰ Most actors kept their names in the movie. Khatra is played by Khatra Ould Abder Kader; Maata by Maata Ould Mohamed Abeid; Abdallah by Mohamed Mahmoud Ould Mohamed; Nana by Nana Diakité; Abdallah's mother (Soukeyna) by Fatimetou Mint Ahmeda; Makan by Makanfing Dabo; Mickaël by Mickaël Onoimweniku; Omar by Cheikh Omar Tembeley; Tchu by Santha Leng and the woman's griot by Nèma Mint Choueikh and her disciple by the little Mamma Mint Lekbeid.
It is worth noting that unlike the other characters in the film, Abdallah did not keep his name (i.e. Mohamed Mahmoud Ould Mohamed) but instead became Abdallah but not Abderhamane, like the director. This detail might indicate that the director sought to create a fictional figure, who resembles him.

¹¹ Alison J. Murray Levine, '"Provoking situations": Abderrahmane Sissako's documentary fiction', *Journal of African Cinemas* 3:1, 2011, 98.

contains the core elements that I will further develop: *watching*, *waiting* and *leaving*. The prologue opens with the sound of a sandstorm and the wind lifting up a clump of brush with the sea in the background. In the next scene we see a rustic clay dwelling (which resembles a colonial outpost) near the seashore. The beach appears as pristine, untouched by human activity. At that moment the sound of the sandstorm is taken over by the sound coming from a radio, hinting at the globalized world and the interconnectedness between both worlds. Next we watch a lonely man sitting, waiting, with his back against the dwelling while listening to the radio. Later we learn his name is Makan, that he comes from Mali, and is a candidate for immigration. A tyre is next to him. He then turns off the radio and buries it in the sand (he first wraps it in a plastic bag and then in a bag made of fabric). After that he moves off to the city, which rises in the distance from the desert, carrying the tyre in one hand. Sissako holds the camera in the direction of the city. Using a deep but static focus shot, we see Makan walking to the city in real time (his back receding from us). Conventional technique would have ended this shot much earlier. By doing so, the film director connects the character to his environment. He also emphasizes the length of the distance (both literal and symbolic) between city life and life at the seashore, and between traditional, restrictive and harsh living conditions, and life in the modern world.

After this prologue, the title of the film *Heremakono*, meaning 'waiting for happiness' in Bambara (the dominant language spoken in Mali) appears, in the background we see the intertidal zone of the beach with the waves slowly drifting. In my analysis I will focus on this ongoing doubling of the beach as literal and symbolic space in which to 'wait for happiness'. I will first discuss Sissako's original way of filming those marginal transitory identities in the section entitled *watching*. Next in the section *waiting* I will demonstrate how the sea functions visually and literally as backdrop for those characters waiting and how the sea is complicit with economic inequalities. In the last section on *leaving*, I will focus on how the beach is a site which contains within it the threat of erasure, exclusion and destruction as much as redemption and potentiality. As such it is a site where life and death are both affirmed less as states but more as processes.

Sissako's film resembles the emerging genre of what might be called *migration cinema*,[12] but he exceeds this genre by highlighting that Nouadhibou also has a creative potential. Indeed if most characters in the film are waiting in the coastal desert city to find a better future somewhere else and if the film highlights the cruelty of migration, some other characters find depth, inspiration and happiness in this environment. While the beach incarnates the place where

---

[12] A notable example of this subject is found in the film *La Pirogue* (2012) [*The Pirogue*] by the Senegalese director Moussa Touré (based on Abasse Ndione's novel *Mbëke Mi. À l'assault des vagues de l'Atlantique* [*Defying the Atlantic Waves*]). It narrates the journey of immigrants, who on a pirogue, try to reach Spain from the Senegalese shore.

both aspects meet, the film takes the representations of these two categories a step further by constantly putting them under contestation.

The idea of liminality (which is implied in the status of waiting) will provide us with a helpful frame to analyze the film drawing, in particular, on Victor Turner's famous implementation of Arnold van Gennep's theory on the three phases of rites of passage: the pre-liminal phase (separation), the liminal phase (transition), and the post-liminal phase (reincorporation). Turner developed the notion of 'betwixt and between,' when one does not belong anymore to the society of which one was previously a part, and one is not yet reincorporated into that society or any other. For Turner, liminality is a middle state 'of ambiguity, even paradox, outside or mediating between customary categories'.[13]

Sissako's comments suggest that he considers his own liminal position of being a foreigner during the time spent in Nouadhibou with his mother fairly explicitly as an advantage which allowed him to see things a local would no longer notice.

> J'ai été très fortement marqué par toutes ces images qui ne parlent pas mais racontent profondément la vie. [...] Ces images qui ont pris possession de moi, j'ai eu envie de les porter à la connaissance des autres comme un témoignage de ces milliers de vies que personne ne raconte.
>
> [I have been very strongly influenced by all those images that do not speak but that recount life intensely. [...] I wanted to bring to the attention of others these images that have taken possession of me, as a testimony of the thousands of life stories that no one tells].[14]

The film director tells us his story through Abdallah's character while developing other stories 'no one tells'. He mixes parts of his own autobiography with biographical elements of other people's lives because for him talking about oneself is 'the best way to approach the other'.[15] Alison J. Murray Levine has convincingly suggested that Sissako makes use of a hybrid narrative form, comprised of documentary and fictional narrative strategies and that this hybrid form makes sense as one element of what she characterizes as 'a poetics of liminality, in which real and metaphorical liminal space signifies broadly for the transformational power of the in-between'.[16] This poetics of liminality permeates his film both thematically and formally (through the genre of documentary fiction).

---

[13] Kathleen M. Ashley (ed.), *Victor Turner and the Construction of Cultural Criticism: Between Literature and Anthropology*, Bloomington, IN: Indiana University Press, 1990, xviii.

[14] Osange Silou, 'Abderrahmane Sissako : "Filmer n'est pas un bonheur"' in *Cinémas africains, une oasis dans le desert?*, CinémAction 106, Éditions Charles Corlet, 2003, 90.

[15] Rachel Gabara, 'Abderrahmene Sissako: Second and Third Cinema in the First Person' in *Global Art Cinema. New Theories and Histories*, edited by Rosalind Galt and Karl Schoonover, Oxford and New York, NY: Oxford University Press, 2010, 326.

[16] Murray Levine, 'Provoking situations', 94.

Throughout the film the documentary aspects which transpire are 'sensed rather than explicit, and they are interwoven with traditional fictional elements'.[17] Jacques Rancière explains the difference between 'documentary' film and 'fiction' film as follows:

> We cannot think of 'documentary' film as the polar opposite of 'fiction' film simply because the former works with images from real daily life and archive documents about events that obviously happened, and the latter with actors who act out an invented story. The real difference between them isn't that the documentary sides with the real against the invention of fiction, it's just that the documentary instead of treating the real as an effect to be produced, treats it as a fact to be understood.[18]

In the film the real is treated both as an effect to be produced and a fact to be understood. Though the narrative seems to drift away (like the sand storms), it is in fact masterfully constructed. However, the film director doesn't impose his vision nor does he provide explanations but lets the emotions speak for themselves so that the spectators form their own responses to what they see. Sissako thus expects the spectators of his film to be what Rancière has called with regard to theatre but applicable here as well: 'emancipated spectators' who are 'both distant spectators and active interpreters of the spectacle offered to them'.[19] He asks the spectator to reflect on what s/he sees by using the technique of inference, because under the surface of the depicted beauty of the film are layers of subtle commentaries on daily life and reflections on what constitutes a human being.

Watching

In Nouadhibou, Sissako shared with his mother a room that had a low window and he spent his time observing people from this vantage point. He has said that he became a film director thanks to the low-window:

> [...] cette fenêtre est l'élément fondamental de mon film. C'est le lieu où j'ai rejoint ma mère, c'est l'endroit d'où est parti mon imaginaire, c'est à partir de là que je suis devenu cinéaste.
>
> [this window is the fundamental element of my film. It is the place where I reconnected with my mother, it is the place where my imagination took off, it is from there that I became a filmmaker].[20]

---

[17] Ibid., 98.

[18] Jacques Rancière, *Film Fables*, trans. Emiliano Battista, Oxford and New York, NY: Berg, 2006, 158.

[19] Jacques Rancière, *The Emancipated Spectator*, trans. Gregory Elliott, London and New York, NY: Verso, 2011, 13.

[20] Silou, op. cit., 92.

Indeed, Sissako uses the low-window as a framing device and by doing so alienates conventional framing and perspectives and forces the spectator to view things differently. He shifts his viewpoint to those occupying 'lower' or forgotten positions within society both literally and figuratively. As a result he focuses on details which are usually secondary or peripheral.

In the film, Abdallah stays with his mother while waiting for his papers to leave legally.[21] He is represented as a stranger: he is dressed in Western attire, and cannot communicate with the inhabitants because he does not know the local language, Hassānīya Arabic. Most of his time he spends looking at what is happening in the courtyard: a female griot teaching a talented little girl how to sing and play the kora and men going to Nana's house, who lives directly opposite. He also reads in the room he shares with his mother, and observes daily life through its low window.

Figure 1. Abdallah spends his time reading and watching through the low-window. *Heremakono* (2002). Screenshot from DVD.

The low window permits Abdallah to see only one part of a person, mainly the shoes. It functions thus as an unusual entry point to get to know people and 'seems to give us a level of quiet intimacy with the local inhabitants'.[22] The same holds true for the drapes, which hang in the courtyard and also show only one part of a person. Some of these people are seen again, and then we get a complete (physical) portrait of them. For example, Abdallah is particularly intrigued to know who enters Nana's dwelling. He notices that one of her visitors wears red

---

[21] The film hints at this fact discretely when Abdallah's mother reminds him that his uncle will help him. The policeman, his mother's friend, says that he will facilitate acquiring a passport for Abdallah.

[22] Victoria Pasley, 'Saharan Architecture in *La vie sur terre* and *Heremakono*', *Camera Lucida Filmski Magazin* 7, 2012, 11.

sneakers and carries a suitcase. Later on in the film, he recognizes this man in the city, thanks to those signs (he realizes that his suitcase contains plastic trinkets and toys that he sells on the streets, and learns that his name is Tchu). Using this method, the director might suggest metaphorically that to get to know people takes time and that at first we only know people from one point of view.

Throughout the film there is a special focus on shoes. Shoes symbolize transit and mobility: one sees shoes walking but also several shoes 'waiting' emphasizing life's static condition. Shoes also distinguish public life from private life. Nana's friends leave their shoes on the sand in the courtyard before stepping into her room. With the exception of Tchu's red sneakers, they all wear different open-toe shoes. The camera lingers at various occasions on pairs of shoes creating in a sense 'still-lives' of shoes. They give us information about their owners and are a way to identify them. Consequently, shoes constitute a piece of a (public) self-portrait, as Meyer Shapiro has said about Van Gogh's paintings of shoes.[23] 'They mark our inescapable position on earth. To "be in someone's shoes" is to be in his predicament or his station in life'.[24]

One scene in the film shows Abdallah watching from the low window while a television (and a refrigerator) are carried on a donkey cart. At that moment we hear the female griot, a repository of oral tradition, singing a song and playing the kora. This juxtaposition of the traditional griot with Abdallah - the future film director and arguably also a modern griot - not only depicts the peaceful coexistence in the same cinematographic space of the traditional and the modern, it also endorses the convergence between the local communities and the global world. Michael Sicinski concurs:

> In this regard Sissako refuses to either promote some pure, untouched pre-modernity or to mourn for some lost social integration. [...] Sissako's primary skill as an artist is his ability to convey total worlds while maintaining a formal porosity that accommodates the displaced, the traveller, and ultimately the impact of the West.[25]

In a later sequence, Abdallah watches, at his uncle's house, the popular French television program, *Des chiffres et des lettres* [*Numbers and letters*], presented by Patrice Laffont and distributed in Mauritania.[26] This insert (the camera lingers

---

[23] 'In isolating his own worn shoes on a canvas, he turns them to the spectator; he makes of them a piece from a self-portrait, that part of the costume with which we tread the earth in which we locate the strains of movement, fatigue, pressure, heaviness – the burden of the erect body in its contact with the ground'. Meyer Shapiro, 'The Still Life as a Personal Object – A Note on Heidegger and van Gogh' in *Theory and Philosophy of Art: Style, Artist, and Society (Selected Papers)*, New York, NY: George Braziller, 1994, 140.

[24] Ibid., 140.

[25] Michael Sicinski, 'A Fragmented Epistemology: The Films of Abderrahmane Sissako', *Cinema Scope* 29, 2007, 17.

[26] Patrice Laffont presented the show from 1972 until 1989. Though antennas appear

for two full minutes on the television program) skilfully highlights the striking difference between the two worlds: the unhurried world of Nouadhibou where a television is delivered by cart and the fast-paced French world where one of the contestants of the show, a postman from Auxerre (a typical, average French city), runs to stay in shape. ('15 km de course à pied pour le loisir car elle maintient en forme' [a 15 km run, for fun, because it keeps you in shape].) Staying in shape is a preoccupation the people in Nouadhibou simply do not have.

Abdallah, whom we see only conversing in French, does not belong to French culture either. When he watches the imported television show sitting alone on a couch in his uncle's living room, he has the same attitude (that of a spectator with no direct interaction with what he sees) as when he watches people from his low window. It is also the same attitude that we, as spectators, have in watching the film, *Heremakono*. As Olivier Barlet insightfully writes: 'Le cinéaste crée de la distance plutôt que de mettre en scène de la proximité'. [The filmmaker creates distance rather than staging proximity].[27] He further explains that by doing so:

> nous devenons spectateurs de corps en mouvement qui ne sont plus nous mais un autre, expérience moderne d'une altérité irréductible, essentielle pour comprendre [...] que l'Afrique n'est pas la projection que l'on croit.
>
> [we become spectators of moving bodies that are no longer us but someone else, a modern experience of an irreducible otherness which is essential to understanding [...] that Africa is not the projection that we think].[28]

Sissako strongly rejects 'a colonial representation of Africa and Africans' and 'a colonial model of documentary representation'.[29]

Waiting

As its title suggests, the film depicts people waiting for a better and happier future, somewhere else. Abdallah is waiting to leave legally by obtaining his papers. During this time, the young Khatra teaches him Hassānīya Arabic through the low window. He stays outside while Abdallah remains in his room. However, Abdallah isn't able to learn the local language. If the low window functions as a learning device for Abdallah's / Sissako's becoming a film director, it also highlights that he will never be part of the other side, of the local community

---

in many scenes, the film features two scenes depicting a television (one is carried by a donkey's cart and one transmits the show *Des chiffres et des lettres*).

[27] Olivier Barlet, *Les cinémas d'Afrique des années 2000. Perspectives critiques*, Paris: l'Harmattan, 2012, 277.

[28] Ibid.

[29] Gabara, op. cit., 331.

which uses Hassānīya as a *lingua franca*. His inability to thrive in this environment is further symbolically underscored by the light bulb in his room, which inexplicably will not light and cannot be repaired by Maata and his apprentice.

Nana, with whom Abdallah can communicate in French, confides in him. While showing him a picture of her daughter Sonya, she tells him how she has been to Europe because of her daughter, whom she had with Vincent, a white Frenchman. Her trip to Perpignan via Spain was to let him know that Sonya had passed away: 'because some things can only be said face to face'.[30] Although she seems to have been able to travel to France without difficulty,[31] once there she was entrapped in an unexpected situation: Vincent paid for her hotel room for only one week. Her psychological confinement is represented metaphorically in a flashback scene, which shows her walking on a street separated by wire fences above railroad tracks. This seems to suggest that, like the relationship she had with Vincent, going to Europe was just a mirage.

The scene of Nana walking above the railroad tracks is followed by the scene showing the Chinese Tchu, the man wearing the red sneakers, walking on dunes above the seashore while humming happily as he advances towards the unobstructed horizon (fig.2). The sea is immaculate.

Figure 2. Tchu walking above the seashore. *Heremakono* (2002). Screenshot from DVD.

It is a long take with the camera slowly following Tchu. The location reflects his sentiments. The colours of his shirt also blend into the landscape. He is serene.

In a previous scene he was in a restaurant on a date with Nana. Indirectly, through the lyrics of a Karaoke song by Chi Zhiqiang, he expressed his feelings

---

[30] Though Nana speaks in French to Abdallah, this sentence she says in Arabic. I have reproduced the text of the English subtitles. Sonya died because of a 'forte fièvre' [high fever], probably a curable disease, which discreetly hints at the difficult life conditions.

[31] Probably because Vincent was her financial guarantor.

for her.

> On this beautiful evening, I am going to sing this song straight from my heart for my friends and loved ones. [...] Doors of iron, windows of iron, chains of iron, through the bars I look outside where life is so beautiful. When will I go home? When will I be able to go home again?[32]

This song about exile and homesickness reflects his own exile (perhaps due to political reasons) in the desert city but unlike the song's lyrics he is in an open space where life can sometimes be beautiful. Like the bells that swung in the video of the Karaoke song, Tchu is in a position of in-between, of uncertainty. The liminal state in which he finds himself is, however, superseded by his hope and /or dream for the fulfilment of his love story with Nana. This is underscored by the fact that in the later sequence, discussed previously, he is walking 'above' the seashore, capable of dominating the future. As metaphor, the beach represents a space of possibility and a launching point for a new life.

Figure 3. Small dugout boat and large industrial ship. *Heremakono* (2002). Screenshot from DVD.

For Makan and Mickaël the beach incarnates literally the prospect of a new life beyond the horizon. Makan lives in poor and difficult conditions in his shed at the seashore: he explains to police officers how he uses the water he keeps in plastic containers. He probably collects seashells, a traditional and labor-intensive but not very profitable occupation. At one moment in the film, Makan comes out of the sea at night with a bag and a knife.

---

[32] I have reproduced the English subtitles of the Chinese song (which is part of the album *Tie chuang lei*). Chi Zhiqiang wrote lyrics about his time in jail during the 1980s. While listening to him, Nana caresses the little stuffed chick Tchu has given her, and smiles.

In one scene we see Mickaël, Makan and Tchu in Makan's dwelling. Tchu gives them both a little present wishing them 'bon voyage'. The camera focuses on Makan testing the fly eye kaleidoscope he has received, which allows him to look at reality in a poetic but deformed way. Then the camera changes direction and lets us, spectators, see the reality they face: a small dugout boat and a very big industrial vessel at sea (fig.3). This contrasts with the image of the pristine sea depicted in the prologue and when Tchu was walking.

This connection evokes the social and economic differences in the world and the huge divergences in people's conditions in life and possibilities for travel. People use dugout boats to do artisanal fishing but also to climb on big vessels to be smuggled to the Canary Islands or the Iberian peninsula.[33] These discrepancies appear again in the scene when Makan sees planes and knows when they arrive (he verifies the time on his watch), but has no access to them.

Like Mickaël, he therefore intends to take the perilous sea route to migrate to Europe. In a later scene in the film shot in the exact same location at the seashore Makan and his friend Omar while looking at the sea wonder where Mickaël is two weeks after his departure ('maybe in Tangiers, maybe already in Spain').[34] This scene recalls all the mothers and wives waiting whose sons or husbands have left illegally by taking the sea road to Europe or any other road to find a better future elsewhere.[35]

In yet another scene shot at Makan's shed, the electrician Maata and his disciple Khatra are having tea. When talking about his previous life as a fisherman, Maata questions the necessity of his current job. He says to Makan: 'You know, I work in electricity now. Do people really need it? They don't pay well. Here I think of the sea, its wonders but also its problems. I think of my boats. I can't forget all that.'[36] The change in profession of Maata, from being a fisherman at the coast to being an electrician in the city, appears to be the consequence of the industrialisation of fishing. Maata didn't choose to become an electrician but very likely changed profession out of necessity. This economic shift replicates the disappearance of fishermen from European coastlines in the 19th and 20th centuries as Jean-Didier Urbain has demonstrated in his account of 'La mort du pêcheur'.[37] This is further emphasized by several still shots in close-up of huge

---

[33] Armelle Choplin and Cheikh Oumar Ba, 'Tenter l'aventure par la Mauritanie', *Autrepart* 36:4, 2005, 23-4. There are three main routes of illegal immigration in Nouadhibou: 1. the most expensive solution is to pay the owners of big fishing vessels (of Chinese, Japanese, Greek, German, Spanish and French origin) to accompany them to the Canary Islands and the Iberian peninsula; 2. to pay a boatman of a dugout to be smuggled at night in those big fishing vessels; 3. the terrestrial road (Ibid., 24-5).

[34] Text reproduced from subtitles.

[35] The core of the novel *Celles qui attendent* [*Those who are Waiting*] by the Senegalese writer Fatou Diome also addresses this issue.

[36] Text reproduced from subtitles.

[37] Jean-Didier Urbain, *Sur la plage. Moeurs et coutumes balnéaires (XIXe – XX siècles)*,

vessels at night, which haunt the seashore. But the film also shows that Maata's material conditions in the city are better than Makan's at the seashore: his room is decorated with colourful wallpaper and is more comfortable. He is also able to buy meat, a much more expensive food product than fish.

Leaving

Mickaël never reaches Europe. The sea rejects his dead body. After a close-up, we see the laced leather shoes of the police officials stepping around the body. Mickaël's face is not shown and he is not wearing shoes. The camera adopts a low viewpoint, which references the viewpoint of the low window. Next, we see the police officers collecting information and evidence on the location: Mickaël's body is stranded in the intertidal space between high and low tides, close to Makan's shed. This liminal space represents literally the tragic outcome of Mickaël's aborted dream for a better future.

The big vessel enshrouded by fog in the background (fig. 4), with its indistinct quality (which recalls watercolours by William Turner), evokes the difficulty of transforming one's aspiration to leave into reality. Its presence underscores here again that some methods of transport are only available to some people. It also indicates that the economic system the ship represents is (directly or indirectly) implicated in the destruction and/or erasure of the people excluded from it. Sissako thus discretely hints at the ravages of globalization.

Figure 4. The police officials document where Mickaël's body has stranded. In the background we see a vessel. *Heremakono* (2002). Screenshot from DVD.

Paris: Petite Bibliothèque Payot, 2002, 71-118.

One of the policemen takes several pictures of Mickaël's body. By doing so, he imitates the gestures of the photographer who took pictures of Mickaël before his departure. Before leaving, he has pictures taken with his friends at a photographer's shop. The background against which they pose is an illuminated Eiffel Tower and the Statue of Liberty, iconic sites incarnating the Western world, happiness and freedom. Another policeman finds these pictures in a plastic bag in his jacket. Now soaked, these photos acquire a new meaning: they immortalize Mickaël but also reify the trauma. As representations, these pictures, second-degree images of Mickaël and of his dead body, take us like the interstice of water and sand, one step further away from the reality of his life and his voyage at sea and him himself. Interestingly these pictures don't permit immediate identification, as photos from an ID or passport would have done.

Figure 5. Makan finds the dead body. *Heremakono* (2002). Screenshot from DVD.

Here we might read the character of Mickaël, who wanted to emigrate, as an incarnation of the accursed figure of the one-time citizen reduced to the 'bare life' of homo sacer, which Giorgio Agamben defines as he 'who may be killed and yet not sacrificed'.[38] He clarifies this as: 'An obscure figure of archaic Roman law, in which human life is included in the juridical order [...] solely in the form of its exclusion (that is, of its capacity to be killed), has thus offered the key by which not only the sacred texts of sovereignty but also the very codes of political power will unveil their mysteries'.[39] Agamben differentiates 'bare life' or *zoë*, which expresses the simple fact of living common to all living beings (animal, men, or gods), and *bios*, which indicates the form or way of living proper to an

---

[38] Giorgio Agamben, *Homo Sacer. Sovereign Power and Bare Life*, trans. Daniel Heller-Roazen, Stanford, CA: Stanford University Press, 1995, 1.

[39] Ibid., 8.

individual or a group' or 'good life'.[40]

Makan does not want to identify the body when the policemen interrogate him in his shed. He says: 'Je n'aime pas regarder ces choses-là'. [I don't like to look at those things]. He describes the friend he has lost as a 'thing', a 'non-person'. At that moment the film shows in flashback Makan watching the body from a distance at sunrise (fig. 5).

The scene is constructed as a triangle with Makan standing in the left angle, Mickaël's dead body in the right angle, and the big vessel at sea in the vertex angle, metaphorically dominating life and death. When the policeman asks Makan if other things have come ashore he answers that one day he recovered a tyre. At the beginning of the film we saw him walking to the city with that tyre. A tyre in the water represents a misplaced mode of transport, suggesting that Mickaël's body at the beach is also incongruous. Like the tyre, Mickaël's life seems 'disposable' to use Achille Mbembe's term[41] or 'ungrievable', 'whose loss is no loss' to draw on Judith Butler's terminology.[42]

When Makan is being asked where the tyre is now, he responds: 'Il n'est plus là' [It is not there anymore]. At that same moment we see through the veil floating at the door's opening that Mickaël's body has been placed in the police jeep. Sissako thus frames the tyre and the body within the same cinematographic space to accentuate their symbolic resemblance and perhaps also to propose a restoring of order: a tyre belongs on a car and the body needs to be identified.

Returning to Agamben, we might further consider his claim that in our contemporary epoch 'the realm of bare life – which is originally situated at the margins of the political order – gradually begins to coincide with the political realm, and exclusion and inclusion, outside and inside, *bios* and *zoë*, right and fact, enter into a zone of irreducible indistinction'.[43] It is possible to read Mickaël, dead, as embodying the realm of bare life entering 'the zone of irreducible indistinction' with the political realm. Indeed, once Mickaël's corpse is officially identified, he will become a political and legal subject (the police officers will list his body). His death might also be read as a sacrifice that was necessary so that Makan (and others amongst his friends) might live. Makan said to his friend Omar that he knew that if he left by taking the sea route he would not come back, which is why he decided to return home, to his Malian village Laandi, which, he explains, is located in the district of Cunya, three kilometres from the physical place called Heremakono.

After the interrogation Makan looks at the police car leaving. The back of the jeep is open showing Mickaël's bare feet. Then the camera, which remains

---

[40] Ibid., 1-2.

[41] Achille Mbembe, 'Necropolitics', trans. Libby Meintjes, *Public Culture* 15:1, 2003, 27.

[42] Judith Butler, *Frames of War. When Is Life Grievable?* London and New York, NY: Verso, 2010, 24.

[43] Agamben, op. cit., 9.

immobile, adopts Makan's point of view watching the trajectory of the jeep in the desert landscape in real-time. Tones of greyish beige dominate the colour palette (the sun has disappeared) accentuating the desolation of this scene. This bareness is further underscored by the horizon, which is obstructed by a large sand hill that the jeep will have to circumnavigate. This scene reflects Makan's melancholy and his reconsideration of his sea journey. It also underscores the difference between authorised modes of transport and transit and unauthorised ones. Thus embodied in the scene is both the impossibility of the terrain as perceived by Makan and the navigability of the jeep as official vehicle.

Unlike Mickaël, whose dead (bare) body was washed up, Maata's body (and death) is sublimated on the beach. Towards the end of the film and in a beautiful scene shot at sunset when the sand is rose (reminiscent of Saint-Exupéry's descriptions), Maata, accompanied by Khatra, goes to Makan's shed and brings electrical light there with a very long cord.[44] That evening, Maata tells Makan and Omar that did not follow Ethmane, who had provided him with a ticket to leave (probably like Mickaël to find a better future beyond the sea), and that he has now lost trace of him. He wonders if that is what weighs on his heart.

At dawn, Maata carries the light to the beach (fig. 6), where he kneels down in meditation, and undergoes a spiritual and/or mystical transformation. In a scene evoking the paintings of Georges de la Tour, with the light he carries illuminating him, he seems to be praying. The beach represents here for him 'a place to retreat from the turmoil of life in order to establish contact with one's inner self'. In solitude the symbolic act of meditation is about entering a liminal space for the purpose of 'setting aside time to attend to the hearth of your inner life.'[45]

After this scene of illumination, Maata lies peacefully on his side in the foetal position. He seems to sleep peacefully. The in-between space of the beach indicates that as Preston-Whyte has suggested, quoting Nisbet:

> [t]he notion of liminality is employed here as a metaphor to facilitate 'a way of proceeding from the known to the unknown', from the accepted symbols of the profane to the blurred, ambiguous, and powerful symbols of the sacred.[46]

The intertidal space of the beach gives access to other realms: a new existence beyond this life on earth. According to Sufi religion (which is practiced in the

---

[44] The electrical light will successfully function in Makan's dwelling at the seashore and replace the lantern whereas Abdallah will use a lantern to read (because electricity could not be restored in his room).

[45] Quoted in Robert Preston-Whyte, 'The Beach as a Liminal Space' in *A Companion to Tourism*, edited by Alan E. Lew, C. Michael Hall and Allan M. Williams, Malden, MA: Blackwell Publishing, 2004, 354.

[46] Robert A. Nisbet, *Social Change and History: Aspects of the Western Theory of Development*, London: Oxford University Press, 1969, 4. Quoted in ibid., 349.

region and to which he likely adheres) death does not represent an end but a start of a new life, entirely different from the life spent on earth.[47] The light bulb next to Maata remains lit. Interestingly Maata still wears his shoes perhaps indicating that his identity has remained intact.

Figure 6. Maata at sunrise goes to the beach where he undergoes a spiritual transformation. *Heremakono* (2002). Screenshot from DVD.

When the sun rises, Khatra runs and discovers his master on the beach.[48] He caresses his face and sings the song 'Petit oiseau' by Paul Niger to him, a song that used to irritate Maata. ('Petit oiseau qui me chante l'amour du pays natal, je te porterai à manger les graines que je choisirai' [Little bird who sings to me the love of the homeland, I will bring you seeds to eat that I will choose for you].) When Khatra realizes that Maata is dead, he unscrews the light bulb. Then Makan and Omar come and together they lean towards the body. In contrast, Makan didn't want to approach or to look at Mickaël's body. Thus Maata's life represents *bios* and the 'good life' in contrast to Mickaël's *bare life*.

In a later sequence (fig. 7), when the sun is in its highest or meridian point of the day, Khatra tries to throw the light bulb into the sea but the waves keep bringing the bulb back. Eventually, Khatra takes it. Without electrical power the bulb has lost its functionality. However, symbolically, we might read the bulb coming back in terms of Maata bequeathing his knowledge to Khatra and so enabling Maata's 'lights' to continue to shine via his disciple from one generation to the next.[49] Maata's legacy thus exceeds his physical existence. Khatra will bear

---

[47] In the film we see Maata praying with the 99 Islam prayer beads.

[48] This scene establishes a visual link between an earlier scene when Khatra lights the face of Maata sleeping after having told Khatra that he was not afraid to die.

[49] In one scene Maata is upset (because Khatra has played with an ouguiya bill) and asks him: 'what would you do without me?' He answers: 'I would be an electrician' (sub-

his wisdom, and like the bird in Niger's song, which sings about his love for the homeland, will bring seeds of knowledge and nourishment to the community in the transitory town.

The rusting shipwrecks, which appear clearly in the background, reveal how globalization impinges on the seashore: Nouadhibou is known to be one of the biggest ship graveyards on earth. The wrecks encapsulate the damages of neo-colonialism on poor countries, which become a dump for multinationals. Sissako might perhaps also indicate that even big vessels don't last forever (in contrast to previous scenes showing big vessels at night dominating the sea). It is worth recalling that Khatra learned from Maata how to transmit electricity but not how to fish.

Figure 7. Khatra throws the light bulb in the sea but the waves bring it back. *Heremakono* (2002). Screenshot from DVD.

At the end of the film, Abdallah leaves his mother's house. His stay in the desert city seems to have come full circle. He is the only character we saw arriving. When he leaves the courtyard, smartly dressed and carrying his suitcase, he takes off his left shoe and walks three steps in his socks. His mother picks up the sand that his left foot has touched. She keeps the sand and puts it in the cloth she is wearing and makes a knot. Following tradition, the sand will be kept in a secret place in the hope the person who has touched the sand will come back safe and sound and not die abroad. However, in the last scene we see Abdallah, he comes down a sand hill before reaching the top. By doing so Sissako keeps the end open because for him the desire to leave, or to think about leaving, is more important than the actual physical act of doing so.[50]

---

titles reproduced from the film).

[50] See interview with Danvers in the DVD extras.

Conclusion

In the final sequence of the film, which functions as an epilogue, Khatra, wearing the electrician's outfit he dreamed of acquiring, walks across a dune, towards us, the spectators. In an earlier scene, he tries to leave by getting on board a train as a stowaway but is kicked off. This contrasts with the prologue where Makan walked to the city away from the spectator.[51]

Figure 8. Final scene of the film showing Khatra wearing an electrician's outfit walking across the dunes. *Heremakono* (2002). Screenshot from DVD.

Unlike Makan who decided to return to his home close to Heremakono, Khatra, we can conclude, has come to realize that his home is in the desert peninsula where he lives. The shape of the dune representing a reclining woman symbolizes his home.[52] He will likely find happiness and thrive there by transmitting light (literally and symbolically). Interestingly this last scene recalls the third-from-last drawing of Saint Exupéry's *Little Prince*.[53]

---

[51] After having seen the film, one can perhaps interpret the prologue as alluding to the fact that Makan will return home to Heremakono (and not take the sea route).

[52] The film's set designer Joseph Kpobly explained Sissako's desire to create a dune that had the shape of a lying female figure. 'On est arrivé à intervenir sur des dunes de sable de façon très spécifique parce que nous voulions obtenir une forme extraordinaire de dune qui reflète l'image d'une femme nue allongée sur le dos'. [We succeeded in intervening on the sand dunes in a very specific way as we wanted to obtain an extraordinary shape of dune reflecting the image of a reclining nude woman]. Souleyman Bilha, 'Un décorateur de cinéma couronné. Entretien avec Joseph Kpobly, Souleyman Bilha Cotonou', *Africultures*, 26 mars 2003. Available: http://www.africultures.com/php/index.php?nav=article&no=2829. Accessed 08/06/2015.

[53] Khatra finds in Abdallah's room some intriguing but rudimentary drawings in the sketchbook they used when he taught Abdallah Hassānīya Arabic. Those drawings made by Abdallah might be linked to Saint Exupéry's enigmatic drawings at the begin-

The drawing illustrates the text where the Little Prince says to the aviator that a snake will bite him so he can go back home 'je rentre chez moi',[54] where he will take care of his beloved pink rose which needs him. He is depicted just before dying. His death on earth is deliberate and calm. 'Ça ne fit même pas de bruit, à cause du sable' [It didn't even make any noise because of the sand].[55] Similar to Maata who went to the beach to die silently, the Little Prince dies and leaves the earth to go back home.

By linking the last image of Khatra with the drawing of the Little Prince and the story of Maata with the story of the Little Prince, Sissako equates a marginal character with a universally recognised one and a story 'no one tells' with one that is widely known.[56] Sissako's openness to other cultures also appears in the textual and musical choices he made in the film's diegesis: the female griot transmits traditional Mauritanian songs to her apprentice but Khatra recites a poem by the Guadeloupian Paul Niger, and Tchu reproduces in karaoke the song by the Chinese Chi Zhiqiang. Thus Sissako adds not only a pan-African but also a transnational dimension to his film.[57]

The film director presents his story to us without relegating other stories to the background. He thus destabilizes the traditional boundaries between filmic genres, autobiography and biography as well as fiction and documentary. He portrays people who are waiting but who don't live in isolation because their everyday lives are insidiously affected by globalization. Its complex effects converge at the beach: the sea took Mickaël's life and rejected his body but the sea also nurtured Khatra by metaphorically bringing back Maata's 'light'. In *Heremakono* nothing is fixed, no one is judged, nothing is certain, no solution is proposed. This open-ended approach and lack of resolution puts the onus on the spectator to think harder about what s/he sees.

Throughout the film Sissako evokes difficult problems of migration and exile while showing a dignified and elegant image of the inhabitants of Nouadhibou's peninsula. This location, marked by international migration, and the beach in particular transmit a sense of violence, uncertainty and questioning while at the same time alluding to the possibility of all kinds of hope and happiness. By doing so, Sissako brings to the fore humanitarian and universal concerns, which he conveys through a personal and also African lens.

---

ning of *The Little Prince* representing a boa digesting an elephant.

[54] Antoine de Saint-Exupéry, *Œuvres complètes,* t. 2, (bibliothèque de la Pléiade) Paris: Gallimard, 1999, 310.

[55] Ibid., 317.

[56] According to the *Le Petit Prince* web page, it has been translated into 265 languages: http://www.lepetitprince.com/70ans/. Accessed 08/06/2015.

[57] The film's soundtrack also draws on various musical traditions featuring music produced by the Congolese Tabu Ley Rochereau, the Malian Oumou Sangaré, the Tunisian Anouar Brahem, the Norwegian saxophonist Jan Garbarek etc.

References

Anderson, Benedict, *Imagined Communities*, London and New York, NY: Verso, 2000.

Agamben, Giorgio, *Homo Sacer. Sovereign Power and Bare Life*, trans. Daniel Heller-Roazen, Stanford, CA: Stanford University Press, 1995.

Appiah, Anthony, '"A screenplay is not a guarantee." Abderrahmane Sissako with Kwame Anthony Appiah', *Through African Eyes: Dialogues with the Directors*, New York, NY: African Film Festival, 2003, 35-42.

Ashley, Kathleen M., ed., *Victor Turner and the Construction of Cultural Criticism: Between Literature and Anthropology*, Bloomington, IN: Indiana University Press, 1990.

Autrand, Michel, 'Le Petit Prince. Notice', *Œuvres completes de Saint Exupéry*, t. 2, (Bibliothèque de la Pléiade) Paris: Gallimard, 1999, 1341-1355.

Ayité, Sitou, 'La quête de l'idéal. *Heremakono*, en attendant le bonheur, de Abderrahmane Sissako', *Africine.org*, 24 December 2006. Available: http://www.africine.org/?menu=art&no=6380. Accessed 09/06/2015.

Barlet, Olivier, *Les cinémas d'Afrique des années 2000. Perspectives critiques*, Paris: L'Harmattan, 2012.

Bilha, Souleyman, 'Un décorateur de cinéma couronné. Entretien avec Joseph Kpobly, Souleyman Bilha Cotonou, le 11 mars 2003', *Africultures*, 26 mars 2003. Available: http://www.africultures.com/php/index.php?nav=article&no=2829. Accessed 08/06/2015.

Burgin, Alice, 'Acculturation and imagination as social practice in *Heremakono*', *Journal of African Cinemas* 3:1, 2011, 51-64.

Butler, Judith, *Frames of War. When Is Life Grievable?*, London and New York, NY: Verso, 2010.

Cavell, Stanley, *The World Viewed*, Cambridge, MA: Harvard University Press, 1979.

Choplin, Armelle and Ba, Cheikh Oumar, 'Tenter l'aventure par la Mauritanie', *Autrepart* 36:4, 2005, 21-42.

Diome, Fatou, *Celles qui attendent*, Paris: Flammarion, 2010.

Downey, Anthony, 'Zones of Indistinction. Giorgio Agamben's "Bare Life" and The Politics of Aesthetics,' *Third Text* 23:2, March 2009, 109-125.

Fawzia, 'Nul n'est prophète dans son pays', *Jeune Afrique*, 15 October 2006. Available: http://www.jeuneafrique.com/216111/archives-thematique/nul-n-est-proph-te-en-son-pays/. Accessed 09/06/2015.

Foucault, Michel, 'Of Other Spaces' in *The Visual Culture Reader*, edited by Nicholas Mirzoeff, London and New York, NY: Routledge, 2002, 229-236.

Gabara, Rachel, 'Abderrahmene Sissako: Second and Third Cinema in the First Person' in *Global Art Cinema. New Theories and Histories*, edited by Rosalind Galt and Karl Schoonover, Oxford and New York, NY: Oxford University Press, 2010, 320-333.

Kessel, Joseph, *Vent de sable*, Paris: Gallimard, 1966.

Lequeret, Elisabeth, 'Scènes de tournage à Nouadhibou,' *Cahiers du cinéma* 560, September 2001, 42-43.

Mbembe, Achille, 'Necropolitics', trans. Libby Meintjes, *Public Culture* 15:1, 2003, 11-40.

Murray Levine, Alison J., '"Provoking Situations": Abderrahmane Sissako's Documentary Fiction', *Journal of African Cinemas* 3:1, 2011, 93-107.

Ndione, Abasse, *Mbëke mi. A l'assaut des vagues de l'Atlantique*, Paris: Gallimard, 2008.

Nisbet, Robert A., *Social Change and History: Aspects of the Western Theory of Development*, London: Oxford University Press, 1969.

Pasley, Victoria, 'Saharan Architecture in *La vie sur terre* and *Heremakono*', *Camera Lucida Filmski Magazin* 7, 2012, 9-11.

Preston-Whyte, Robert, 'The Beach as a Liminal Space' in *A Companion to Tourism*, edited by Alan E. Lew, C. Michael Hall and Allan M. Williams, Malden, MA: Blackwell Publishing, 2004, 349-359.

Rancière, Jacques, *The Emancipated Spectator* trans. Gregory Elliott, London and New York, NY: Verso, 2011.

_____ , *Film Fables* trans. Emiliano Battista, Oxford and New York, NY: Berg, 2006.

Saint-Exupéry, Antoine de, *Terre des hommes*, Paris: Gallimard, 1939.

_____ , *Œuvres complètes*, 2 vols, (Bibliothèque de la Pléiade) Paris: Gallimard, 1994-1999.

Shapiro, Meyer, 'The Still Life as a Personal Object – A Note on Heidegger and van Gogh' in *Theory and Philosophy of Art: Style, Artist, and Society (Selected Papers)*, New York, NY: George Braziller, 1994, 135-142.

Sicinski, Michael, 'A Fragmented Epistemology: The Films of Abderrahmane Sissako', *Cinema Scope* 29, 2007, 16-19.

Silou, Osange, 'Abderrahmane Sissako : "Filmer n'est pas un Bonheur"' in *Cinémas africains, une oasis dans le désert*, *CinémAction* 160, Éditions Charles Corlet, 2003, 88-92.

Streiff-Fénart, Jocelyne and Poutignat Philippe, 'Nouadhibou "ville de transit"? Le rapport d'une ville à ses étrangers dans le contexte des politiques de contrôle des frontières de l'Europe', *Revue européenne des migrations nationales* 24:2, 2008, 193-217.

_____ , 'De l'aventurier au commerçant transnational, trajectoires croisées et lieux intermédiaires à Nouadhibou (Mauritanie)', *Cahiers de la Méditerranée* 73, December 2006, 129-149.

Urbain, Jean-Didier, *Sur la plage. Moeurs et coutumes balnéaires (XIXe – XX siècles)*, Paris: Petite Bibliothèque Payot, 2002.

Filmography

Danvers, Louis, dir., *Partir, Revenir, Voyages d'un cineaste*, DVD bonus feature to *Heremakono* directed by Abderrahmane Sissako, DVD, Filmfreak Distributie Tiger releases, 2004.

Sissako, Abderrahmane, dir., *Heremakono*, DVD, Filmfreak Distributie Tiger releases, 2004 [2002].

Touré, Moussa, dir., *La pirogue*, DVD, Orange Studio, 2012.

INDEX

Accad, Evelyne, 162-169, 171-2
Adnan, Etel, 162-4, 169-172
Agamben, Giorgio, 134, 206-7
alienation, 8, 13n, 15, 23, 24, 26, 28, 57, 59-60, 117, 163
  self-alienation, 180
Antilles, 141, 151
Atlantic Coast, 90n, 121, 138, 189
Augé, Marc, 4, 101, 135-7, 138, 143
authenticity, 18, 19, 22, 23, 25, 28-9, 53, 56, 91, 119, 123, 136-7, 179
Bardot, Brigitte, 105-6, 118-19, 121-3, 124n, 177
barricades, 20-2
Barthes, Roland, 35-9, 40-6, 146n, 147
Bataille, Georges, 41, 43, 57
Baudelaire, Charles, 16, 18-20
beachscape, 114-117, 119, 121-2, 124
Beauvoir, Simone de, 122-3
Beirut, 1, 159-65, 169-72
biopolitics, 134
Blanchot, Maurice, 41, 52
body, 5, 71, 77, 103, 113, 114, 124, 127, 134, 144, 170, 179, 181-3, 188, 205-9, 212
  ageing, 180, 185-6
  female, 115-16, 118-19, 122-3, 130, 160, 185, 187
bodily sensation, 180-1, 187
Bougainville, Louis Antoine de, 143-4
Breillat, Catherine, 113-15, 121-6, 128, 130
  À ma sœur, 114-15, 121-4, 126n, 128
  Sex is Comedy, 125, 128
camp, 133-5, 139, 142, 155
Camus, Albert, 3n, 49-51, 53-4, 57, 60, 63, 182

Cannes, 90, 96, 101n, 118, 123, 129, 193
capitalism, 2, 19, 22, 26, 29-30, 61-2
  late, 6, 8, 50, 58, 63, 134-5, 143, 153, 179
Caribbean, 91, 141
Chamoiseau, Patrick, 8
Charlie Hebdo, 2
childhood, 24-5, 82, 89, 92-4, 114, 136
Chtcheglov, Ivan, 20
cinema, 1, 6, 72, 84, 90, 92, 95, 97, 100, 101n, 102n, 114-16, 124-6, 160, 188, 194, 200, 207
  art-house, 116-17, 119, 120, 121, 130
  du corps, 113
  European, 115-19, 121, 122n, 123, 130
  history of, 89, 90, 102
  migration, 196
city, 1, 21, 96, 114, 116-17, 143, 146, 159-72, 193-4, 196, 199, 201, 203-5, 207, 210-11
cityscape, 162, 164, 169
cliff; cliffs, 86, 96, 105-6, 166, 186-7
Club Med, 1, 15, 27, 63, 90-1. 97, 99, 133-5, 139-55, 177
  Blitz, Gérard, 139-40, 142, 144, 148-9, 155
  Trigano, Gilbert, 139, 142, 148-9
consumerism, 25, 62, 90, 136-7, 139-40, 146-7, 151, 154, 177, 184
Corbin, Alain, 2-3, 102, 117n, 177
Corsica, 90, 98
cynicism, 15, 55, 59, 135, 152, 154, 179
death, 53, 59, 75, 80, 83-4, 116, 120, 123, 133, 134n, 168, 171, 190, 194, 196, 207-8, 212
  of Man, 39
Debord, Guy, 13, 16-18, 23, 26, 28-30

decolonization, 140, 145, 178
Deleuze, Gilles, 41n, 44, 45-6, 135
   and Félix Guattari, 115
Derrida, Jacques, 41n, 86, 93, 96n, 97
desert, 1, 114, 193-4, 196, 203, 207, 210, 211
   island, 91
détournement, 21, 27, 30
documentary, 95, 102n, 188, 197-8, 201, 212
   fiction, 197
dune; dunes, 83, 98, 123, 126, 182, 194, 202, 211
Duras, Marguerite, 5, 162
El Saadawi, Nawal, 171
empire, 6, 147, 154
   French, 178
   Ottoman, 161
ennui, 19, 136
Eustache, Jean, 91
existentialism, 5, 18-19, 23-4, 27, 36-7, 39, 49-50-5, 57-8, 60-1, 63, 69, 182, 187-9
fisherman; fisherman, 4, 68, 71, 73, 80, 159, 195, 204
flânerie; *flâneur*, 116-17, 180
flesh, 57, 114-16, 118-22, 124, 167, 188, 190
foam, 96, 102, 104, 194n
   line of, 36n, 44
Foucault, Michel, 36-7, 39-41, 43-6, 51-2, 56, 96n, 166
frame, 3, 67, 77, 86, 96, 98-9, 105-7, 115, 117, 178
Frères Lumière, 89-90, 102
gaze, 78, 82, 164
   male, 102
   tourist, 136-7
globalization, 134, 136-7, 148, 150-1, 153-4, 178, 184, 196, 200, 205, 210, 212
Godard, Jean-Luc, 96, 101, 107, 154
   Film Socialisme, 1
   Le Mepris [*Contempt*], 105, 119, 121, 123
   Numéro deux, 127
   Pierrot le fou, 96n, 116

   Weekend, 1, 136
Hegel, Georg Wilhelm Friedrich, 17, 23, 133
horizon, 40, 96, 114, 115, 170, 172, 178, 184-5, 189, 190, 202, 203, 208
Houellebecq, Michel, 5-7, 49, 58-63, 136, 179-82, 184, 190
   La carte et le territoire, 61, 62
   Extension du domaine de la lutte, 50, 58-61, 180-3, 189
   Lanzarote, 5, 180, 182-3, 189
   Les Particules élémentaires, 5, 60
   Platforme, 62, 154, 180, 182, 184
   Poésies, 180-1, 188-9, 190
   La Possibilité d'une île, 1, 60, 179-80, 184-90
   Soumission, 6
identity, 3, 6, 7, 18, 29, 70, 75, 83, 151, 153-4, 161-3, 209
   national, 7, 147-8, 150, 154, 159, 161
Jameson, Frederic, 56
jetty, 68, 70, 80, 89
Kassir, Samir, 160
La Baule, 1, 4, 136, 138
Le Clèzio, J.M.G., 49-50, 56-7
   Le Procès-verbal, 50, 56-7
Leconte, Patrice, 133, 135-6, 149, 154
   Les Bronzés, 133, 135-6, 148
leisure, 2, 13n, 15, 19, 22, 25, 27, 68-9, 71, 73, 91, 117n, 122n, 133-4, 138, 148, 150, 160, 177-8
Letterist International, 16-18
liminal; liminality, 50, 62, 67, 72, 77, 82, 90, 93, 94, 96, 99, 117, 135, 163-4, 166, 178, 181, 197, 203, 205, 208
limit, 1, 4, 36, 39, 43-4, 46, 56, 93, 96, 98-100, 133, 140, 146, 154, 160, 182, 190
   limit-texts, 41
   limitless, 54, 83, 180
Little Miss Sunshine, 69-70
Mallarmé, Stéphane, 40-1, 45
Martinique, 140-1, 151

Marx, Karl, 17, 28, 133
Marxist, 18
May 1968, 13-15, 16-17, 19-23, 29, 91
Mediterranean, 2, 7, 121, 140, 142, 145, 159, 163, 188
metaphor, 24, 25, 36-7, 39, 43-6, 50-4, 63, 67-8, 71, 73, 80, 83, 94, 118, 135, 162, 164, 165, 167, 181, 183, 186, 197, 200, 202, 203, 207, 208, 212
migration, 2, 134, 137, 142, 178, 195-6, 204n, 212
  see also cinema
mirror, 7, 85, 137, 181, 185, 186
mission civilisatrice, 137, 138, 140-1, 143, 145, 148-50, 152, 154
myth, 2, 6, 38, 51, 53-4, 75, 91, 129, 130, 135, 143, 145-7, 149, 151, 154, 165, 189
  mythology, 25, 39, 117, 120
    Greek, 75, 107, 119
naked, 7, 114-15, 119-20, 128, 184
  see also nudity
Nietzsche, Friedrich, 40-1, 69n
  Nietzschean, 39, 69
nostalgia, 116, 136, 178-80, 184, 188-9
Nouadhibou, 1, 193-8, 201, 204n, 210, 212
nouveau roman, 42, 50-1, 55, 57, 62-3
nudity, 115, 119-20, 123, 211n
  see also naked
Other; Otherness, 2, 3-4, 8, 39, 45, 50, 143, 160, 179
Ozon, François, 6, 113-15, 124-30
  5x2, 114, 125-9
  Jeune et jolie, 129
  Sous le sable [Under the Sand], 115, 124-5, 128
Paris, 20, 22, 26, 68, 71, 77, 78, 83, 89-90, 98, 127, 146, 182
  Disneyland, 136, 149
postmodernism, 7, 56, 135, 154
promenade, 76, 85, 159
Proust, Marcel, 6, 7, 67-86
  Albertine, 67, 71-2, 79-80, 81-6

Balbec, 1, 67-8, 70, 71, 73-86
  Elstir, 67, 71-3, 79-81, 85-6
Rancière, Jacques, 94, 198
rape, 6, 49, 56, 58, 114-17, 119-21, 123-4, 127-9, 162, 167, 170
  see also violence; sexual
refugee, 2, 133
resort, 1, 5, 6, 62-3, 70, 77-8, 89, 118, 127-8, 133-5, 137-8, 140-2, 145-6, 151-3, 159, 161, 188
Robbe-Grillet, Alain, 42-3, 45, 49, 51, 53-7, 60
  Le Voyeur, 42, 49, 50, 55-7
  Pour un nouveau roman, 51
Robinson Crusoe, 8, 91-2, 96n
Ross, Kristin, 38
Rozier, Jacques, 6, 90-107
  Adieu Philippine, 90, 92-3, 97, 99, 100-3, 106
  Blue Jeans, 90, 92, 96-8, 101n, 102, 107
  Du Côté d'Orouët, 91-2, 95, 98, 101, 103-4, 106-7
  Fifi Martingale, 90
  Maine Océan, 91-2, 95, 100, 103n
  Les naufragés de l'île de la Tortue, 91, 95, 101
  Le Parti des choses, 105-6
  Rentrée des classes, 90, 92-4, 99, 102n
ruins; ruination, 165, 190
Saint-Exupéry, Antoine de, 193-4, 208, 212
same, 4-5, 45, 178
sand, 1, 2, 4, 6, 25, 39, 43, 50, 60, 70, 75-7, 82, 83, 86, 97, 100, 102, 114-15, 123, 124-6, 160, 177, 178 180, 187, 189, 193n, 194, 196, 200, 206, 208, 210-12
  face in the, 36, 39, 44-5
sandstorms, 194-6, 198
  see also dune; dunes
Sartre, Jean-Paul, 6, 19n, 35-9, 49, 50-5, 57, 62
  La Nausée, 35-9, 49, 52, 54
  see also existentialism

INDEX   219

screen, 6, 67, 68, 72, 75, 76, 77, 79, 84, 96, 125, 187
sea [*mer*], 2, 3, 4, 5, 35-9, 41-4, 45n, 46, 50-4, 60, 67-9, 71-6, 80, 83-6, 95-7, 98-103, 105, 114, 117, 119, 120, 125-9, 138, 139, 145, 155, 159-64, 165-72, 177-8, 182, 185, 187-90, 194, 196, 202-10, 212
seashore, 67, 195-6, 202-5, 208n, 210
sea-wall, 68, 70, 71, 77-85
sex, 62, 114, 119, 128, 129, 133, 144, 154
sexual desire, 26, 62, 113, 124, 126, 171, 188
sexual encounter, 7, 68, 83, 91, 121, 124, 129, 136, 144, 177, 183
sexual fantasy, 75, 91, 107, 116, 144, 182, 184, 188
see also transgression
violence; sexual
sexuality, 36, 43, 53n, 83, 86, 102-3, 113-15, 118, 121, 127-30, 160, 162, 163
shipwreck, 3, 5, 169, 171, 210
Sissako, Abderrahmane, 7, 194-98, 200-1, 205, 207, 210-12
Situationist International, 13-16, 18-25, 29
sky, 50, 53, 54, 57, 71, 72, 80, 96, 127
strand, 104-5
structuralism, 36-7, 50-1
sun, 5, 16, 26, 52-4, 57, 60, 75, 80, 84, 102, 125-7, 134, 160, 181, 183, 190, 207-9
sunbathing, 118, 123, 144, 187
Surrealism, 16-18, 20, 24, 28, 41, 162
tabula rasa, 95, 146
Thailand, 63, 152, 178
tourism, 4, 6, 15, 25-6, 28, 62, 74, 89, 122n, 133-41, 143, 145, 147, 150-55, 160-1, 177
dark, 133-4
transgression, 6, 50, 63, 68, 83, 93, 96, 98-9, 116-17, 129, 134, 163-4, 169
Trente glorieuses, Les [Thirty Glorious Years], 25, 140, 146
Truffaut, François, 1, 100, 116, 117, 118-19, 122, 123
Les 400 Coups [*The 400 Blows*], 1, 100, 103, 116, 117
Urbain, Jean-Didier, 2-5, 68, 92n, 96n, 101, 124, 143, 144, 204
utopian, 45, 116, 134
vacation, 4-5, 89-92, 107, 126n, 128, 133-142, 145-7
grandes vacances, 94, 137
Varda, Agnès, 7
violence, 4-6, 26, 49, 56, 58, 117, 123-4, 133-4, 162-3, 164, 166, 171-2, 182, 212
sexual, 8, 114, 116, 123-4, 128, 163, 164, 166, 172
see also rape
Virilio, Paul, 5, 138, 140, 143, 154
war, 2, 6, 7, 133-5, 138, 140, 142, 144, 146, 154, 159, 161-4, 166, 167, 169, 172, 194n
Algerian War, 92, 93, 100
post-war, 2, 3, 19, 26, 50, 122n, 134, 139, 154-5, 177
First World War, 78n, 138n, 139, 161
Second World War, 25, 138-9
wave; waves, 1, 39, 43-4, 46, 76, 84, 89, 96n, 97, 100, 101-7, 122, 125, 166, 178, 189, 196, 209-10
Žižek, Slavoj, 55

www.ingramcontent.com/pod-product-compliance
Lightning Source LLC
Chambersburg PA
CBHW061246230426
43662CB00021B/2446